ALSO BY CHRISTOPHER CERF AND VICTOR S. NAVASKY

THE EXPERTS SPEAK:
THE DEFINITIVE COMPENDIUM OF AUTHORITATIVE MISINFORMATION

CHRISTOPHER CERF

THE OFFICIAL POLITICALLY CORRECT DICTIONARY AND HANDBOOK (WITH HENRY BEARD)

THE GULF WAR READER (WITH MICAH L. SIFRY)

THE IRAQ WAR READER (WITH MICAH L. SIFRY)

THE PENTAGON CATALOG: ORDINARY PRODUCTS AT EXTRAORDINARY PRICES (WITH HENRY BEARD)

THE EIGHTIES: A LOOK BACK
(EDITED, IN 1979, WITH TONY HENDRA AND PETER ELBLING)

VICTOR S. NAVASKY

NAMING NAMES

KENNEDY JUSTICE

A MATTER OF OPINION

MISSION ACCOMPLISHED!

Or How We Won the War in Iraq

The Experts Speak

CHRISTOPHER CERF
and VICTOR S. NAVASKY

Simon & Schuster Paperbacks
New York London Toronto Sydney

Simon & Schuster Paperbacks
A Division of Simon & Schuster, Inc.
1230 Avenue of the Americas
New York, NY 10020

First Simon & Schuster trade paperback edition March 2008

For information about special discounts for bulk purchases, please contact Simon & Schuster Special Sales at 1-800-456-6798 or business@simonandschuster.com

Designed by Nancy Singer

Manufactured in the United States of America

10 9 8 7 6 5 4 3 2 1

Library of Congress Cataloging-in-Publication Data

Cerf, Christopher.
Mission accomplished! or how we won the war in Iraq: the experts speak / Christopher Cerf and Victor S. Navasky.
p. cm.
Includes bibliographical references.
1. Iraq War, 2003—Campaigns—United States. 2. Iraq War, 2003—Military intelligence—United States. 3. United States—Politics and government—2001- 4. Quotations, English. I. Navasky, Victor S. II. Title.

DS79.764.U6C47 2007
956.7044'3—dc22 2007049315

ISBN-13: 978-1-4165-6993-0
ISBN-10: 1-4165-6993-6

To Joseph W. Aidlin,

who buys when the experts sell

You need somebody in office who will tell the truth.

George W. Bush, Republican candidate for the
U.S. presidency, October 17, 2000

CONTENTS

INTRODUCTION xv

PROLOGUE xxiii

PART I: SADDAM HUSSEIN: "A FORCE FOR PEACE IN THE MIDDLE EAST" xxiii

PART II: PREMONITIONS OF LIBERATION xxv

VOLUME I: THE GATHERING STORM 1

WEAPONS OF MASS DESTRUCTION: DOES SADDAM REALLY HAVE THEM? (ONLY A FOOL—OR POSSIBLY A FRENCHMAN—COULD CONCLUDE OTHERWISE) 3

Does Saddam Have Nukes? "We Don't Want the Smoking Gun to be a Mushroom Cloud!" 8

Aluminum Tubes 9

"16 Little Words" 9

Chemical and Biological Weapons 10

Biological Vans: Cooking Everything but the Books? 12

Anthrax: "Let's All Take a Deep Breath" 16

The Loyal Opposition Speaks 20

THE MISSING LINK 22
Mohammed Atta's Trip to Prague: An "Undisputed Fact" 27
AN IMMINENT THREAT? 28
Postscript: On the Imminency of Nonimminency 29
UNIMPEACHABLE SOURCES: THE WORLD ACCORDING TO JUDITH MILLER 29
THE SEARCH FOR A DIPLOMATIC SOLUTION 34
Inspecting the Inspectors (or The Search for Rosie O'Donnell's Stretch Marks) 34
Cheese-Eating Surrender Monkeys 35
War or Peace? "The Decider Has Yet to Decide" 39

VOLUME II: THEIR FINEST HOUR: AMERICA READIES ITSELF TO FREE THE IRAQI PEOPLE 42
CAKEWALK! 45
HOW MANY TROOPS WILL BE NEEDED? 46
Postscript: What About Casualties? 48
A BURNING QUESTION: WHAT'S OIL GOT TO DO WITH IT? 49
HOW MUCH WILL IT COST? A WAR THAT WILL PAY FOR ITSELF! 52
HOW LONG WILL IT LAST? (OR WHEN DO WE GET TO DINE IN THE GASLIGHT DISTRICT?) 56
And Wait . . . There's Even *More* Good News! 60
Postscript: "The Rush to Peace" 60

VOLUME III: THE GRAND ALLIANCE 62
Part I: The Coalition of the Willing Invades Iraq 62
THE COALITION OF THE WILLING 65
"GOD IS GRILLING THEIR STOMACHS IN HELL!" 67
"THE GREATEST HEROINE OF ALL TIME": SAVING PRIVATE LYNCH 69

Part II: Mission Accomplished 75

POSTSCRIPT: AND YOU KNOW WHAT? THINGS COULD HAVE GONE EVEN BETTER! 81

VOLUME IV: THE HINGE OF FATE 82

LOOTING: "A NATURAL PROCESS" AND "A RELIEF TO COLLEGE STUDENTS EVERYWHERE" 85

Postscript: Keeping Our Priorities Straight 88

RESISTANCE? WHAT RESISTANCE? 88

WHY BAGHDAD IS JUST LIKE MANHATTAN (OR IS IT CALIFORNIA?) 93

THE NEXT (OR NEXT TO LAST) WORD ON WMDS 96

Postscript: So We Didn't Find the WMDs. Big Deal! 100

A "BUNCH OF BULL": THE "IRRELEVANT" DEBATE OVER THE "16 LITTLE WORDS" 101

Revisionist History 101

THE VALERIE PLAME AFFAIR 104

TORTURE: THE NEW PARADIGM 105

Optional Reading: The Geneva Convention 105

Welcome to Guantánamo! 106

Postscript: Should Guantánamo Prison Be Shut Down? 109

The Case for Torture 110

Postscript: The President Calls the World to Action 114

The Comforts of Abu Ghraib 115

ALL HAIL THE VICEROY: JERRY BREMER AND THE CPA 121

Reconstruction, American-Style 125

Postscript: Money Players 129

Perspectives on Chaos 130

COMING REAL SOON NOW: THE NEW, DE-BA'ATHIFIED IRAQI SECURITY FORCES! 132

CONTRACTORS: "SKYDIVERS AND MOTORCYCLISTS" 136
"An Uptick in Local Engagements" 136
The Ambush in Fallujah: What Really Happened? 139
"Humane Democracy" in Nisour Square 141
See No Evil, Hear No Evil 144
Postscript: The Cookie and Buzzy Show 148
A CIVIL WAR? NOT BLOODY LIKELY! 149
MISSION ACCOMPLISHED REVISITED 151

VOLUME V: CLOSING THE RING: THE END GAME? 152
MEASURING THE IRAQ WAR IN "FRIEDMAN UNITS" 155
TURNING POINTS 158
VIGILANCE, THE PRICE OF LIBERTY 161
Some Dare Call It Treason: America's Fifth Column 161
Fear Itself: The Bush Administration Reassures America 165
Things We Mustn't Do (So the Terrorists Won't Win) 167
Postscript: The Hunt for Osama bin Laden 168

VOLUME VI: TRIUMPH OR TRAGEDY? AMERICA LOOKS BACK AT FIVE YEARS OF CONFLICT 170
WHY WE FIGHT 173
PLANTING THE SEEDS OF FREEDOM (THE DEVIL IS IN THE DETAILS) 175
History's Judgment 175
"Resolve, Constancy and Unity of Purpose" 176
PROFILES IN COMPASSIONATE CONSERVATISM 176
RUMSFELD'S PERFORMANCE: THE DECIDER DECIDES 178
NOTHING FAILS LIKE SUCCESS! 180
WHO, ME? 181

THE NEW CRUSADERS 183
God Is on Our Side 184
Postscript: God Is on Their Side, Too 185
PAX AMERICANA 186
In Closing: A Message of Unity and Hope from President George W. Bush 189

EPILOGUE: FINALLY, AN EXPERT WHO WAS RIGHT 191

ACKNOWLEDGMENTS 195

NOTES 199

INDEX 253

THE INSTITUTE OF EXPERTOLOGY 267

ABOUT THE AUTHORS 269

SPECIAL BONUS SECTION: A SNEAK PREVIEW OF OUR FORTHCOMING BOOK, *THE EXPERTS SPEAK ABOUT IRAN* 271

INTRODUCTION

It is, of course, twenty-four years since the Institute of Expertology issued its first findings. For those who may have been too young to see our study, or are too old to remember it, we recall that, notwithstanding the best efforts of the Institute's worldwide cadre of researchers, we were unable to identify a single expert who was right. At the time, despite these findings, our scholarly integrity compelled us to concede the statistical probability that in theory the experts might be right as much as half the time. It was simply that we hadn't found any.

And this was despite our expansive definition of who qualifies as an expert. We use the term *expert* to designate people who, by virtue of celebrity, official status, formal title (military or civilian), academic degree, professional license, public office, journalistic beat, quantity of publications, and/or use of highly technical jargon, are presumed to know what they are talking about. Trust us, they don't.

However, when we decided to undertake a scholarly monograph with the working title "Expertology and the Iraq War: How Could So Many Have Been Misled by So Few?," we began to fear that our hypothesis—that once again the experts got it wrong—was erroneous. Our researchers deluged us with information, all of which showed such a historic unanimity of opinion on the war questions that the intellectual foundations of the Institute itself were shaken.

Certainly, indeed clearly, as Secretary of State Rice (one of the typically articulate experts represented in this particular volume) likes to say, we can state without fear of contradiction, based on a careful review of the Institute of Expertology archives, that never before in history has there been such a distinguished cast of experts as the one we have assembled here on the Iraq War. These are not your average experts. Our database consists of the highest government officials, diplomats, cabinet officers, four-star generals, bigfoot pundits, prize-winning Middle East scholars, top think-tank strategists, heads of congressional committees, the leadership of the Central Intelligence Agency, and such. Moreover, the database is transpartisan, featuring leading neoconservatives and liberals alike.

Thus, as responsible scholars, we tentatively had to consider the possibility that our scores of highly trained expertise experts at the Institute of Expertology were wrong in saying the experts were never right. In the case of America's adventure in Iraq, we seemed to have a clear exception to the Iron Law of Expertise. For never before in history has such a large and diverse group of experts been so unanimously in favor of a particular national policy as has this group in the case of the U.S. invasion of Iraq. Could it be that we at the Institute were wrong?

Let us say in our defense that our work in the past covered many fields of expertise, including science, religion, music, literature, and economics. In those cases, the problems of identifying expertise were more complex and multifaceted. Frequently the experts disagreed with one another. In this study, however, we are concerned with but a single question: the wisdom of the United States invading and waging war in Iraq. On this clear question, we have uncovered an astonishing level of unanimity across the board. In the face of such unanimity, how could we, as scientific expertologists, say, "The experts were wrong"?

The temptation was to succumb to the weight of what appeared to be the evidence. Moreover, as patriotic Americans, we were as eager as our fellow countrymen to take pride in our country's triumphs so persuasively proclaimed by our brilliant, keenly intelligent, high-IQ, perspicacious homegrown opinion leaders—"Made in the USA."

Of course, as scrupulous scholars, we planned to report and not suppress the fact that there was and is a small group of dissenters from this Great Consensus, but they are for the most part ordinary citizens or extreme left (and far right) wingers who really don't count, and so we don't count them. They would, in truth, only pollute our sample.

But after having completed our in-depth study and analysis of five years of expert commentary on the Iraq War, despite the near-unanimity and the high status and IQ of our subjects, we now must allow for the possibility that (with one exception, discussed below), the experts all got it wrong. We should have been suspicious of these overachievers based on our earlier studies. (Indeed, in our previous report we quoted Arthur R. Jensen, professor emeritus of educational psychology at Berkeley, who said, "The most important fact about intelligence is that we can measure it.") The fact that the Iraq experts all agreed with each other should have been the tip-off.

In the interests of objectivity, what we have decided to do, therefore, is publish this interim report, leaving open the possibility that the experts may all be right or they may all be wrong. We are confident that we will not have long to wait to learn precisely which faction was right and which was wrong. Indeed, we expect the answer in six months. A leading expert, the *New York Times* columnist Thomas Friedman, has assured us that, as he said in 2003 (and again in 2004, 2005, etc.), "The next six months in Iraq" will settle the case once and for all.

By the way, we should mention here that we are more than cognizant that our critics and enemies will object that many of those we quote have changed their opinions over time and that we do not note this in our text. For example, we do not note that Richard Cohen, a *Washington Post* columnist who wrote in February 2003 that the evidence Colin Powell presented to the United Nations proved so conclusively that Iraq retained weapons of mass destruction that "only a fool—or possibly a Frenchman—could conclude otherwise," later changed his mind about the war. He could stand in for many others. However, we do not include them in our sample for the same reason we don't count the original opponents of the war: namely, they would pollute our sample. Changing one's mind is an example of what is called in the field "negative expertology" and is the subject of a separate scientific study.

In any case, it is not for us, who are, after all, impartial social scientists, to pass judgment on the motives or character of those who supported the war and later retracted. No doubt many did so from high-minded motives, but we leave that determination to scholars in future studies that will set the record straight pundit by pundit.

On the other hand, much of the press—like the columnist Cal Thomas, who wrote that Saddam Hussein was in such breach of UN resolutions "that only the duped, the dumb and the desperate could ignore it," or Laura Ingraham, who reported that "Hans Blix couldn't find stretch marks on Rosie O'Donnell"—held firm to their convictions. Were they right in doing so? The next six months will definitively tell the story.

Finally, we wish to draw the reader's attention to our epilogue. One of the outcomes of the Iraq study—whatever its final findings—is that it did produce one expert who was right. To avoid presenting this expert out of context, we resist the temptation to quote him here. (On the matter of context, we are the first to concede that some of the quotations in this book may be said to be out of context. But that is only because the context itself was constantly changing: Why did we go into Iraq in the first place, for instance: WMDs? To bring democracy to the Middle East? Regime change? To combat terrorism? Oil?)

We can, however, assert with confidence that anyone who gets as far as the epilogue will have to agree that our study—whatever its final findings—has produced one expert on whose foresight both the experts and we expertologists are in unanimous agreement.

Christopher Cerf
Victor S. Navasky
Founders, the Institute of Expertology

A REPRESENTATIVE SAMPLE OF OUR SAMPLE OF EXPERTS

George W. ("Mission Accomplished") **Bush,**
President of the United States of America

★

Dick ("The streets of Baghdad are sure to erupt in joy")
Cheney, Vice President of the United States of America

★

Condoleezza ("We don't want the smoking gun to be a mushroom cloud") **Rice,** U.S. Secretary of State

★

Donald ("Stuff Happens") **Rumsfeld,**
U.S. Secretary of Defense

★

Richard ("Saddam will take the UN down with him") **Perle,**
Chairman, Defense Policy Board

★

Tom ("The next six months will tell the story") **Friedman,**
New York Times columnist

★

George ("It's a slam dunk!") **Tenet,** Director,
Central Intelligence Agency

★

L. Paul ("Insurgents pose no strategic threat") **Bremer III,**
Director of the Coalition Provisional Authority

★

Fred ("We know beyond a shadow of a doubt that Saddam Hussein has been pursuing aggressively weapons of mass destruction") **Barnes,** editor, *The Weekly Standard*

★

Colin ("Every statement I make [at the UN] is backed up by sources, solid sources"] **Powell,** U.S. Secretary of State

(MORE)

Jacob ("The interesting question is why pessimism continues to flourish in the face of military success") **Weisberg,** *Slate* reporter

Paul ("Iraq was the logical place to begin") **Berman,** *International Herald Tribune* reporter

☆

Bill ("Military action will not last more than a week") **O'Reilly,** *The O'Reilly Factor* host

☆

David ("The blood of hundreds of thousands of Americans is on the hands of the anti-war activists") **Horowitz,** *Los Angeles Times* reporter

☆

William ("Democratizing the country should not be too tall an order for the world's sole superpower") **Kristol,** *Weekly Standard* editor

☆

Douglas J. ("This month will be a turning point") **Feith,** U.S. Undersecretary of Defense for Policy

☆

Mitch ("Iraq will not require sustained aid") **Daniels,** U.S. Budget Director

☆

Hazin ("We will cut off their hands and behead them") **Shaalan,** Iraqi Minister of Defense

☆

Charles ("We must be prepared to torture") **Krauthammer,** syndicated columnist

☆

Alberto ("I don't recall") **Gonzales,** U.S. Attorney General

John ("Reasonable people will disagree about when torture is justified") **Yoo,**
Former Deputy Assistant Attorney General

Rush ("Abu Ghraib is no different from what happens at the Skull and Bones initiation") **Limbaugh,**
The Rush Limbaugh Show host

Ann ("We should kill their leaders, and convert them to Christianity") **Coulter**

PROLOGUE

PART I

Saddam Hussein: "A Force for Peace in the Middle East"

RUMSFELD'S GIFTS

In 1983 and 1984, Donald Rumsfeld, then a special envoy for the Reagan administration, traveled to Baghdad for meetings with President Saddam Hussein designed to "improve understanding" between the United States and Iraq. Rumsfeld brought Hussein several gifts, including a set of medieval spiked hammers and a pair of golden cowboy spurs. In its report on these meetings, the *Christian Science Monitor* noted that, as a sign of warming relations between the two nations, the U.S. government had recently "removed Iraq's name from a list of countries alleged to support terrorism."[1]

Access to Persian Gulf oil and the security of key friendly states . . . are vital to U.S. national security. . . . Normal relations between the United States and Iraq would serve our longer-term interests and promote stability in the Gulf and the Middle East.

President George H. W. Bush, National Security Directive 26, paving the way for $1 billion in new U.S. loan guarantees to Iraq, October 2, 1989[2]

I have been sitting here and listening to you for about an hour, and I am now aware that you are a strong and intelligent man and that you want peace. I believe, Mr. President, that you can be a very influential force for peace in the Middle East.

Senator Howard Metzenbaum (D-OH), speaking to Iraqi President Saddam Hussein at a meeting between Hussein and American senators in Mosul, Iraq, April 12, 1990[3]

I enjoy meeting candid and open people [like you].

Senator Alan K. Simpson (R-WY), Republican Whip of the Senate, speaking to Iraqi President Saddam Hussein at a meeting between Hussein and American senators in Mosul, Iraq, April 12, 1990[4]

Access to Persian Gulf oil and the security of key friendly states are vital to U.S. national security. . . . Iraq . . . is clearly a power with interests inimical to our own.

President George H. W. Bush, National Security Directive 54, launching the First Gulf War, January 15, 1991[5]

PART II

Premonitions of Liberation

BOOM BOX 1.

BOOM BOX 2.

Editors' Note: Pedants may argue that these "premonitions of liberation" more properly belong on page 42, where the attitudes of authoritative Americans on the eve of invasion are presented. Perhaps such objections would be justified.

Indeed, if this were a work of formal scholarship, we would have used the following few pages to present an abstract of our study. But we are, of course, committed to making our data comprehensible to the lay community. Therefore, rather than provide an obfuscatory précis, we herewith present what nonscientists might think of as a preview of coming attractions.

Dancing in the streets of Baghdad will be even more joyous than that in Kabul after its liberation.

Kenneth Adelman, member of the Defense Policy Board at the U.S. Department of Defense, February 13, 2002[6]

After liberation, the streets in Basra and Baghdad are sure to erupt in joy.

Vice President Dick Cheney, August 26, 2002[7]

If we come to Baghdad, Damascus and Tehran as liberators, we can expect overwhelming popular support.

Michael Ledeen, Freedom Scholar at the American Enterprise Institute, September 2002[8]

We shall be greeted, I think, in Baghdad and Basra with kites and boom boxes.

Fouad Ajami, professor of Middle East studies at Johns Hopkins University, assessing the likely outcome of an American invasion of Iraq, October 7, 2002[9]

There will . . . occur in Iraq a . . . [show of military force] rapid and accurate and overwhelming enough to deal with an army or a country many times the size of Iraq. . . . And that will be greeted by the majority of Iraqi people and Kurdish people as a moment of emancipation, which will be a pleasure to see. . . . Bring it on.

Christopher Hitchens, journalist, January 28, 2003[10]

I think they will be greeted with sweets and flowers in the first months and simply have very, very little doubts that that is the case. . . . This is a remarkable situation in which the population of a country that's about to have a war waged over its head positively wants the war.

Kanan Makiya, Islamic scholar, March 17, 2003[11]

I don't want to make a prediction . . . but you're going to find, and this is very important, you're going to find Iraqis out cheering American troops.

Paul Wolfowitz, U.S. Deputy Secretary of Defense, February 23, 2003[12]

The terrified and brutalized people of Iraq will rejoice at the downfall of Saddam Hussein. And when we finally smash his evil regime suddenly those countries that doubt us will have their eyes opened.

Richard Perle, Chairman, Defense Policy Board, February 23, 2003[13]

The Iraqi people understand what this crisis is about. Like the people of France in the 1940s, they view us as their hoped-for liberator.

Paul Wolfowitz, U.S. Deputy Secretary of Defense, March 11, 2003[14]

My belief is we will, in fact, be greeted as liberators.

Vice President Dick Cheney, March 16, 2003[15]

I believe . . . that the Iraqi people will greet us as liberators.

Senator John McCain (R-AZ), March 20, 2003[16]

IN FACT

A poll commissioned by the Coalition Provisional Authority in May 2004, just thirteen months after U.S. troops entered Baghdad, showed that Iraqis who viewed American-led forces as "liberators" numbered only 2 percent of those polled.[17]

VOLUME I

THE GATHERING

STORM

From a marketing point of view, you don't introduce new products in August.

Andrew Card, White House Chief of Staff, explaining why the Bush administration's coordinated effort to convince the world of the urgent danger presented by Saddam Hussein's WMDs had to wait until after Labor Day, September 7, 2002[1]

WEAPONS OF MASS DESTRUCTION: DOES SADDAM REALLY HAVE THEM?

(ONLY A FOOL—OR POSSIBLY A FRENCHMAN—COULD CONCLUDE OTHERWISE)

There is no doubt that Saddam Hussein now has weapons of mass destruction. There is no doubt he is amassing them to use against our friends, against our allies, and against us. And there is no doubt that his aggressive regional ambitions will lead him into future confrontations with his neighbors—confrontations that will involve both the weapons he has today, and the ones he will continue to develop with his oil wealth.

Vice President Dick Cheney, speech at the Veterans of Foreign Wars' 103rd National Convention, August 26, 2002[2]

There is already a mountain of evidence that Saddam Hussein is gathering weapons [of mass destruction] for the purpose of using them. And adding additional information is like adding a foot to Mount Everest.

Ari Fleischer, White House Press Secretary, responding to a question about whether there was any "new evidence" that the threat from Saddam's WMDs was "getting worse," September 6, 2002[3]

[Saddam's] regime has amassed large clandestine stocks of biological weapons, including anthrax and botulism toxin and possibly smallpox. His regime has amassed large clandestine stockpiles of chemical weapons, including VX and sarin and mustard gas.

Donald H. Rumsfeld, U.S. Secretary of Defense, September 18, 2002[4]

Some of these weapons are deployable within 45 minutes of an order to use them.

Tony Blair, Prime Minister of Great Britain, in the foreword to *The Iraq Dossier*, a document issued by the British government assessing the case for weapons of mass destruction in Iraq, September 24, 2002[5]

[Saddam's] facilities are mobile; they have been widely dispersed to a number of locations; [he has] vast underground networks and facilities, and sophisticated denial and deception techniques. In addition, [weapons and military facilities] have been placed in close proximity to hospitals, schools and mosques.

Donald H. Rumsfeld, U.S. Secretary of Defense, September 27, 2002[6]

They have chemical weapons; they have biological weapons; they're trying to acquire nuclear weapons.

Colin Powell, U.S. Secretary of State, October 22, 2002[7]

President Bush has said Iraq has weapons of mass destruction; Tony Blair has said Iraq has weapons of mass destruction; Donald Rumsfeld has said Iraq has weapons of mass destruction; Richard Butler [former chairman of the U.N. weapons inspection organization in Iraq] has said they do; the United Nations has said they do; the experts have said they do. Iraq says they don't. You can choose who you want to believe.

Ari Fleischer, White House Press Secretary, December 5, 2002[8]

Don't worry, it's a slam dunk!

George Tenet, Director of the Central Intelligence Agency, assuring President George W. Bush that the intelligence that Iraq possessed weapons of mass destruction was foolproof, December 21, 2002[9]

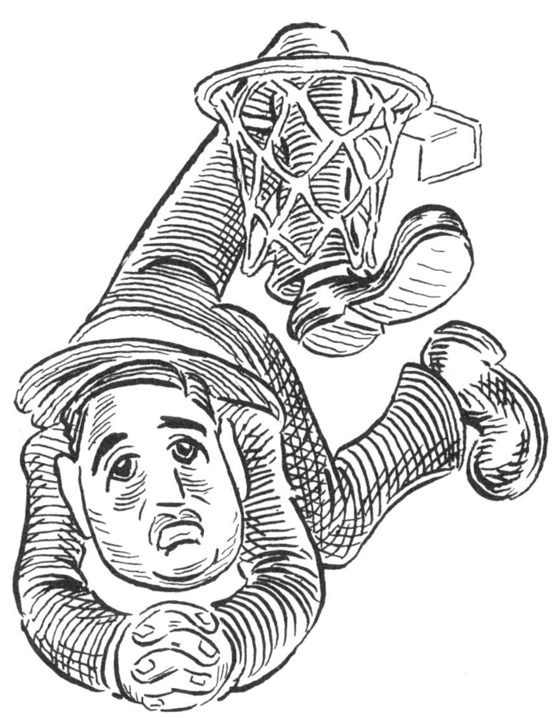

PROGRESS REPORT

FEBRUARY 7, 2003

"IT IS NOT KNOWABLE IF FORCE WILL BE USED, BUT IF IT IS TO BE USED, IT IS NOT KNOWABLE HOW LONG THAT CONFLICT WOULD LAST. IT COULD LAST, YOU KNOW, SIX DAYS, SIX WEEKS. I DOUBT SIX MONTHS."

★ SECRETARY OF DEFENSE DONALD RUMSFELD[P1]

We have first-hand descriptions of biological weapons factories on wheels and on rails. Our conservative estimate is that Iraq today has a stockpile of between one hundred and five hundred tons of chemical weapons agents. . . . [Saddam] remains determined to acquire nuclear weapons. . . . What I want to bring [to] your attention today is the much more sinister nexus between Iraq and the Al Qaeda terrorist network. . . .

Ladies and gentlemen, these are not assertions. These are facts, corroborated by many sources, some of them sources of the intelligence services of other countries.

Colin Powell, U.S. Secretary of State, offering "proof" to the UN Security Council to back up his claims of Iraq's possession and surreptitious concealment of weapons of mass destruction and Iraq's connection to Al Qaeda, February 5, 2003[10]

The evidence [Colin Powell] presented to the United Nations—some of it circumstantial, some of it absolutely bone-chilling in its detail—had to prove to anyone that Iraq not only hasn't accounted for its weapons of mass destruction but without a doubt still retains them. Only a fool—or possibly a Frenchman—could conclude otherwise.

Richard Cohen, *The Washington Post*, February 6, 2003[11]

To continue to say that the Bush administration has not made its case, you must now believe that Colin Powell lied in the most serious statement he will ever make, or was taken in by manufactured evidence. I don't believe that. Today, neither should you.

Jim Hoagland, *The Washington Post*, February 6, 2003[12]

Speaking to the U.N. Security Council last week, Secretary of State Colin Powell made so strong a case that Iraqi dictator Saddam Hussein is in material breach of U.N. resolutions that only the duped, the dumb and the desperate could ignore it.

Cal Thomas, syndicated column, February 6, 2003[13]

If the Americans go in and overthrow Saddam Hussein and it's clean—he has nothing—I will apologize to the nation, and I will not trust the Bush administration again.

Bill O'Reilly, American political commentator, March 18, 2003[14]

IN FACT

The American invasion of Iraq, which commenced with a bombing attack on the evening of the day after O'Reilly's *Good Morning America* appearance, failed to find any evidence of weapons of mass destruction. Eleven months later, egged on by *Good Morning America* host Charlie Gibson, O'Reilly issued an apology. "I was wrong. I am not pleased about it at all," he said. "What do you want me to do, go over and kiss the camera?"

MARCH 23, 2003

"THIS CONFLICT IS . . . GOING TO BE RELATIVELY SHORT."

★ SENATOR JOHN MCCAIN[P2]

DOES SADDAM HAVE NUKES? "WE DON'T WANT THE SMOKING GUN TO BE A MUSHROOM CLOUD!"

We know that he has the infrastructure, nuclear scientists to make a nuclear weapon. And we know that when the inspectors assessed this after the Gulf War, he was far, far closer to a crude nuclear device than anybody thought, maybe six months from a crude nuclear device. . . .

There will always be some uncertainty about how quickly he can acquire nuclear weapons. But we don't want the smoking gun to be a mushroom cloud.

Condoleezza Rice, National Security Advisor to President George W. Bush, commenting on Iraq's nuclear capabilities and the case for preemptive war, September 8, 2002[15]

The first time we may be completely certain he has nuclear weapons is when, God forbid, he uses one. We owe it to all our citizens to do everything in our power to prevent that day from coming.

President George W. Bush, address to the United Nations General Assembly, September 12, 2002[16]

America must not ignore the threat gathering against us. Facing clear evidence of peril, we cannot wait for the final proof—the smoking gun—that could come in the form of a mushroom cloud.

President George W. Bush, October 7, 2002[17]

Aluminum Tubes

Our intelligence sources tell us that [Saddam] has attempted to purchase high-strength aluminum tubes suitable for nuclear weapons production.

President George W. Bush, State of the Union message, January 28, 2003[18]

IN FACT

On January 9, 2003, almost three weeks before Mr. Bush's address, International Atomic Energy Agency Director General Dr. Mohamed El Baradei reported to the UN Security Council that the IAEA had concluded: "The aluminum tubes sought by Iraq in 2001 and 2002 were not directly suitable" for uranium enrichment. Months earlier, technical experts at the U.S. Department of Energy had reached the same conclusion—as had intelligence specialists at the State Department.

"16 Little Words"

The British government has learned that Saddam Hussein recently sought significant quantities of uranium from Africa.

President George W. Bush, State of the Union message, January 28, 2003[19]

JULY 3, 2003

"I THINK THE NEXT FEW MONTHS WILL BE CRUCIAL."

 SENATOR PAT ROBERTS[P3]

IN FACT

By the time President Bush uttered these "16 little words" (as they would later come to be known), his administration had already been cautioned by the CIA that the intelligence behind them was not credible. Indeed, as a result of such warnings, the claim had been excised from the President's October 7, 2002, Cincinnati speech presenting the case for Iraqi possession of WMD.

[See also "A Bunch of Bull": The "Irrelevant" Debate over the "16 Little Words," page 101.]

WHO SAYS SADDAM HAS NUCLEAR WEAPONS?

We know [Saddam has] been absolutely devoted to trying to acquire nuclear weapons, and we believe he has, in fact, reconstituted nuclear weapons.

Vice President Dick Cheney, March 16, 2003[20]

I don't know anybody that I can think of who has contended that the Iraqis had nuclear weapons.

Donald H. Rumsfeld, U.S. Secretary of Defense, June 24, 2003[21]

CHEMICAL AND BIOLOGICAL WEAPONS

They have weaponized chemical weapons, we know that.

Donald H. Rumsfeld, U.S. Secretary of Defense, June 10, 2002[22]

Our conservative estimate is that Iraq today has a stockpile of between 100 and 500 tons of chemical weapons agent. That is enough agent to fill 16,000 battlefield rockets. Even the low end of 100 tons of agent would enable Saddam Hussein to cause mass casualties across more than 100 square miles of territory, an area nearly five times the size of Manhattan.

Colin Powell, U.S. Secretary of State, address to the UN Security Council, February 5, 2003[23]

IN FACT

To hammer home the point that Iraq possessed the ability to disperse all the "lethal poisons and diseases" he had just described, Secretary Powell showed the Security Council members a photo, which he said had been obtained by UN inspectors "some years ago," of an Iraqi Mirage F-1 jet aircraft spraying "200 liters of simulated anthrax."

All the world has now seen the footage of an Iraqi Mirage aircraft with a fuel tank modified to spray biological agents over wide areas. Iraq has developed spray devices that could be used on unmanned aerial vehicles with ranges far beyond what is permitted by the Security Council. A UAV [unmanned aerial vehicle] launched from a vessel off the American coast could reach hundreds of miles inland.

President George W. Bush, on the day after Secretary Powell's presentation to the UN Security Council, February 6, 2003[24]

SEPTEMBER 10, 2003

"I WOULD ARGUE THAT THE NEXT THREE TO SIX MONTHS WILL BE CRITICAL."

 SENATOR JOHN MCCAIN[P4]

IN FACT

The President—in addition to referring, as Secretary Powell had the day before, to a picture of an Iraqi jet that had been taken years earlier—failed to mention the conclusion of the U.S. agency most expert on the subject of UAVs, the Air Force's National Air and Space Intelligence Center. "[The] U.S. Air Force does not agree," the agency had written the previous October, "that Iraq is developing UAVs primarily intended to be delivery platforms for chemical and biological warfare (CBW) agents. The small size of Iraq's new UAV strongly suggests a primary role of reconnaissance."[25]

Biological Vans: Cooking Everything but the Books?

An Iraqi major, who defected, confirmed that Iraq has mobile biological research laboratories. . . . We have diagrammed what our sources reported about these mobile facilities.

Here you see both truck and rail car–mounted mobile factories. The description our sources gave us of the technical features required by such facilities are [*sic*] highly detailed and extremely accurate. As these drawings based on their description show, we know what the fermenters look like, we know what the tanks, pumps, compressors and other parts look like. We know how they fit together. We know how they work. And we know a great deal about the platforms on which they are mounted.

Colin Powell, U.S. Secretary of State, address to the UN Security Council, February 5, 2003[26]

We know he continues to hide biological and chemical weapons, moving them to different locations as often as every 12 to 24 hours, and placing them in residential neighborhoods.

Donald H. Rumsfeld, U.S. Secretary of Defense, March 11, 2003[27]

COLIN'S CARTOONS

IN FACT

In late April, approximately a month after coalition forces had actually invaded Iraq, Kurdish forces near Irbil, in northern Iraq, seized a trailer that bore a resemblance to the drawings displayed by Powell. A second, similar trailer was found by U.S. forces near Mosul in May. The Bush administration was quick to hail the discoveries as, to quote the *Washington Post*, "a vindication of the decision to go to war."[28]

NOVEMBER 30, 2003

"THE NEXT SIX MONTHS IN IRAQ—WHICH WILL DETERMINE THE PROSPECTS FOR DEMOCRACY-BUILDING THERE—ARE THE MOST IMPORTANT SIX MONTHS IN U.S. FOREIGN POLICY IN A LONG, LONG TIME."

★ THOMAS FRIEDMAN, *NEW YORK TIMES* COLUMNIST[PS]

The mobile vans that you may have been reading about, it is becoming clear that these vans can have no other purpose than the production of biological weapons.

Colin Powell, U.S. Secretary of State, May 22, 2003[29]

Colin Powell, if you may recall, at the UN mentioned the existence of . . . mobile biological laboratories and two of those are now in our custody.

Donald H. Rumsfeld, U.S. Secretary of Defense, May 27, 2003[30]

Already, we've discovered, uh, uh, trailers, uh, that look remarkably similar to what Colin Powell described in his February 5th speech, biological weapons production facilities.

Condoleezza Rice, National Security Advisor, reporting progress in the search for weapons of mass destruction in Iraq, June 8, 2003[31]

I can assure you that if those biological vans were not biological vans, when I said they were on the 5th of February, on the 6th of February Iraq would have hauled those vans out, put them in front of a press conference, gave them to the UNMOVIC [UN Monitoring, Verification and Inspection Commission] inspectors to try to drive a stake in the heart of my presentation. They did not. The reason they did not is they knew what they were.

Colin Powell, U.S. Secretary of State, June 8, 2003[32]

One item I showed was cartoons of the mobile biological van. They were cartoons, artist's renderings, because we had never seen one of these things, but we had good sourcing on it, excellent sourcing on it. And we knew what it would look like when we found it, so we made those pictures. And I can assure you I didn't just throw those pictures up without having quite a bit of confidence. And we waited. And it took a couple of months, and it took until after the war, until we found a van and another van that pretty much matched what we said it would look like. And I think that's a pretty good indication that we were not cooking the books.

Colin Powell, U.S. Secretary of State,
July 10, 2003[33]

IN FACT

On October 2, 2003, David Kay, head of the Iraq Survey Group, a CIA-led team sent to Iraq after the invasion to search for Saddam's WMDs, told a joint congressional committee, "When you look at these two trailers, while [they] had capabilities in many areas, their actual intended use was not for the production of biological weapons. . . . [They] were actually designed to produce hydrogen for weather balloons."[34]

During a visit to Baghdad the previous July, Hamish Killip, a British member of the Iraq Survey Group, had also offered an opinion about the vans. "The equipment was singularly inappropriate for biological weapons," he said. "We were in hysterics over this. You'd have better luck putting a couple of dust bins on the back of the truck and brewing it in there."[35]

DECEMBER 1, 2003

"THE NEXT SIX TO SEVEN MONTHS ARE CRITICAL."

 SENATOR HILLARY RODHAM CLINTON[P6]

Anthrax: "Let's All Take a Deep Breath"

On October 4, 2001, a nation still jittery from the 9/11 attacks learned that a Palm Beach County, Florida, photo editor named Bob Stevens had been hospitalized with inhalation anthrax, a disease that many countries have experimented with for use as a bioweapon and that is so rare that no American cases had been reported for a full twenty-five years.

It appears that this is just an isolated case. There's no evidence of terrorism. . . . So people should not go out and do anything different than what they're doing.

Tommy Thompson, U.S. Secretary of Health and Human Services, speaking at a White House news conference, October 4, 2001[36]

IN FACT

Secretary Thompson's reassurances notwithstanding, it became clear almost immediately that the incident was neither isolated nor unrelated to terrorism. Indeed, a series of letters containing potentially deadly anthrax spores were being received at newspaper, broadcasting, and government offices around the United States. Among those to whom the letters were addressed were NBC news anchor Tom Brokaw and Democratic senators Tom Daschle and Patrick Leahy. Both the letters sent to the senators featured the words "Death to America, Death to Israel, Allah is Great." All told, twenty-two people became ill, and five of them died.

American investigators probing anthrax outbreaks in Florida and New York . . . have named Iraq as prime suspect as the source of the deadly spores. . . . According to sources in the Bush administration, investigators are talking to Egyptian authorities who say members of the al-Qaeda network, detained and interrogated in Cairo, had obtained phials of anthrax [from an Iraqi] in the Czech Republic.

The Observer (London), October 14, 2001[37]

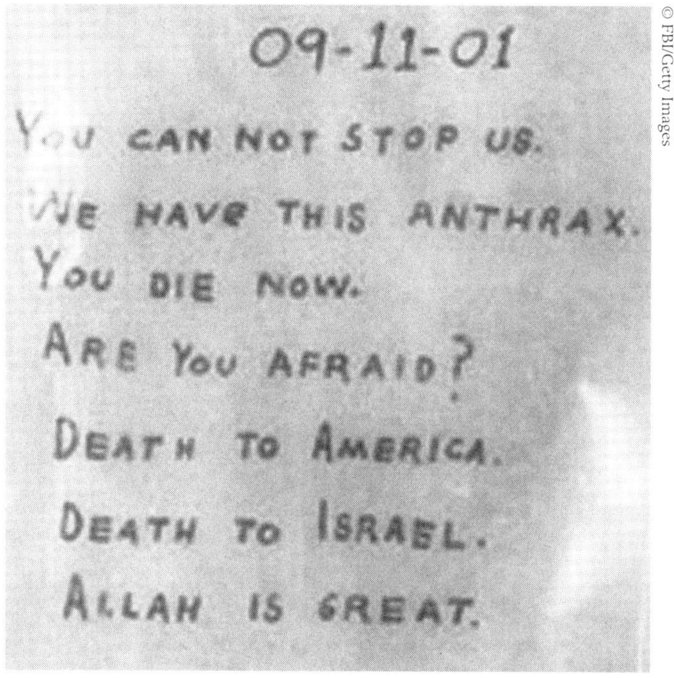

© FBI/Getty Images

A facsimile of the handwritten message accompanying the anthrax mailed to Senator Tom Daschle in October 2001.

It's possible that many months ago anthrax, a small quantity of it, was handed over in Prague to [9/11 ringleader] Mohamed Atta.

Richard Butler, former Chairman of the UN Iraq weapons inspection effort (UNSCOM), suggesting a link between Iraq, Al Qaeda, and recent anthrax-by-mail attacks in the United States, October 15, 2001[38]

DECEMBER 16, 2003

"THE SITUATION IN IRAQ APPEARS TO BE LOOKING UP?"

★ MAX BOOT, *LOS ANGELES TIMES* COLUMNIST[P7]

I don't put it past Iraq. We know they have been working on this kind of terror weapon, and we keep a very close eye on them. . . . [But] frankly . . . it would be wise for all of us to take a deep breath and let our investigative agencies figure this out before we go rushing in front of television sets to present these rumors . . . and get the country all excited.

Colin Powell, U.S. Secretary of State, October 21, 2001[39]

America is now getting a taste of the havoc biological weapons can wreak. . . . Such a weapon in the hands of a thug is untenable . . . Saddam and his bloody bugs have to go.

Richard Cohen, *The Washington Post*, October 18, 2001[40]

According to Israeli security sources . . . Atta was handed a vacuum flask of anthrax by his Iraqi contact. From Prague, it is believed Atta flew to Newark. From New Jersey, letters laced with anthrax were sent to broadcasters and politicians in New York.

The Times (London), citing a report in the previous day's edition of the German mass-circulation newspaper *Bild*, October 27, 2001[41]

Saddam has enormous quantities of anthrax. In 1995 before U.N. weapons inspectors were expelled from Iraq, they estimated that he had produced . . . enough to kill every person on earth. . . . Saddam knows that the only way he can survive is if others are blamed for the terrorist attacks on America, at least for now. So initial attacks have been small, but much larger attacks are being planned.

Laurie Mylroie, former Pentagon Defense Consultant and Adjunct Fellow of the American Enterprise Institute, interviewed by *NewsMax,* October 29, 2001[42]

NewsMax followed up Mylroie's remarks by asking her how, if she were president of the United States, she would respond to this threat:

First, I'd do everything possible to minimize casualties and risk. I'd ground all crop dusters and round up everyone who might be responsible. Then I'd go after Iraq. I'd bomb the Special Republican Guard that keeps Saddam in power. I'd bomb his 40 palaces and anyplace else he might be. I'd work with the Iraqi resistance to get rid of his corrupt regime. I'd do whatever it takes to put Saddam in his grave. . . . The State Department doesn't want to do it. Bush doesn't want to do it. But we have to do it, and the sooner the better. The only alternative is to wait until Saddam launches a massive biological or nuclear attack on the U.S. that kills millions.

Laurie Mylroie, October 29, 2001[43]

JANUARY 4, 2004

"THE IMPORTANT THING IS TO REALIZE WE ARE ABOUT TO ENTER INTO A VERY CRITICAL SIX MONTHS."

☆ TONY BLAIR, PRIME MINISTER OF GREAT BRITAIN[P8]

The anthrax in the mail turns out to be weapons-grade, finely ground and with electrostatic charges eliminated to facilitate aerial spread. . . . Similarly, the Czech interior minister confirms that Mohamed Atta met with a ranking Iraqi spy on his route to the United States. This should be a scales-from-the-eyes moment. . . . Yes, other scenarios are conceivable, but why ignore the elephant standing in the corner of the room? To wit, Saddam Hussein.

Robert L. Bartley, Pulitzer Prize–winning editorial page director of *The Wall Street Journal*, October 29, 2001[44]

Was someone unrelated to bin Laden's people ready to mail anthrax spores immediately after Sept. 11 just for the fun and chaos of it? . . . We can try to close our eyes to the truth about Iraq in the service of the "coalition" and "patience." But we cannot win a real war on terrorism with our eyes closed.

William Kristol, *The Washington Post*, October 30, 2001[45]

IN FACT

As of fall 2007, the mystery of who mailed the anthrax remains unsolved. But, since late 2001, FBI investigators have consistently leaned toward the theory that the perpetrator was a male domestic loner with a knowledge of New Jersey (all the letters were mailed from Princeton) and at least limited experience working with laboratory equipment.

THE LOYAL OPPOSITION SPEAKS

Saddam Hussein in effect has thumbed his nose at the world community. The President is approaching this in the right fashion.

Senator Harry Reid (D-NV), September 18, 2002[46]

We know that [Saddam] has stored secret supplies of biological and chemical weapons throughout his country.

Former Vice President Al Gore, September 23, 2002[47]

We have known for many years that Saddam Hussein is seeking and developing weapons of mass destruction.

Senator Edward Kennedy (D-MA), September 27, 2003[48]

Saddam Hussein certainly has chemical and biological weapons. There's no question about that.

Representative Nancy Pelosi (D-CA), November 17, 2002[49]

I don't think there can be any question about Saddam's conduct. He has systematically violated, over the course of the past 11 years, every significant UN resolution that has demanded that he disarm and destroy his chemical and biological weapons, and any nuclear capacity. This he has refused to do. He lies and cheats; he snubs the mandate and authority of international weapons inspectors; and he games the system to keep buying time against enforcement of the just and legitimate demands of the United Nations, the Security Council, the United States and our allies. Those are simply the facts.

Representative Henry Waxman (D-CA), addressing the U.S. Senate, October 10, 2002[50]

MARCH 24, 2004

"IRAQ NOW FACES A CRITICAL MOMENT."

★ PRESIDENT GEORGE W. BUSH[P9]

In the four years since the inspectors left, intelligence reports show that Saddam Hussein has worked to rebuild his chemical and biological weapons stock, his missile delivery capability, and his nuclear program. He has also given aid, comfort, and sanctuary to terrorists, including Al Qaeda members.... It is clear ... that if left unchecked, Saddam Hussein will continue to increase his capacity to wage biological and chemical warfare, and will keep trying to develop nuclear weapons.

Senator Hillary Rodham Clinton (D-NY), addressing the U.S. Senate in support of a resolution to authorize the use of U.S. armed forces against Iraq, October 10, 2002[51]

Without question, we need to disarm Saddam Hussein. He is a brutal, murderous dictator, leading an oppressive regime.... He presents a particularly grievous threat because he is so consistently prone to miscalculation.... And now he is miscalculating America's response to his continued deceit and his consistent grasp for weapons of mass destruction.

Senator John Kerry (D-MA), January 23, 2003[52]

I support the president's efforts to disarm Saddam Hussein. I think he was right on in his speech tonight.

Senator Evan Bayh (D-IN), commenting on President George W. Bush's televised ultimatum to Saddam Hussein, March 17, 2003[53]

THE MISSING LINK

I think Iraq is, actually, the big unspoken elephant in the room today. There's a fair amount of evidence that Iraq had very close associations with Osama bin Laden in the past.

William Kristol, Editor of *The Weekly Standard*, interviewed on National Public Radio's *All Things Considered* the day after the 9/11 attacks, September 12, 2001

I don't think there's any doubt about . . . contacts between the people who became the hideous terrorists here and Iraqi intelligence months ago.

Richard Butler, former Chairman of the UN Iraq weapons inspection effort (UNSCOM), October 15, 2001[54]

Did Saddam have a direct hand in the attacks on America that began on Sept. 11? The evidence at our disposal is circumstantial but suggestive. We do know that he has not just the motive and malevolence, but the means. And we also know that Iraqi intelligence officials have met at critical times with members of the al Qaeda network.

Senator Joe Lieberman (D-CT), October 29, 2001[55]

Bin Laden and Hussein work together. Bin Laden provides the ideology, he recruits the foot soldiers, and he provides a smokescreen. Iraqi intelligence provides the direction and training for the terrorism.

Laurie Mylroie, former Pentagon Defense Consultant and Adjunct Fellow of the American Enterprise Institute, interviewed on *CNN Chatroom*, October 29, 2001[56]

We've learned that Iraq has trained al-Qaida members in bomb-making and poisons and deadly gases. And we know that after September 11 Saddam Hussein's regime gleefully celebrated the terrorist attacks on America.

President George W. Bush, speech at the Cincinnati Museum Center, October 7, 2002[57]

APRIL 8, 2004

"[DESPITE] THE HORRIFIC BARBARISM IN FALLUJAH AND THE GUN-TOTING AND KILLING BY THE SHIITES, THE UNITED STATES IS EVER SO STEADILY ESTABLISHING A CONSENSUAL GOVERNMENT."

★ VICTOR DAVIS HANSON, *NATIONAL REVIEW ONLINE* COLUMNIST[P10]

THE PRESIDENT PROVIDES NEW INSIGHT INTO SADDAM'S LINKS TO TERRORISM

The war on terror involves Saddam Hussein because of the nature of Saddam Hussein, the history of Saddam Hussein, and his willingness to terrorize himself.

President George W. Bush, during a speech about Medicare Reform in Grand Rapids, Michigan, January 29, 2003[58]

What I want to bring to your attention today is the . . . sinister nexus between Iraq and the Al Qaeda terrorist network, a nexus that combines classic terrorist organizations and modern methods of murder.

Colin Powell, U.S. Secretary of State, address to the UN Security Council, February 5, 2003[59]

Secretary Powell . . . presented, not opinions, not conjecture, but facts demonstrating Iraq's . . . ties to terrorist networks, including al-Qaeda-affiliated cells operating in Baghdad. . . . The threat is there to see.

Donald H. Rumsfeld, U.S. Secretary of Defense, address to the Munich Conference on European Security Policy, February 8, 2003[60]

There are al Qaeda terrorists who operate in and out of Iraq. Secretary Powell was quite explicit about some of them in his speech to the United Nations. That by itself would be justification for military action. Not as openly as they did in Afghanistan, for obvious reasons. Saddam is not quite as foolish as the Taliban. But the support for terrorism is clear-cut. The support for al Qaeda is clear-cut.

Paul Wolfowitz, U.S. Deputy Secretary of Defense, March 5, 2003[61]

We know that [Saddam] has a long-standing relationship with various terrorist groups, including the al-Qaeda organization.

Vice President Dick Cheney, March 16, 2003[62]

We haven't really had the time yet to pore through all those records in Baghdad. We'll find ample evidence confirming the link, that is the connection if you will between al Qaida and the Iraqi intelligence services. They have worked together on a number of occasions.

Vice President Dick Cheney, interview, *Rocky Mountain News*, January 10, 2004[63]

You know, one of the hardest parts of my job is to connect Iraq to the war on terror.

President George W. Bush, September 6, 2006[64]

MAY 14, 2004

"THE AMAZING THING REMAINS NOT THAT WE HAVE SEEN A DEPRESSING YEAR OF CHAOS, BUT THAT THE FORCES OF CHANGE ARE STILL IN OUR FAVOR."

★ VICTOR DAVIS HANSON, *NATIONAL REVIEW ONLINE* COLUMNIST[P11]

IN FACT

As James Risen of *The New York Times* reported on January 14, 2004, Saddam Hussein "warned his Iraqi supporters to be wary of joining forces with foreign Arab fighters entering Iraq to battle American troops, according to a document found with the former Iraqi leader when he was captured." Additionally, CIA interrogators "elicited from the top Qaeda officials in custody" that, before the American-led invasion, Osama bin Laden had rejected entreaties from some of his lieutenants to work jointly with Mr. Hussein. It seems as if the only connection between Al Qaeda and Hussein's Ba'ath Party was mutual disdain.[65]

EPISTEMOLOGY 101 WITH DONALD RUMSFELD

At a Defense Department news briefing on February 13, 2002, a reporter challenged the Bush administration's claims about Saddam's associations with Al Qaeda, noting, "There are reports that there is no evidence of a direct link between Baghdad and some of these terrorist organizations." The charge elicited the following comment from Secretary of Defense Donald Rumsfeld:

> Reports that say that something hasn't happened are always interesting to me, because as we know, there are known knowns; there are things we know we know. We also know there are known unknowns; that is to say we know there are some things we do not know. But there are also unknown unknowns—the ones we don't know we don't know.[66]

MOHAMMED ATTA'S TRIP TO PRAGUE: AN "UNDISPUTED FACT"

The undisputed fact connecting Iraq's Saddam Hussein to the Sept. 11 attacks is that Mohamed Atta, who died at the controls of an airliner-missile, flew from Florida to Prague to meet on April 8 of this year with Ahmed Al-Ani, the Iraqi consul.

William Safire, *The New York Times*, November 12, 2001[67]

It's been pretty well confirmed that [Atta] did go to Prague and he did meet with a senior official of the Iraqi intelligence service in Czechoslovakia last April.

Vice President Dick Cheney, December 9, 2001[68]

We know that Mohamed Atta, the ringleader of September 11th, went out of his way to meet with an Iraqi intelligence official a few months before he flew a plane into the WTC.

Robert Kagan and William Kristol, contributor to and editor of *The Weekly Standard*, January 21, 2002[69]

Several workers at Prague airport identified Atta following 9/11 and remember him traveling with his brother Farhan Atta.

Slide prepared by the "Iraqi Intelligence Cell" under the direction of Douglas Feith, U.S. Undersecretary of Defense for Policy, presented at White House briefing, September 16, 2002[70]

MAY 18, 2004

"IT'S HARD WORK IN IRAQ. OUR EFFORTS ARE APPROACHING A CRUCIAL MOMENT."

★ PRESIDENT GEORGE W. BUSH[P12]

IN FACT

By the time Feith's briefers presented this information, the CIA and the FBI had already concluded that the Prague meeting had never taken place. In fact, Atta did not even have a brother. All this led one member of the 9/11 Commission to remark, "Are you sure Elvis wasn't there also?"[71]

AN IMMINENT THREAT?

We have no time to lose. Saddam must be removed from office. Every day that goes by is a day in which we are exposed to dangers on a far larger scale than the tragedy of September 11.

Richard Perle, Chairman of the Pentagon's Defense Policy Board, July 11, 2002[72]

Some have argued that the nuclear threat from Iraq is not imminent—that Saddam is at least 5–7 years away from having nuclear weapons. I would not be so certain. And we should be just as concerned about the immediate threat from biological weapons. Iraq has these weapons.

Donald H. Rumsfeld, U.S. Secretary of Defense, September 18, 2002[73]

The danger to our country is grave. . . . According to the British government, the Iraqi regime could launch a biological or chemical attack in as little as 45 minutes after the orders were given.

President George W. Bush, September 26, 2002[74]

WOLF BLITZER: Is [Saddam] an imminent threat to U.S. interests, either in that part of the world or to Americans right here at home?

DAN BARTLETT: Well, of course he is.

Dan Bartlett, White House Communications Director, January 26, 2003[75]

I think some in the media have chosen to use the word "imminent." Those were not words we used.

Scott McClellan, White House Press Secretary, rejecting intimations by reporters that the Bush administration had portrayed Saddam as an imminent threat in order to justify an invasion of Iraq, January 27, 2004[76]

POSTSCRIPT: ON THE IMMINENCY OF NONIMMINENCY

I believe it is essential that when we see a threat, we deal with those threats before they become imminent. It's too late if they become imminent.

President George W. Bush, February 8, 2004[77]

UNIMPEACHABLE SOURCES: THE WORLD ACCORDING TO JUDITH MILLER

Judith Miller, a Pulitzer Prize–winning *New York Times* correspondent with special expertise on WMDs in Iraq, had unique lines of communication to members and former members of the Iraqi military and political establishment, principally Ahmed Chalabi, who had last set foot in Iraq forty-seven years before.

Chalabi left Iraq with his family when he was twelve years old and had spent most of the rest of his life living in the United States and England, and in Jordan, where he was indicted for bank fraud.

MAY 25, 2004

"[IN TERMS OF THE TIMELINE FOR THE PRESENCE OF MULTINATIONAL FORCES,] I THINK IT WILL BE A QUESTION OF MONTHS RATHER THAN YEARS."

★ ALI ALLAWI, DEFENSE MINISTER FOR IRAQ[P13]

In 1992, he was installed as head of the Iraqi National Congress (INC), an umbrella group of Iraqi exiles.[78]

Based largely on the extraordinary sources made available to her by Chalabi, abetted by tips offered her by contacts she had developed at the highest levels of the executive branch, Miller scored a series of scoops that no other journalist was able to match. Here is a small sampling:

JUDITH MILLER

Iraq has stepped up its quest for nuclear weapons and has embarked on a worldwide hunt for materials to make an atomic bomb.

Judith Miller and Michael Gordon, *The New York Times,* September 8, 2002[79]

In the last 14 months, Iraq has sought to buy thousands of specially designed aluminum tubes . . . intended as components of centrifuges to enrich uranium.

Judith Miller and Michael Gordon, *The New York Times,* September 8, 2002[80]

The dominant view [is] that the tubes [are] for Iraq's nuclear program . . . only one of several indications that Iraq [is] reconstituting and expanding its effort to acquire nuclear weapons.

Judith Miller and Michael Gordon, *The New York Times,* September 13, 2002[81]

IN FACT

The Iraq Survey Group, in a comprehensive report delivered on September 30, 2004, to the CIA, determined that the best explanation for the tubes' use was to produce conventional 81mm rockets.

[See also "Aluminum Tubes," p. 9.]

Iraq obtained a particularly virulent strain of smallpox from a Russian scientist, Nelja N. Maltseva, a virologist who worked for more than 30 years at the Research Institute for Viral Preparations in Moscow.

Judith Miller, *The New York Times,* December 2, 2002[82]

IN FACT

Miller's story was based, in her own words, on "an informant whose identity has not been disclosed." No evidence has been found in Iraq to support the existence of the smallpox program she described.

An Iraqi defector [Adnan Ihsan Saeed al-Haideri] who described himself as a civil engineer said he personally worked on renovations of secret facilities for biological, chemical and nuclear weapons in underground wells, private villas and under the Saddam Hussein Hospital in Baghdad as recently as a year ago. . . . Government experts said yesterday that . . . his information seemed reliable and significant. The interview with Mr. Saeed was arranged by the Iraqi National Congress, the main Iraqi opposition group, which seeks the overthrow of Mr. Hussein. If verified, Mr. Saeed's allegations would provide ammunition to officials within the Bush administration who have been arguing that Mr. Hussein should be driven from power partly because of his unwillingness to stop making weapons of mass destruction, despite his pledges to do so.

Judith Miller, *The New York Times,* December 20, 2001[83]

JUNE 1, 2004

"IT'S THE BEGINNING OF THE END OF THE BAD NEWS."

★ CHARLES KRAUTHAMMER, SYNDICATED COLUMNIST[P14]

IN FACT

When members of the Iraq Survey Group took Saeed back to Iraq after the invasion, Jonathan S. Landay of Knight-Ridder newspapers reported in 2004, he "was unable to identify a single site associated with illegal weapons."[84]

Iraq has ordered large quantities of a drug that can be used to counter the effects of nerve gas, mainly from suppliers in Turkey.

Judith Miller, *The New York Times,* November 12, 2002[85]

Iraq destroyed chemical weapons and biological warfare equipment only days before the war began.

Judith Miller, *The New York Times,* April 21, 2003[86]

IN FACT

Judith Miller attributed the information in this story, which she wrote while embedded with a unit in Iraq that was searching for WMDs, to a man in a baseball cap whom she was "permitted to see . . . from a distance at the sites where he said that material from the arms program was buried." Nothing was ever heard about this man—or the illegal weapons to which he had allegedly led the U.S. military—again.

My job was not to collect information and analyze it independently, my job was to tell readers of the *New York Times* **. . . what people inside the government, . . . who were not supposed to talk to me, were saying.**

Judith Miller, appearing on National Public Radio's *The Connection*, February 3, 2004[87]

I didn't feel that I had anything to apologize for with my WMD coverage. . . . I had done the best I could at the time with the information that was available to me.

Judith Miller, interview, July 13, 2005[88]

[Judith Miller] was caught over and over basically retyping Chalabi without fact checking.

Marc Fisher, *The Washington Post*, January 25, 2007[89]

IN FACT

Subsequently, Judith Miller was subpoenaed by the special prosecutor, Patrick Fitzgerald, who was investigating the leak of the identity of CIA covert agent Valerie Plame. Miller had not written a story about it, but nevertheless, rather than reveal her source, she went to prison. "Having been summoned by the grand jury, I went to jail instead, to protect my source—Mr. Libby," she later wrote.[90]

Eighty-five days thereafter she emerged, saying, "I am leaving jail today because my source has now voluntarily and personally released me from my promise of confidentiality." But her source's counsel, Joseph Tate, claimed he had released her from her promise before she went to jail, a fact disputed by Floyd Abrams, Miller's counsel at the time.[91]

JUNE 3, 2004

"IT MIGHT BE OVER IN A WEEK, IT MIGHT BE OVER IN A MONTH, IT MIGHT BE OVER IN SIX MONTHS, BUT WHAT'S THE RUSH? CAN WE LET THIS PLAY OUT, PLEASE?"

★ THOMAS FRIEDMAN, *NEW YORK TIMES* COLUMNIST[F15]

THE SEARCH FOR A DIPLOMATIC SOLUTION

INSPECTING THE INSPECTORS (OR THE SEARCH FOR ROSIE O'DONNELL'S STRETCH MARKS)

The inspectors are not going to find anything. . . . Because [Saddam} controls the territory and the terms of the inspections, we're never going to find anything of consequence. . . . So he will go on with a clandestine nuclear program. He'll go on with chemical and biological weapons. . . . In the meantime, the illusion that we are accomplishing something with the inspectors is really quite dangerous.

Richard Perle, Chairman of the Defense Policy Board, a Pentagon advisory group, and former Assistant Secretary of Defense during the Reagan administration, interviewed by James Rubin on PBS's *Wide Angle*, July 11, 2002[92]

Scott Ritter [former chief UN weapons inspector] . . . is over there playing footsie with Saddam Hussein.

Michael Smerconish, Philadelphia radio talk show host and newspaper columnist, appearing as guest host of *CNN Talkback Live*, September 19, 2002[93]

UN weapons inspectors are being seriously deceived. . . . It reminds me of the way the Nazis hoodwinked Red Cross officials inspecting the concentration camp at Theresienstadt in 1944.

Richard Perle, "Take Out Saddam—It's the Only Way," *News of the World*, February 23, 2003

Did it ever occur to Blix that you can't see a smoking gun if it is hidden?

Janet Parshall, nationally syndicated radio network talk-show host, explaining in an interview in *Insight on the News* why UN inspectors in Iraq, led by Hans Blix, had yet to find any WMDs, February 17, 2003

[Hans Blix] couldn't find a stretch mark on Rosie O'Donnell.

Laura Ingraham, nationally syndicated radio host, on the *Imus in the Morning* radio program, discussing UN inspectors' failure to find weapons of mass destruction in Iraq, February 23, 2003[94]

CHEESE-EATING SURRENDER MONKEYS

After France made it clear that it intended to veto a UN resolution that would have explicitly authorized the use of force to disarm Saddam Hussein, American politicians and journalists responded quickly and forcefully. Among the terms that gained currency for describing the French was "cheese-eating surrender monkeys," a reference to France's behavior during the Second World War that had first been used by Groundskeeper Willie on *The Simpsons* TV show and was quickly adopted as a rallying cry by *National Review Online* editor Jonah Goldberg.

JUNE 25, 2004

"U.S. GENERAL (CASEY) SAYS NEXT FEW MONTHS KEY TO IRAQ'S FUTURE"

 *BOSTON GLOBE* HEADLINE[P16]

Since the inception of this column, I have been adhering to Al Bundy's immortal fatwah, "It is good to hate the French." I have made *The Simpsons*–derived epithet "Cheese-Eating Surrender Monkeys" an accepted term in official diplomatic channels around the globe. OK, maybe not, but if you ever do hear Kofi Annan refer to the Cheese-Eating Surrender Monkeys, I will deserve much of the credit.

Jonah Goldberg, *National Review Online*, April 6, 2001[95]

The gist of the disagreement between Europe and America is the 'peens think they achieved lasting peace through endless conversations in Swiss hotels with bottles of bubbly water and plates of runny cheese scattered about the table.

Jonah Goldberg, *National Review Online*, July 31, 2002[96]

IN FACT

Goldberg was far from alone. On March 11, 2003, Republican congressmen Bob Ney (R-OH) and Walter Jones (R-NC) held a press conference to trumpet their success in having the word *French* expunged from the menu in the three House cafeterias. Hence, they decreed, "French fries" would be called "Freedom fries" and "French toast" would become "Freedom toast."

This action today is a small, but symbolic effort to show the strong displeasure of many on Capitol Hill with the actions of our so-called ally, France.

Representative Bob Ney, Chairman of the House Administration Committee, March 11, 2003[97]

FREEDOM FRIES

I represent a district with multiple military bases that have deployed thousands of troops. As I've watched these men and women wave good-bye to their loved ones, I am reminded of the deep love they have for the freedom of this nation and their desire to fight for the freedom of those who are oppressed overseas. Watching France's self-serving politics of passive aggression in this effort has discouraged me more than I can say.

Representative Walter Jones, March 11, 2003[98]

JULY 22, 2004

"THE NEXT FEW MONTHS WILL BE CRITICAL."

★ SENATOR RICHARD G. LUGAR[P17]

AXIS OF WEASEL—GERMANY AND FRANCE WIMP OUT ON IRAQ

Front-page headline, *New York Post*, January 24, 2003

Where are the French now, as Americans prepare to put their soldiers on the line to fight today's Hitler, Saddam Hussein? Talking appeasement. Wimping out. How can they have forgotten?

Steve Dunleavy, *New York Post*, February 10, 2003[99]

One of the reasons why France and Germany [are] a little bit cautious here is because they're afraid folks are going to go into Iraq and they're going to see stamped "made in Germany" or "made in France" on some of [Saddam's weapons of mass destruction], and they don't want that to be found.

Janet Parshall, nationally syndicated radio talk-show host, February 14, 2003[100]

We are tempted to comment, in these last days before the war, on the U.N., and the French, and the Democrats. But the war itself will clarify who was right and who was wrong about weapons of mass destruction. It will reveal the aspirations of the people of Iraq, and expose the truth about Saddam's regime. . . . History and reality are about to weigh in, and we are inclined simply to let them render their verdicts.

William Kristol, *The Weekly Standard* editor, March 17, 2003[101]

WAR OR PEACE? "THE DECIDER HAS YET TO DECIDE"

The president has not decided on a military option. . . . Nobody wants war as a first resort. . . . Nobody is looking for a war if it can be avoided.

Colin Powell, U.S. Secretary of State, "U.S. Policy toward Iraq: Hearing before the U.S. House Committee on International Relations," September 19, 2002[102]

Hopefully, we can do this peacefully—don't get me wrong. War is not my first choice . . . it's my last choice.

President George W. Bush, November 7, 2002[103]

SEPTEMBER 26, 2004

"NOW, HOWEVER, 18 MONTHS AFTER ENTERING, I SEE TANGIBLE PROGRESS. IRAQI SECURITY ELEMENTS ARE BEING REBUILT FROM THE GROUND UP."

 GENERAL DAVID PETRAEUS[P18]

This is our attempt to work with the world community to create peace. And the best way for peace is for Mr. Saddam Hussein to disarm. It's up to him to make his decision.

President George W. Bush, commenting to reporters about the UN inspection process in Iraq, December 4, 2002[104]

[Bush is] not particularly interested in going to war, I don't believe. He wants to see compliance.

General George Harrison, CNN military analyst, December 21, 2002[105]

You said we're headed to war in Iraq—I don't know why you say that. I hope we're not headed to war in Iraq. I'm the person who gets to decide, not you.

President George W. Bush, remarks on Iraq and North Korea, December 31, 2002[106]

But Saddam Hussein is—he's treated the demands of the world as a joke up to now, and it was his choice to make. He's the person who gets to decide war and peace.

President George W. Bush, February 7, 2003[107]

I've not made up my mind about military action.

President George W. Bush, address to the nation, March 6, 2003[108]

We are doing everything we can to avoid war in Iraq.

President George W. Bush, radio address, March 8, 2003[109]

Should Saddam Hussein choose confrontation, the American people can know that every measure has been taken to avoid war, and every measure will be taken to win it.

President George W. Bush, address to the nation, March 17, 2003

The American people can take comfort in knowing that their country has done everything humanly possible to avoid war and to secure Iraq's peaceful disarmament.

Donald H. Rumsfeld, U.S. Secretary of Defense, March 20, 2003[110]

IN FACT

On May 1, 2005, *The Times* of London published the hitherto secret minutes of a July 23, 2002, meeting between British Prime Minister Tony Blair and several other government officials, including Richard Dearlove, the British head of foreign intelligence, who had just returned to London after consultations with representatives of the U.S. intelligence community in Washington.

"Military action was now seen as inevitable," the minutes—which became known as the "Downing Street Memo"—cited Dearlove as reporting. "Bush wanted to remove Saddam, through military action, justified by the conjunction of terrorism and WMD. But the intelligence and facts were being fixed around the policy."[111]

OCTOBER 3, 2004

"WHAT WE'RE GONNA FIND OUT. . . IN THE NEXT SIX TO NINE MONTHS IS WHETHER WE HAVE LIBERATED A COUNTRY OR UNCORKED A CIVIL WAR."

★ THOMAS FRIEDMAN, *THE NEW YORK TIMES* COLUMNIST[P19]

VOLUME II

THEIR FINEST

AMERICA READIES

HOUR

ITSELF TO FREE THE IRAQI PEOPLE

CAKEWALK!

I believe demolishing Hussein's military power and liberating Iraq would be a cakewalk.

Kenneth Adelman, member of the Pentagon's Defense Policy Board, February 13, 2002[1]

Support for Saddam, including within his military organization, will collapse after the first whiff of gunpowder.

Richard Perle, Chairman of the Pentagon's Defense Policy Board, July 11, 2002[2]

Desert Storm II would be a walk in the park. . . . The case for "regime change" boils down to the huge benefits and modest costs of liberating Iraq.

Kenneth Adelman, member of the Pentagon's Defense Policy Board, August 29, 2002[3]

ADELMAN'S CAKEWALK

Having defeated and then occupied Iraq, democratizing the country should not be too tall an order for the world's sole superpower.

William Kristol, *Weekly Standard* editor, and Lawrence F. Kaplan, *New Republic* senior editor, February 24, 2003[4]

[See also "How Long Will It Last?," page 56.]

HOW MANY TROOPS WILL BE NEEDED?

I would be surprised if we need anything like the 200,000 figure that is sometimes discussed in the press. A much smaller force, principally special operations forces, but backed up by some regular units, should be sufficient.

Richard Perle, Chairman of the Pentagon's Defense Policy Board, July 11, 2002[5]

I don't believe that anything like a long-term commitment of 150,000 Americans would be necessary.

Richard Perle, Chairman of the Pentagon's Defense Policy Board, speaking at a conference on "Post-Saddam Iraq" sponsored by the American Enterprise Institute, October 3, 2002[6]

I would say that what's been mobilized to this point—something on the order of several hundred thousand soldiers are probably, you know, a figure that would be required.

General Eric Shinseki, testimony before the Senate Armed Services Committee, February 25, 2003[7]

The idea that it would take several hundred thousand U.S. forces, I think, is far from the mark.

Donald H. Rumsfeld, U.S. Secretary of Defense,
February 27, 2003[8]

I am reasonably certain that they will greet us as liberators, and that will help us keep [troop] requirements down. . . . We can say with reasonable confidence that the notion of hundreds of thousands of American troops is way off the mark . . . wildly off the mark.

Paul Wolfowitz, U.S. Deputy Secretary of Defense,
testifying before the House Budget Committee,
February 27, 2003[9]

It's hard to conceive that it would take more forces to provide stability in post-Saddam Iraq than it would take to conduct the war itself and to secure the surrender of Saddam's security forces and his army. Hard to imagine.

Paul Wolfowitz, U.S. Deputy Secretary of Defense,
testifying before the House Budget Committee,
February 27, 2003[10]

NOVEMBER 28, 2004

"IMPROV TIME IS OVER. THIS IS CRUNCH TIME. IRAQ WILL BE WON OR LOST IN THE NEXT FEW MONTHS. BUT IT WON'T BE WON WITH HIGH RHETORIC. IT WILL BE WON ON THE GROUND IN A WAR OVER THE LAST MILE."

★ THOMAS FRIEDMAN, *NEW YORK TIMES* COLUMNIST[P20]

If our commanders on the ground say we need more troops, I will send them.

But our commanders tell me they have the number of troops they need to do their job. Sending more Americans would undermine our strategy of encouraging Iraqis to take the lead in this fight.

And sending more Americans would suggest that we intend to stay forever, when we are, in fact, working for the day when Iraq can defend itself and we can leave.

President George W. Bush, June 28, 2005[11]

The debate over troop levels will rage for years; it is . . . beside the point.

Rich Lowry, syndicated columnist, April 19, 2006[12]

POSTSCRIPT: WHAT ABOUT CASUALTIES?

Oh, no, we're not going to have any casualties.

President George W. Bush, response attributed to him by the Reverend Pat Robertson, when Robertson warned the President to prepare the nation for "heavy casualties" in the event of an Iraq War, March 2003[13]

Robertson, who recounted this exchange during an October 19, 2004, interview on CNN, went on to note that, while Bush's response turned out to be a mistake, God has blessed the President anyhow.

Why should we hear about body bags and deaths. Oh, I mean, it's not relevant. So why should I waste my beautiful mind on something like that?

Barbara Bush, former First Lady (and the current president's mother), on *Good Morning America,* March 18, 2003[14]

I think the level of casualties is secondary. . . . [A]ll the great scholars who have studied American character have come to the conclusion that we are a warlike people and that we love war. . . . What we hate is not casualties but losing.

Michael Ledeen, Freedom Scholar, the American Enterprise Institute, March 25, 2003[15]

A BURNING QUESTION: WHAT'S OIL GOT TO DO WITH IT?

In the Middle East and Southwest Asia, our overall objective is to remain the predominant outside power in the region and preserve U.S. and Western access to the region's oil.

Paul Wolfowitz, U.S. Undersecretary of Defense for Policy, and I. Lewis "Scooter" Libby, Deputy Undersecretary of Defense for Policy, under U.S. Secretary of Defense Dick Cheney, February 18, 1992[16]

The fabulous—and they are fabulous—oil resources of Iraq . . . will be ultimately in the control of a Government of Free Iraq.

Paul Wolfowitz, Dean of the Paul H. Nitze School of Advanced International Studies at Johns Hopkins University, testimony before the House National Security Committee, September 16, 1998[17]

DECEMBER 9, 2004

"FALLUJAH, A BATTLE THAT MIGHT PROVE A TURNING POINT. . . ."

★ MAX BOOT, *NATIONAL REVIEW ONLINE* COLUMNIST[P21]

Saddam Hussein's main supporters in the Security Council, France and Russia, I think could be expected to follow their commercial noses when they saw—forgive the mixed metaphors—which way the oil wind was blowing.

Paul Wolfowitz, Dean of the Paul H. Nitze School of Advanced International Studies at Johns Hopkins University, testimony before the House National Security Committee, September 16, 1998[18]

American companies will have a big shot at Iraqi oil.

Ahmed Chalabi, leader, Iraqi National Congress, suggesting that, under a post-Saddam, INC-led government, Iraq might abandon current deals with French and Russian oil companies in favor of new ones with U.S. corporations, September 15, 2002[19]

The key issue is oil, and a regime change in Iraq would facilitate an increase in world oil.

Lawrence Lindsey, White House Economic Advisor, explaining why a war in Iraq would drive down world oil prices, September 19, 2002[20]

IN FACT

The average price for a barrel of crude oil during September 2002 was $26.82. By October 31, 2007, the price had nearly quadrupled, to $96.24.

[See also "How Much Will It Cost? A War That Will Pay for Itself!," page 52; and "Why We Fight," page 173.]

We basically feel that [Saddam Hussein] is a threat to our oil supply there.

Bill O'Reilly, American political commentator, January 14, 2003[21]

GET READY FOR "THE WORLD'S BIGGEST OIL BONANZA"!

The world's biggest oil bonanza in recent memory may be just around the corner, giving U.S. oil companies huge profits and American consumers cheap gasoline for decades to come. And it all may come courtesy of a war with Iraq.

Robert Collier, "Oil Firms Wait as Iraq Crisis Unfolds," San Francisco Chronicle, *September 29, 2002*

IN FACT

In March 2003, just before the invasion, Iraq was producing 2.5 million barrels of oil per day. Once the war began, oil production fell off dramatically; two years later, it had recovered to only 2 million barrels per day. During 2005, as a result of repeated sabotage by insurgents and poor project management, production fell to 1.1 million barrels per day, the lowest output since American and British troops arrived in Iraq.

The United States is not interested in the oil in that region from Iraq. That's just utter nonsense.

Donald H. Rumsfeld, U.S. Secretary of Defense, interview with Al Jazeera TV, February 25, 2003[22]

FEBRUARY 22, 2005

"THE GOVERNMENT BELIEVES THAT IRAQ IS VERY MUCH AT A TILTING POINT."

★ JOHN HOWARD, AUSTRALIAN PRIME MINISTER[P22]

The president or no one else ever said that this war was going to result in cheaper gas prices.

Dan Bartlett, counselor to President George W. Bush, April 19, 2006[23]

I am saddened that it is politically inconvenient to acknowledge what everyone knows, the Iraq war is largely about oil.

Alan Greenspan, former Chairman of the U.S. Federal Reserve Board of Governors, September 2007[24]

HOW MUCH WILL IT COST? A WAR THAT WILL PAY FOR ITSELF!

Iraq is a very wealthy country. Enormous oil reserves. They can finance, largely finance the reconstruction of their own country. And I have no doubt that they will.

Richard Perle, Chairman of the Pentagon's Defense Policy Board, July 11, 2002[25]

The likely economic effects [of a war in Iraq] would be relatively small. . . . Under every plausible scenario, the negative effect will be quite small relative to the economic benefits.

Lawrence Lindsey, White House Economic Advisor, September 16, 2002[26]

It is unimaginable that the United States would have to contribute hundreds of billions of dollars and highly unlikely that we would have to contribute even tens of billions of dollars.

Kenneth M. Pollack, former Director for Persian Gulf Affairs, U.S. National Security Council, September 2002[27]

The costs of any intervention would be very small.

Glenn Hubbard, White House Economic Advisor, October 4, 2002[28]

When it comes to reconstruction, before we turn to the American taxpayer, we will turn first to the resources of the Iraqi government and the international community.

Donald H. Rumsfeld, U.S. Secretary of Defense, March 27, 2003[29]

There is a lot of money to pay for this that doesn't have to be U.S. taxpayer money, and it starts with the assets of the Iraqi people. We are talking about a country that can really finance its own reconstruction and relatively soon.

Paul Wolfowitz, U.S. Deputy Secretary of Defense, testifying before the Defense Subcommittee of the House Appropriations Committee, March 27, 2003[30]

WOLFIE - IRAQI ASSETS

JUNE 24, 2005

"THIS IS A VERY CRITICAL PERIOD IN IRAQ."

★ SCOTT MCCLELLAN, WHITE HOUSE PRESS SECRETARY[P23]

MORE AMBITIOUS THAN THE MARSHALL PLAN— AT 1/57 THE PRICE!

On April 23, 2003, approximately one month after the U.S. invasion of Iraq, Andrew Natsios, appointed by the Bush administration to run the U.S. Agency for International Development (USAID), was interviewed by Ted Koppel on the ABC news program *Nightline.* Koppel asked Natsios if he agreed that the reconstruction of Iraq, which USAID had been assigned to oversee, would be a "much bigger project" than the administration had implied.

TED KOPPEL:	I understand that more money is expected to be spent on this than was spent on the entire Marshall Plan for the rebuilding of Europe after World War II.
ANDREW NATSIOS:	No, no. This doesn't even compare remotely with the size of the Marshall Plan.
TED KOPPEL:	The Marshall Plan was $97 billion.
ANDREW NATSIOS:	This is $1.7 billion.
TED KOPPEL:	. . . You're not suggesting that the rebuilding of Iraq is gonna be done for $1.7 billion?
ANDREW NATSIOS:	Well, in terms of the American taxpayers' contribution, I do; this is it for the U.S. The rest of the rebuilding of Iraq will be done by other countries who have already made pledges, Britain, Germany, Norway, Japan, Canada, and Iraqi oil revenues, eventually in several years, when it's up and running and there's a new government that's been democratically elected, will finish the job with their own revenues. They're going to get in $20 billion a

year in oil revenues. But the American part of this will be $1.7 billion. We have no plans for any further-on funding for this. . . . That is our plan and that is our intention. And these figures, outlandish figures I've seen, I have to say, there's a little bit of hoopla involved in this.[31]

IN FACT

In the year 2004 alone, U.S. taxpayer funds committed for reconstruction projects in Iraq amounted to more than $9.6 billion. Of this amount, $2.8 billion was awarded by USAID to Bechtel for surveying and repairing Iraq's infrastructure. Natsios had worked with Bechtel before; the company was also the principal contractor on Boston's "Big Dig" project which Natsios had managed before moving on to his USAID assignment.

By October 2007, total U.S. expenditures for Iraq reconstruction had reached more than $45 billion, just under 27 times Natsios's original estimate. The transcript of Natsios's *Nightline* interview was originally posted on the USAID website, but was removed shortly thereafter. Natsios left his USAID assignment in 2005; as of this writing, he is President Bush's special envoy for Darfur.[32]

JUNE 29, 2005

"I THINK THE NEXT NINE MONTHS ARE CRITICAL."

☆ ZALMAY KHALILZAD, U.S. AMBASSADOR TO THE UN[P24]

The United States is committed to helping Iraq recover from the conflict, but Iraq will not require sustained aid.

Mitchell Daniels, Director, White House Office of Management and Budget, April 21, 2003[33]

Iraq has tremendous resources that belong to the Iraqi people. And so there are a variety of means that Iraq has to be able to shoulder much of the burden for their own reconstruction.

Ari Fleischer, White House Press Secretary, February 18, 2003[34]

The allies [have] contributed $14 billion in direct aid.

Dick Cheney, Vice Presidential debate with Democratic candidate John Edwards, October 5, 2004[35]

IN FACT

Actually, only $13 billion was pledged, and, on the date Mr. Cheney spoke, only $1 billion had arrived.[36] As of October 28, 2007, the National Priorities Project estimated that the share of Iraq War costs that had been borne by U.S. taxpayers exceeded $463 billion.

HOW LONG WILL IT LAST? (OR WHEN DO WE GET TO DINE IN THE GASLIGHT DISTRICT?)

Now, it isn't going to be over in 24 hours, but it isn't going to be months either.

Richard Perle, Chairman of the Pentagon's Defense Policy Board and former Assistant Secretary of Defense during the Reagan administration, July 11, 2002[37]

The idea that it's going to be a long, long, long battle of some kind I think is belied by the fact of what happened in 1990. Five days or five weeks or five months, but it certainly isn't going to last any longer than that.

Donald H. Rumsfeld, U.S. Secretary of Defense, November 15, 2002[38]

I will bet you the best dinner in the gaslight district of San Diego that military action will not last more than a week. Are you willing to take that wager?

Bill O'Reilly, American political commentator, January 29, 2003[39]

JULY 18, 2005

"I THINK THE NEXT 18 MONTHS ARE CRUCIAL."

★ RETIRED GENERAL BARRY R. MCCAFFREY[P25]

It is unknowable how long that conflict will last. It could last six days, six weeks. I doubt six months.

Donald H. Rumsfeld, U.S. Secretary of Defense, addressing U.S. troops in Aviano, Italy, February 7, 2003[40]

It won't take weeks. . . . Our military machine will crush Iraq in a matter of days and there's no question that it will.

Bill O'Reilly, American political commentator, February 10, 2003[41]

There is zero question that this military campaign . . . will be reasonably short. . . . Like World War II for about five days.

General Barry R. McCaffrey, national security and terrorism analyst for NBC News, February 18, 2003[42]

The Iraq fight itself is probably going to go very, very fast. The shooting should be over within just a very few days from when it starts.

David Frum, former White House speechwriter, *National Review*, February 24, 2003[43]

Our military superiority is so great—it's far greater than it was in the Gulf War, and the Gulf War was over in 100 hours after we bombed for 43 days. . . . Now they can bomb for a couple of days and then just roll into Baghdad. . . . The odds are there's going to be a war and it's going to be not for very long.

Former President Bill Clinton, March 6, 2003[44]

I think it will go relatively quickly . . . weeks rather than months.

Vice President Dick Cheney, March 16, 2003[45]

"A SHORT, SHORT CONFLICT": GENERAL MYERS SPEAKS

What you'd like to do is have it be a short, short conflict. . . . Iraq is much weaker than they were back in the '90s, when its forces were routed from Kuwait.

General Richard B. Myers, Chairman of the U.S. Joint Chiefs of Staff, at a breakfast with reporters, March 4, 2003[46]

GEN. MYERS

Nobody ever promised a short war. . . . Nobody should have any illusions that this is going to be a quick and easy victory.

General Richard B. Myers, Chairman of the U.S. Joint Chiefs of Staff, interviewed on NBC's Meet the Press, March 30, 2003[47]

OCTOBER 5, 2005

"THE DEVELOPMENTS OVER THE NEXT SEVERAL MONTHS WILL BE CRITICAL."

★ GENERAL DAVID PETRAEUS, FORMER COMMANDER, MULTINATIONAL TRANSITION COMMAND IRAQ AND NATO TRAINING MISSION IRAQ[P26].

AND WAIT . . . THERE'S EVEN MORE GOOD NEWS!

Saddam Hussein . . . will go quickly but not alone: in a parting irony, he will take the U.N. down with him. . . . As we sift the debris, it will be important to preserve, the better to understand, the intellectual wreckage of the liberal conceit of safety through international law administered by international institutions.

Richard Perle, Chairman of the Pentagon's Defense Policy Board, March 21, 2003[48]

POSTSCRIPT: "THE RUSH TO PEACE"

I think that if President Bush is to be faulted for anything in this so far, it's that he's taken much too long to get on with it, much too long.

Michael Ledeen, Freedom Scholar at the American Enterprise Institute, August 19, 2002[49]

The sooner the fighting begins in Iraq, the nearer we are to its imminent end. Which means, in other words, that this "rush to war" should really be seen as the ultimate "rush to peace."

David Frum, former White House speechwriter, February 24, 2003[50]

FRUM-RUSH TO PEACE

AUGUST 18, 2005

"THESE NEXT SIX MONTHS ARE GOING TO BE VERY CRITICAL IN IRAQ."

★ SENATOR CHUCK HAGEL[P27]

VOLUME III

THE GRAND

PART I: The Coalition of the

ALLIANCE

Willing Invades Iraq

THE COALITION OF THE WILLING

Should [Saddam] not disarm, the United States will lead a coalition of the willing to disarm him.

President George W. Bush, remarks during a joint press conference with Czech President Vaclav Havel at Prague Castle, Czech Republic, November 20, 2002[1]

The coalition against Iraq, called Operation Iraqi Freedom, is large and growing. This is not a unilateral action, as [it] is being characterized in the media. Indeed, the coalition in this activity is larger than the coalition that existed during the Gulf War in 1991.

Donald H. Rumsfeld, U.S. Secretary of Defense, U.S. Department of Defense news briefing on the day after the Iraq War began, March 20, 2003[2]

President Bush is assembling a Coalition that has already begun military operations to disarm Iraq of its weapons of mass destruction, and enforce 17 UNSC [UN Security Council] resolutions.

The Coalition will also liberate the Iraqi people from one of the worst tyrants and most brutal regimes on earth. . . .

Forty-nine countries are publicly committed to the Coalition.

Press release posted on the official White House website, March 27, 2003[3]

IN FACT

Among the forty-nine members of the Coalition of the Willing listed by the White House were Tonga, which deployed 49 troops in July 2004 and withdrew them the following December; Moldavia, which deployed 24 troops, 12 of whom were still serving as 2007 began; Armenia, which deployed 46 troops in January 2005; Kazakhstan, which deployed 29 ordnance disposal engineers; Iceland, whose deployed forces, at peak strength, totaled two troops (who have since been withdrawn); Mongolia, whose total annual defense budget is less than the cost of the Tomahawk cruise missiles the United States launched on the opening night of the war; Costa Rica, which contributed no troops at all and asked, in 2004, to no longer be considered a member; Micronesia, the Marshall Islands, and Palau, none of which could have sent troops even if they had wanted to, since they had no military forces; and the Solomon Islands, whose government, after hearing that it had joined the Coalition, insisted it was "completely unaware" of this action on its part and, as a result, wished "to disassociate itself from the report." In fact, the invasion of Iraq was almost totally a U.S. and British operation, with no other country, with the exception of Australia, contributing meaningful numbers of troops.[4]

COALITION UPDATE!

The success of Iraq matters to every civilized nation. We thank the 36 nations that have troops on the ground in Iraq.

President George W. Bush, expressing his gratitude to the countries that had been willing to remain in the Coalition, September 13, 2007[5]

IN FACT

Actually, only twenty-five nations had troops on the ground in Iraq on September 13, 2007. Iceland's one remaining soldier left Iraq the following day, reducing the active membership in the Coalition of the Willing to twenty-four.

"GOD IS GRILLING THEIR STOMACHS IN HELL!"

As the Coalition Army approached, and then entered, Baghdad during the third week of the war, Iraqi Information Minister Mohammed Saeed al-Sahaf appeared on television in a series of briefings to help his people—and the entire world—understand what was happening.

AUGUST 25, 2005

"THESE REMAINING MONTHS ARE REALLY THE MAKE OR BREAK OF IRAQ."

 HOSHYAR ZEBARI, IRAQI FOREIGN MINISTER[P28]

We butchered the force present at the airport. We have retaken the airport! There are no Americans there!

Mohammed Saeed al-Sahaf, Iraqi Information Minister, televised press briefing, April 6, 2003[6]

We have killed most of the coalition infidels, and I think we will finish off the rest soon.

Mohammed Saeed al-Sahaf, Iraqi Information Minister, briefing held outside the Palestine Hotel, Baghdad, April 7, 2003[7]

The infidels are committing suicide by the hundreds on the gates of Baghdad. God has given victory to the soldiers in Iraq. . . . Be assured, Baghdad is safe, protected.

Mohammed Saeed al-Sahaf, Iraqi Information Minister, briefing held outside the Palestine Hotel, Baghdad, April 7, 2003[8]

The Americans are not there. They're not in Baghdad. There are no troops there. Never. They're not at all.

Mohammed Saeed al-Sahaf, Iraqi Information Minister, briefing held outside the Palestine Hotel, Baghdad, April 7, 2003[9]

As Saeed al-Sahaf made this statement, the sound of American machine-gun fire could be plainly heard in the background.

As our leader Saddam Hussein said, "God is grilling their stomachs in hell."

Mohammed Saeed al-Sahaf, Iraqi Information Minister, Iraqi Information Ministry briefing held outside the Palestine Hotel, Baghdad, April 7, 2003[10]

IN FACT

Mohammed Saeed al-Sahaf's news conferences proved so entertaining that the Western press began to refer to him as "Comical Ali" (a reference to Ali Hassan al-Majid, a former Ba'athist defense minister whose alleged role in the gassing of villages in northern Iraq led the Kurds to nickname him "Chemical Ali").

"THE GREATEST HEROINE OF ALL TIME": SAVING PRIVATE LYNCH

During the first week after the invasion of Iraq, on March 23, 2003, the U.S. Army's 507th Ordnance Maintenance Company in Iraq, part of a six-hundred-vehicle convoy, took a wrong turn and accidentally entered the town of Nasiriyah, where it ran into an ambush. When the smoke cleared, eleven soldiers had been killed, another nine were wounded, and nine, including Pfc. Jessica Lynch, were captured. But before news of these events could dent the nation's morale, there came media reports of a spectacular mission to rescue Private Lynch, and of equally spectacular feats of heroism performed by the nineteen-year-old supply clerk herself.

AUGUST 4, 2005

"I HAVE LONG BEEN INVESTED WITH ENSURING THE DEVELOPMENT OF A PEACEFUL, DEMOCRATIC IRAQ. WE ARE NEARING THE RESOLUTION OF THAT PROCESS, AND THE NEXT MONTHS WILL BE CRITICAL."

★ JOHN BOLTON, U.S. AMBASSADOR TO THE UN[P29]

Pfc. Jessica Lynch, rescued Tuesday from an Iraqi hospital, fought fiercely and shot several enemy soldiers after Iraqi forces ambushed the Army's 507th Ordnance Maintenance Company, firing her weapon until she ran out of ammunition. . . . Lynch, a 19-year-old supply clerk, continued firing at the Iraqis even after she sustained multiple gunshot wounds and watched several other soldiers in her unit die around her in fighting 11 days ago.

Susan Schmidt and Vernon Loeb, citing unidentified "U.S. officials," *The Washington Post*, April 3, 2007[11]

[Pfc. Lynch] was fighting to the death. She did not want to be taken alive.

Susan Schmidt and Vernon Loeb, citing an unidentified "U.S. official," *The Washington Post*, April 3, 2007

Lynch was also stabbed when Iraqi forces closed in on her position. . . . Initial intelligence reports indicated that she had been stabbed to death.

Susan Schmidt and Vernon Loeb, *The Washington Post*, April 3, 2007

Lynch's rescue at midnight local time Tuesday was a classic Special Operations raid, with U.S. commandos in Blackhawk helicopters engaging Iraqi forces on their way in and out of the medical compound. . . . Acting on information from CIA operatives . . . a Special Operations force of Navy SEALS, Army Rangers and Air Force combat controllers touched down in blacked-out conditions. An AC-130 gunship, able to fire 1,800 rounds a minute from its 25mm cannon, circled overhead, as did a reconnaissance aircraft providing real-time overhead video imagery of the operation as it unfolded.

Susan Schmidt and Vernon Loeb, *The Washington Post*, April 3, 2007

Jessica was being tortured. That was the urgent word from an Iraqi man who alerted American troops where to find Pfc. Jessica Lynch—and her injuries seem to bear out the allegation. . . .

Her broken bones are a telltale sign of torture, said Amy Waters Yarsinske, a former Navy intelligence officer and an expert on POW and MIA treatment. "It's awfully hard to break both legs and an arm in a truck accident," Yarsinske said.

Maki Becker, "POW Jessica Was Tortured," *New York Daily News*, April 3, 2003

God, what a kid! If we had five of her I don't think we would lose to anybody.

Bobby Knight, legendary Texas Tech basketball coach, expounding on Jessica Lynch's heroism after his team defeated Minnesota in a National Invitation Tournament consolation game, April 3, 2003[12]

[Jessica Lynch is the] greatest heroine of all time. She has surpassed Joan of Arc. Look where France is today. I'd take Jessica Lynch over ten Joan of Arcs.

Bobby Knight, April 3, 2003[13]

ST. JESSICA

SEPTEMBER 25, 2005

"I THINK WE'RE IN THE END GAME NOW. . . ."

 THOMAS FRIEDMAN, *NEW YORK TIMES* COLUMNIST[P30]

On the day after the *Washington Post* reported on Lynch's Rambo-like exploits, the Armed Forces Press Service, the official news service of the U.S. Department of Defense, issued an article about the heroics of the Iraqi (later identified as Nasiriyah-based lawyer Mohammed Odeh al-Rehaief) who had risked his life to tell "shocked" U.S. Marines the location of the hospital where Jessica Lynch lay "under the watchful eyes of more than 40 murderous gunmen." The story also presented Odeh al-Rehaief's firsthand account of the abuse the injured soldier allegedly suffered at the hands of her captors.

Peering through the room's window, [Odeh al-Rehaief] saw a sight he claims will stay with him for life: An Iraqi colonel slapped the soldier, who had been captured after a fierce firefight March 23—first with his palm, then with his backhand. . . . "My heart stopped," he said in a soft tone. "I knew then I must help her be saved."

Sergeant Joseph R. Chenelly, U.S. Marine Corps
American Forces Press Service, April 4, 2003[14]

Officials have refused to say why so many of Lynch's bones were broken, but it's likely she was tortured.

Owen Moritz, "Jessica Took Awful Beating," *New York Daily News*, April 5, 2003

IN FACT

It was eventually revealed that Pfc. Lynch had been neither shot nor stabbed. Rather, she had sustained her injuries when the Humvee she was riding in crashed into a tractor-trailer. Furthermore, wrote David D. Kirkpatrick in the November 7, 2003, edition of the *New York Times*, "subsequent investigations determined that . . . her weapon jammed before she could fire, the Iraqi doctors treated her kindly, and the hospital was already in friendly hands when her rescuers arrived."

"It hurt in a way that people would make up stories that they had no truth about," Jessica Lynch told Diane Sawyer in an exclusive interview broadcast by ABC on November 11. In the interview, Lynch also refuted Mohammed Odeh al-Rehaief's claim that he had seen an Iraqi slap her. "From the time I woke up in that hospital, no one beat me, no one slapped me, no one, nothing," she said. "I'm so thankful for those people," she continued, referring to the Iraqis who had cared for her before her rescue, "because that's why I'm alive today."[15]

These revelations notwithstanding, Mohammed Odeh al-Rehaief was granted asylum by the U.S. government, received a $300,000 book advance from Rupert Murdoch's HarperCollins for his version of the Lynch story, and was given a job with the Livingston Group, a Washington public relations and lobbying firm that also employed Lauri J. Fitz-Pegado, best known for her involvement in a bogus story, promulgated during Operation Desert Storm, about Iraqi soldiers murdering Kuwaiti babies by pulling them out of incubators. Indeed, Fitz-Pegado was assigned the task of promoting Odeh al-Rehaief's book.

SEPTEMBER 28, 2005

"MAYBE THE CYNICAL EUROPEANS WERE RIGHT. MAYBE THIS NEIGHBORHOOD IS JUST BEYOND TRANSFORMATION. THAT WILL BECOME CLEAR IN THE NEXT FEW MONTHS AS WE SEE JUST WHAT KIND OF MINORITY THE SUNNIS IN IRAQ INTEND TO BE."

★ THOMAS FRIEDMAN, *NEW YORK TIMES* COLUMNIST[P31]

Jessica Lynch, for her part, received a $1 million advance for a book—a sum she split equally with her ghostwriter, former *New York Times* reporter Rick Bragg, who was suspended from the paper in May 2003 for taking credit for a story he didn't write. He subsequently resigned.

Void of all facts and absolutely ridiculous.

Bryan Whitman, Pentagon spokesperson, responding to a BBC report charging that the Lynch rescue was "one of the most stunning pieces of news management ever conceived," May 19, 2003[16]

PART II

Mission Accomplished

The man who slept through many classes at Yale and partied the nights away stands revealed as a profound and great leader who will reshape the world for the better. The United States is lucky once again.

Mona Charen, syndicated columnist, March 23, 2003[17]

IRAQ IS ALL BUT WON; NOW WHAT?

Los Angeles Times headline, April 10, 2003

[General] Tommy Franks and the coalition forces have demonstrated the old axiom that boldness on the battlefield produces swift and relatively bloodless victory. The three-week swing through Iraq has utterly shattered skeptics' complaints.

Tony Snow, host of *Fox News Sunday*, Fox News, April 13, 2003[18]

Liberal writers for ideologically driven magazines like *The Nation* and for less overtly political ones like *The New Yorker* did not predict a defeat, but the terrible consequences many warned of have not happened. Now liberal commentators must address the victory at hand and confront an ascendant conservative juggernaut that asserts United States might can set the world right.

David Carr, *The New York Times*, April 16, 2003[19]

KRAUTHAMMER-VICTORY

The only people who think this wasn't a victory are Upper West Side liberals, and a few people here in Washington.

Charles Krauthammer, *Inside Washington*, WUSA-TV, April 19, 2003[20]

Now that the war in Iraq is all but over, should the people in Hollywood who opposed the president admit they were wrong?

Alan Colmes, *Hannity & Colmes*, Fox News, April 25, 2003[21]

Congress returns to Washington this week to a world very different from the one members left two weeks ago. The war in Iraq is essentially over and domestic issues are regaining attention.

Bob Edwards, National Public Radio, April 28, 2003[22]

OCTOBER 5, 2005

"THE DEVELOPMENTS OVER THE NEXT SEVERAL MONTHS WILL BE CRITICAL—AS GENERAL CASEY AND GENERAL ABIZAID AND THE SECRETARY MADE VERY CLEAR OVER THE COURSE OF LAST WEEK."

★ GENERAL DAVID PETRAEUS[P32]

"The United States [has] committed itself . . . to reshaping the Middle East, so the region [will] no longer be a hotbed of terrorism, extremism, anti-Americanism, and weapons of mass destruction. . . . The first two battles of this new era are now over. The battles of Afghanistan and Iraq have been won decisively and honorably.

William Kristol, *The Weekly Standard*, April 28, 2003[23]

AND PERHAPS LIGHT UP A CIGARETTE?

From start to finish, President Bush has led the United States and its coalition partners to the most important military victory since World War II. . . . This was a war worth fighting. It ended quickly with few civilian casualties and with little damage to Iraq's cities, towns or infrastructure. . . . It ended . . . without the quagmire [the war's critics] predicted. . . . Iraqis are freer today and we are safer. Relax and enjoy it.

Richard Perle, Chairman of the Pentagon's Defense Policy Board, May 1, 2003[24]

PERLE RELAXES IN QUAGMIRE

We ought to look in a mirror and get proud, and stick out our chests, and suck in our bellies, and say, "Damn, we're Americans!"

General Jay Garner, director of American reconstruction and humanitarian assistance efforts in Iraq, April 30, 2003[25]

It is amazing how thorough the victory in Iraq really was in the broadest context.

Jeff Birnbaum, *The Washington Post,* May 2, 2003[26]

Major combat operations in Iraq have ended. In the battle of Iraq, the United States and our allies have prevailed.

President George W. Bush, dressed in aviator gear and standing under a "Mission Accomplished" banner on the deck of the aircraft carrier USS *Lincoln,* May 2, 2003[27]

And a year from now, I'll be very surprised if there is not some grand square in Baghdad that is named after President Bush. There is no doubt that, with the exception of a very small number of people close to a vicious regime, the people of Iraq have been liberated and they understand that they've been liberated.

Richard Perle, Chairman of the Pentagon's Defense Policy Board, September 22, 2003[28]

[See also "Mission Accomplished Revisited," page 151.]

NOVEMBER 27, 2005

"WE'VE GOT TO STAY FIRM FOR THE NEXT SIX MONTHS. IT IS A CRITICAL PERIOD. . . . YOU'LL HAVE TO WAIT. YOU SHOULDN'T SPECULATE. WE'LL HAVE TO WAIT FOR THOSE SIX MONTHS."

★ SENATOR JOHN WARNER[P33]

"ONE OF THE GREAT MOMENTS IN THE HISTORY OF LIBERTY"

The toppling of Saddam Hussein's statue in Baghdad will be recorded, alongside the fall of the Berlin Wall, as one of the great moments in the history of liberty.

President George W. Bush, speaking to troops at Fort Hood, Texas, April 11, 2005[29]

The previous July, the *Los Angeles Times* had published an article citing a U.S. Army report that it was "a marine colonel—not joyous Iraqi civilians, as was assumed from TV images—who decided to topple the statue." A "marine recovery vehicle" had toppled the statue with a chain, the *Times* reported, "but the effort appeared to be Iraqi-inspired because" an Army psychological team had "managed to pack the vehicle with cheering Iraqi children."[30]

POSTSCRIPT: AND YOU KNOW WHAT? THINGS COULD HAVE GONE EVEN BETTER!

There is a school of thought that says we should have given the citizens of Baghdad forty-eight hours to get out of Dodge by dropping leaflets and going with the AM radios and all that. Forty-eight hours, you've got to get out of there, and flatten the place. Then the war would be over. We could have done that in two days. . . . You flatten Baghdad, you flatten all the troops, we know where they go, there's nowhere to hide in the desert. We know where everybody's moving. And you know as well as I do, this war could have been over in two days. . . . It's just frustrating for everybody to know that we have been fighting this war with one hand behind our back.

Bill O'Reilly, American political commentator,
March 26, 2003[31]

NOVEMBER 30, 2005

"WE SHOULD NOT AT THIS TIME IN THESE CRITICAL FOUR TO SIX MONTHS BE WORRYING ABOUT A TIMETABLE TO WITHDRAW OR EVEN TALKING ABOUT IT."

★ SENATOR JOHN WARNER[P34]

VOLUME IV

THE HINGE

OF FATE

BRING 'EM ON

NOT A GOOD SIGN

The enemy we're fighting is a bit different than the one we war gamed against.

Lieutenant General William Wallace, Commander of U.S. Army Forces in the Persian Gulf, speaking to reporters at Forward Operating Base Shell, a U.S. refueling depot in the Iraqi desert, March 28, 2003

Wallace was referring to the unexpected importance of enemy militia units in the "real" war in Iraq. "In fact," wrote Fred Kaplan in *Slate*, "militia fighters did play a crucial role in a major war game designed to simulate combat in Iraq—but the Pentagon officials who managed the game simply disregarded or overruled the militias' most devastating moves."[1]

LOOTING: "A NATURAL PROCESS" AND "A RELIEF TO COLLEGE STUDENTS EVERYWHERE"

We don't get involved in that. It's a natural process. There are some very, very angry people out there and we need to step back from that.

Lieutenant Colonel Eric Schwartz, Commander of U.S. Task Force 1–64, explaining why his unit was doing nothing to prevent what was reported to be widespread looting of businesses and government offices that had begun in Baghdad hours after the American takeover of the city, April 10, 2003[2]

There were originally reports of looting, and there was, indeed, looting in Basra and other cities in the south. And as the security situation stabilized, the looting did, indeed, decline.

Ari Fleischer, White House Press Secretary, responding to a statement by UN Secretary General Kofi Annan that uncontrolled looting had erupted in Baghdad, April 10, 2007[3]

IN FACT

By the next day, U.S. newspapers were filled with reports of uncontrolled chaos in Baghdad, including the widespread, and apparently systematic, looting of Iraqi institutions. Among the buildings ransacked was the Iraqi National Museum, where, according to the museum's deputy director, as many as 170,000 priceless antiquities, some dating back thousands of years to the dawn of civilization in Mesopotamia, were either stolen or destroyed.

Stuff happens.

Donald H. Rumsfeld, U.S. Secretary of Defense, commenting on reports of uncontrolled looting in Baghdad, April 11, 2003[4]

Freedom's untidy.... Free people are free to make mistakes and commit crimes and do bad things.

Donald H. Rumsfeld, U.S. Secretary of Defense, continuing his commentary on the disorder in Baghdad, April 11, 2003[5]

IN FACT

Eleanor Robson, a specialist in the history of mathematics in the ancient Near East and an Oxford fellow, said, "You'd have to go back centuries, to the Mongol invasion of Baghdad in 1258, to find looting on this scale." Paul Zimansky, a Boston University archaeologist, called the looting "the greatest cultural disaster of the last 500 years."[6]

Let me say one other thing. The images you are seeing on television you are seeing over, and over, and over, and it's the same picture of some person walking out of some building with a vase, and you see it 20 times, and you think, "My goodness, were there that many vases?" (Laughter.) "Is it possible that there were that many vases in the whole country?"

Donald H. Rumsfeld, U.S. Secretary of Defense, April 11, 2003[7]

I don't think that anyone anticipated that the riches of Iraq could be looted by the Iraqi people.

Brigadier General Vincent Brooks, official spokesperson for U.S. Central Command, April 15, 2007[8]

IN FACT

It was soon revealed that, less than three weeks before U.S. troops had entered Baghdad, the Pentagon had sent an internal memo to Coalition Command listing, in order of importance, sixteen sites that were crucial to protect. Perhaps remembering that nine of Iraq's thirteen regional museums had been looted during Operation Desert Storm in 1991, the Defense Department had placed the Iraqi National Museum in Baghdad second on the list.

DECEMBER 4, 2005

"WE WILL PROBABLY SEE SIGNIFICANT PROGRESS IN THE NEXT SIX MONTHS TO A YEAR."

 SENATOR JOHN MCCAIN[P35]

The war was so successful, [liberals] don't have any arguments left. . . . Just two weeks ago, they claimed American troops were caught in another Vietnam quagmire. That didn't happen. Now the biggest mishap liberals can seize on is that some figurines from an Iraqi museum were broken—a relief to college students everywhere who have ever been forced to gaze upon Mesopotamian pottery.

Ann Coulter, "Liberals Meet Unexpected Resistance," April 30, 2003[9]

POSTSCRIPT: KEEPING OUR PRIORITIES STRAIGHT

At a Department of Defense news briefing six months after the invasion of Iraq, Walt Slocombe, the Special Advisor on Security and Defense for the Coalition Provisional Authority, was asked if, in retrospect, he thought there was any way that the systematic looting that swept Iraq immediately after the fall of Baghdad—specifically, the wholesale plundering of military bases—could have been anticipated and prevented.

I suppose if you'd made it your highest priority, you could have protected a couple of facilities. . . . I'm not sure that that would have made any sense as the highest priority anyway. Anyway, it's a hypothetical question.

Walt Slocombe, Coalition Provisional Authority Special Advisor on Security and Defense, September 17, 2003[10]

RESISTANCE? WHAT RESISTANCE?

There is no longer any organized . . . military resistance to the U.S. push into Baghdad.

A "senior [U.S.] Army colonel in the field," quoted by CNN correspondent Walt Rodgers, embedded with the 37th Cavalry on the "outskirts of Baghdad," April 8, 2003[11]

IN FACT

Rodgers went on to opine that he found the colonel's statement a "bit misleading." "There is resistance," he reported. "Sometimes that resistance is very fierce. One soldier says it appears as if every Iraqi citizen has a rocket-propelled grenade or shoulder-fired artillery piece as his calling card."

The war was the hard part. The hard part was putting together a coalition, getting 300,000 troops over there and all their equipment and winning. And it gets easier. I mean, setting up a democracy is hard, but it is not as hard as winning a war.

Fred Barnes, editor, *The Weekly Standard*, Fox News, April 10, 2003[12]

Pockets of dead-enders are trying to reconstitute. Gen. [Tommy] Franks and his team are rooting them out.

Donald H. Rumsfeld, U.S. Secretary of Defense, June 18, 2003[13]

Although major combat operations have concluded, our soldiers are involved in almost daily contact with noncompliant forces, former regime members and common criminals. . . . But I really qualify it as militarily insignificant. They are very small. They are very random. They are very ineffective.

Major General Ray Odierno, Commander of the U.S. Army's 4th Infantry Division, briefing Pentagon reporters in a video conference from Iraq, June 18, 2003[14]

[Insurgents] pose no strategic threat to the United States or to the coalition forces.

L. Paul Bremer III, Director of the Coalition Provisional Authority, August 26, 2003[15]

DECEMBER 17, 2005

"THE LAST TWO WEEKS . . . MAY BE SEEN AS A TURNING POINT."

★ SENATOR JOSEPH LIEBERMAN[P36]

I keep reading stories about it's a country in chaos. This is simply not true. It is not a country in chaos, and Baghdad's not a city in chaos.

L. Paul Bremer III, Director of the Coalition Provisional Authority, August 27, 2003[16]

There is obviously violence. . . . But you're talking about specific, isolated acts just like you would get in an American city.

Michael O'Hanlon, Senior Fellow, Foreign Policy Studies, Brookings Institution, interviewed by Liane Hansen on NPR's *Weekend Edition* after returning from a Defense Department–sponsored tour of Iraq, September 28, 2003[17]

Safety and security have been achieved [in Baghdad].

Major General Martin Dempsey, Commander, U.S. First Army Division, at a ceremony officially reopening the Fourteenth of July Bridge in Baghdad, October 25, 2003[18]

IN FACT

Fifteen hours after General Dempsey made his remarks, insurgents drove across the newly reopened bridge and fired eight Katyusha rockets into the Al Rashid Hotel inside the supposedly impenetrable Green Zone, killing a staffer of the Coalition Provisional Authority, wounding fifteen others, and narrowly missing U.S. Deputy Secretary of Defense Paul Wolfowitz, who was staying at the hotel.

BARELY MISSING WOLFOWITZ

It is a last ditch—I think it is a desperate effort by these terrorists. It's not representative of a significant guerrilla force that's fighting the United States there.

Fred Barnes, editor, *The Weekly Standard*,
commenting on terrorist attacks across Baghdad,
October 27, 2003[19]

These dead-enders are few in number and have little ability to inspire a broader following among the Iraqi people.

Michael O'Hanlon and Stephen J. Solarz,
Brookings Institution, *The Washington Times*,
February 17, 2004[20]

Any remaining violence [in Iraq] is due to thugs, gangs, and terrorists.

Donald H. Rumsfeld, U.S. Secretary of Defense,
CNN Late Edition, March 14, 2004[21]

DECEMBER 18, 2005

"THE NEXT SIX MONTHS ARE GOING TO TELL THE STORY."

★ SENATOR JOSEPH BIDEN[P37]

CHENEY'S LAST THROES

I think they're in the last throes, if you will, of the insurgency.

Vice President Dick Cheney, interviewed on *The Larry King Show*, June 20, 2005[22]

ASSUMING THERE ACTUALLY IS AN INSURGENCY, HOW BIG IS IT?

I would say that the force of people actively armed and operating against us does not exceed 5,000.

General John Abizaid, Commander of U.S. forces in Iraq, November 13, 2005[23]

I think the resistance is more than 200,000 people.

General Mohammed Abdullah Shahwani, Director of the Iraqi intelligence service, January 3, 2005[24]

WHY BAGHDAD IS JUST LIKE MANHATTAN (OR IS IT CALIFORNIA?)

Go[ing] through the city of Baghdad is like being in Manhattan. I'm talking about shopping centers . . . restaurants . . . video stores. . . . You would never know there was a war going on.

Representative Peter King (R-NY), speech at Merrick Jewish Center, Merrick, New York, October 17, 2006[25]

[The state of the war in Iraq] reminded me, as I listened to these briefings, of what I faced in New York City when we had tremendously high levels of crime.

Rudy Giuliani, former Mayor of New York City and Republican candidate for president, January 11, 2007[26]

Basically, um, it is like California with Baghdad as L.A. with Hispanics, white and blacks. . . . You have the Crips and the Bloods in Baghdad. That's where all the fighting is.

Ann Coulter, *Hannity & Colmes*, January 17, 2007[27]

DECEMBER 18, 2005

"I THINK THE NEXT SIX MONTHS REALLY ARE GOING TO DETERMINE WHETHER THIS COUNTRY IS GOING TO COLLAPSE INTO THREE PARTS OR MORE OR WHETHER IT'S GOING TO COME TOGETHER."

☆ THOMAS FRIEDMAN, *NEW YORK TIMES* COLUMNIST[P38]

There are neighborhoods in Baghdad where you and I could walk through those neighborhoods today. The U.S. is beginning to succeed in Iraq.

Senator John McCain (R-AZ), Republican candidate for president, interviewed on the Bill Bennett radio program, March 26, 2007[28]

To prove his point, McCain, accompanied by Senator Lindsay Graham (R-SC), Representative Mike Pence (R-IN), and several other members of Congress, made a surprise visit to Baghdad the very next weekend. McCain was photographed strolling with his congressional colleagues through the open-air Shorja market, where massive bombings had killed 137 people less than two months before.

After their open-air outing, McCain and his colleagues held an upbeat news conference in the heavily fortified Green Zone.

Things are better and there are encouraging signs. I have been here many years—many times over the years. Never have I been able to drive from the airport, never have I been able to go out into the city as I was today. The American people are not getting the full picture of what's happening here.

Senator John McCain, Republican candidate for president, at a news conference in the Green Zone after completing a "walking tour" of the Shorja market, April 1, 2007[29]

[It was] like a normal outdoor market in Indiana in the summertime.

Representative Mike Pence, at a news conference in the Green Zone after completing a "walking tour" of the Shorja market, April 1, 2007[30]

IN FACT

On the evening after the news conference, NBC's *Nightly News* provided further details about McCain's and Pence's guided tour. The congressmen were accompanied, the network reported, by "100 American soldiers, with three Blackhawk helicopters, and two Apache gunships overhead." In addition, the network said, still photographs provided by the military revealed that McCain and his colleagues had been wearing body armor during their entire afternoon stroll.[31]

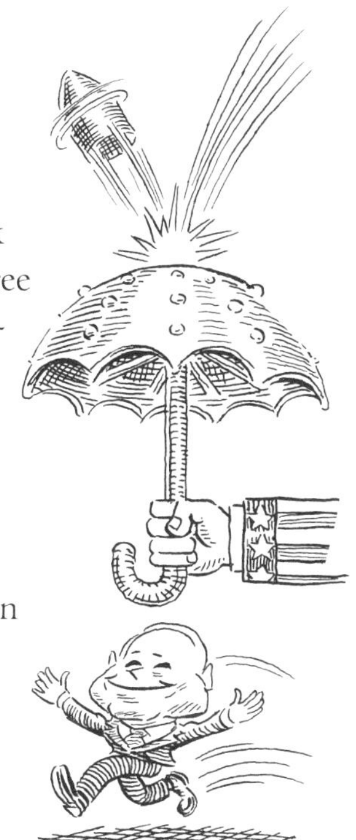

In a *New York Times* interview published on April 3, 2007, Amir Raheem, thirty-two, a floor carpeting merchant at the Shorja market, provided further background on McCain's and Pence's encouraging visit. "Just yesterday," he reported, "an Iraqi soldier was shot in his shoulder by a sniper, and the day before, two civilians were shot by a sniper as well."[32]

DECEMBER 20, 2005

"WE'RE AT THE BEGINNING OF I THINK THE DECISIVE I WOULD SAY SIX MONTHS IN IRAQ."

★ THOMAS FRIEDMAN, *NEW YORK TIMES* COLUMNIST[P39]

UMM QASR ES SU QASR

Umm Qasr is a city similar to Southampton.

Geoff Hoon, British Defense Minister, describing, in the House of Commons, a tiny port settlement just across the border from Kuwait where U.S. and British marines encountered "stern resistance" shortly after the invasion of Iraq, March 26, 2003[33]

IN FACT

According to the British newspaper *The Independent,* a marine patrolling the still-embattled port responded, "He's either never been to Southampton, or he's never been to Umm Qasr." "There's no beer, no prostitutes and people are shooting at us," added another. "It's more like Portsmouth."[34]

THE NEXT (OR NEXT TO LAST) WORD ON WMDS

There is no doubt that the regime of Saddam Hussein possesses weapons of mass destruction. And . . . as this operation continues, those weapons will be identified [and] found, along with the people who have produced them and who guard them.

General Tommy Franks, three days after the invasion of Iraq, March 22, 2003[35]

We know where they are. They're in the area around Tikrit and Baghdad and east, west, south and north somewhat.

Donald H. Rumsfeld, U.S. Secretary of Defense, pinpointing, after troops invading Iraq had failed to find them after ten days of warfare, the location of the weapons of mass destruction, March 30, 2003[36]

On weapons of mass destruction, we know that the regime has them, we know that as the regime collapses we will be led to them.

Tony Blair, British Prime Minister, April 8, 2003[37]

Make no mistake—we have high confidence that [the Iraqis] have weapons of mass destruction. That is what this war was about and it is about. And we have high confidence [they] will be found.

Ari Fleischer, White House Press Secretary, April 10, 2003[38]

We're not going to find just a smoking gun, but a smoking cannon.

Chief Warrant Officer Richard L. Gonzales, head of a Defense Department WMD search team in Iraq, expressing unshaken confidence in his mission despite failing to find evidence of unconventional weapons during a weeklong survey of a munitions plant near Karbala, April 16, 2003[39]

On May 18, 2003, the *Washington Post*'s Barton Gelman published the saga of another highly trained search team that had spent the past eight weeks tracking down "high priority intelligence" leads in search of illegal Iraqi weaponry. Thus far, Gelman reported, the team had "dug up a playground, raided a distillery, seized a research paper from a failing graduate student and laid bare a swimming pool where an underground chemical weapons stash was supposed to be." Among their other discoveries were "a cache of vacuum cleaners," a factory filled with thousands of old metal license plates, and "suspi-

DECEMBER 21, 2005

"THE NEXT SIX MONTHS WILL TELL US A LOT. I REMAIN GUARDEDLY HOPEFUL."

 THOMAS FRIEDMAN, *NEW YORK TIMES* COLUMNIST[P40]

cious glass globes" that turned out to be filled with cleaning fluid. The one thing they had not found was weapons of mass destruction.

But just eleven days later, while on a trip to Poland, President Bush made a startling announcement.

We found the weapons of mass destruction. We found biological laboratories. You remember when Colin Powell stood up in front of the world, and he said, Iraq has got laboratories, mobile labs to build biological weapons. They're illegal. They're against the United Nations resolutions, and we've so far discovered two. And we'll find more weapons as time goes on. But for those who say we haven't found the banned manufacturing devices or banned weapons, they're wrong, we found them.

President George W. Bush, responding to a reporter from TVP, Poland, who had asked how Mr. Bush could justify the invasion of Iraq now that no weapons of mass destruction had been found, May 29, 2003[40]

IN FACT

The "mobile labs" turned out not to be devices for building biological weapons. Rather, they were constructed to manufacture hydrogen for weather balloons. (See page 15.)

I'm not willing at all at this point to buy the proposition that somehow Saddam Hussein . . . had no WMD and some guy out at the CIA, because I called him, cooked up a report saying he did. That's crazy.

Vice President Dick Cheney, September 14, 2003[41]

We are still looking. We are still searching.

Colin Powell, U.S. Secretary of State, January 14, 2004[42]

It's going to take some additional considerable period of time in order to look in all the cubbyholes and ammo dumps and all the places in Iraq where you'd expect to find something like that.

Vice President Dick Cheney, January 24, 2004[43]

As of this writing, the search continues.

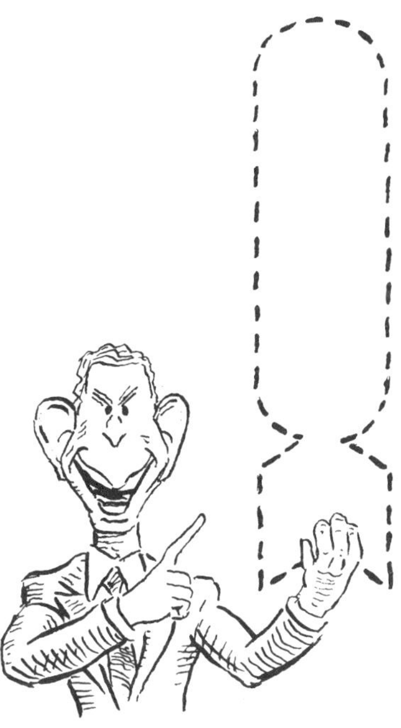

DECEMBER 27, 2005

"WE'VE HAD A LOT OF THESE STATEMENTS OF PROGRESS JUST AROUND THE CORNER . . . BUT 2006 IS THE CRUCIAL YEAR."

★ ANDREW KREPINEVICH, DEFENSE ANALYST AT THE CENTER FOR STRATEGIC AND BUDGETARY ASSESSMENTS[P41]

WHY THE WMD TRAIL REACHED A DEAD END: A FAIR AND BALANCED EXPLANATION

Let us assume for the sake of argument that Saddam or his two sons gave the order to bury the stuff that they had just before the war started in the sand somewhere in the Iraqi desert. If they did . . . conceivably the people who did it were then either assassinated by Saddam Hussein himself or killed in the war. We now know that two of those three people are dead. The sons are now dead. So therefore, the people who had the knowledge of exactly where this stuff would be, in a country that's the size of California—they may no longer have the capacity to give up the information because they're not alive anymore.

Mansoor Ijaz, Fox News correspondent, analysis presented on On the Record with Greta van Susteran, *September 18, 2003*

POSTSCRIPT: SO WE DIDN'T FIND THE WMDS. BIG DEAL!

As far as I'm concerned, we do not need to find any weapons of mass destruction to justify this war. . . . Mr. Bush doesn't owe the world any explanation for missing chemical weapons (even if it turns out that the White House hyped this issue).

Thomas Friedman, *The New York Times*, April 27, 2003[44]

Weapons of mass destruction or uranium from Niger are little elitist issues that do not bother most of the people.

Robert Novak, syndicated political columnist, on *Meet the Press*, July 6, 2003[45]

I'm not concerned about weapons of mass destruction.... I didn't come [to Iraq] in a search for weapons of mass destruction.

Paul Wolfowitz, U.S. Deputy Secretary of Defense, talking to reporters after a five-day tour of Iraq, July 22, 2003[46]

A "BUNCH OF BULL": THE "IRRELEVANT" DEBATE OVER THE "16 LITTLE WORDS"

REVISIONIST HISTORY

IN FACT

The British government has learned that Saddam Hussein recently sought significant quantities of uranium from Africa.

Those "16 little words"—included, despite CIA warnings, in George W. Bush's 2003 State of the Union message—were meant to help clinch the case that Saddam was reconstituting his nuclear weapons program. But on June 6, 2003, Joseph Wilson, a former U.S. ambassador to Niger who had been sent to Africa to investigate Bush's claim, published an op-ed piece in the *New York Times,* followed by an appearance on *Meet the Press,* that started a vigorous public debate about the president's veracity.

JUNE 9, 2006

"IF THIS IS THE TIPPING POINT, THEN THINGS JUST TIPPED TOWARD A POLITICAL SETTLEMENT. THIS WILL BECOME CLEARER OVER THE NEXT FEW DAYS."

★ STRATEGIC FORECASTING, INC.[P42]

Based on my experience with the administration in the months leading up to the war, I have little choice but to conclude that some of the intelligence related to Iraq's nuclear weapons program was twisted to exaggerate the Iraqi threat.

Joseph Wilson, *The New York Times*, July 6, 2003[47]

My judgment on this is that if they were referring to Niger when they were referring to uranium sales from Africa to Iraq, that information was erroneous and that they knew about it well ahead of both the publication of the British White Paper and the president's State of the Union address. . . . They were using the selective use of facts and intelligence to bolster a decision in a case that had already been made, a decision that had been made to go to war.

Joseph Wilson, on *Meet the Press,* July 6, 2003[48]

IN FACT

Over the next few days, a National Security Council spokesperson, Michael N. Anton, admitted that the agency now knew that the "documents alleging a transaction between Iraq and Niger had been forged," and CIA Director George Tenet dutifully took the blame for letting the "16 little words" stay in the speech and for not warning the President about them directly.

The president is pleased that the director of central intelligence acknowledged what needed to be acknowledged. The president has moved on. And I think, frankly, much of the country has moved on as well.

Ari Fleischer, White House Press Secretary, July 12, 2003[49]

End of story.

Donald H. Rumsfeld, U.S. Secretary of Defense, July 13, 2003[50]

I think the bottom has been gotten to.

Ari Fleischer, White House Press Secretary, July 14, 2003[51]

But critics continued to insist that the revelation of the fact that the President knew, or should have known, that the "16 little words" were misleading undermined the administration's entire case for invading Iraq. At a White House press briefing, Ari Fleischer angrily disagreed.

This revisionist notion that somehow this is now the core of why we went to war, a central issue of why we went to war, a fundamental underpinning of the president's decisions, is a bunch of bull.

Ari Fleischer, White House Press Secretary, July 14, 2003[52]

JUST IN CASE YOU DIDN'T UNDERSTAND WHAT MR. FLEISCHER MEANT

There are some who would like to rewrite history—revisionist historians is what I like to call them.

President George W. Bush, denouncing critics who claimed that the threat of unconventional weapons in Iraq was inflated before the war, June 16, 2003[53]

JULY 7, 2006

"THE SITUATION IN IRAQ IS A LOT BETTER . . . THAT'S PROGRESS."

★ SENATOR JOE LIEBERMAN[P43]

IN FACT

On the same day that Ari Fleischer made his remark about historical revisionism, columnist Robert Novak published "Mission to Niger," disclosing that Ambassador Joseph Wilson's spouse was a CIA "operative" named Valerie Plame. Since Plame's agency identity had been classified prior to its appearance in Novak's column, its revelation resulted in a special prosecution, a grand jury, a criminal trial, a civil suit, any number of books, *and* . . .

THE VALERIE PLAME AFFAIR

If there's a leak out of my administration, I want to know who it is. And if the person has violated the law, the person will be taken care of.

President George W. Bush, discussing the possibility that a member of his administration had leaked the name of covert CIA operative Valerie Plame to the press in response to evidence, offered by Plame's husband, Joseph Wilson, that the administration had intentionally misrepresented intelligence about Saddam's alleged purchase of nuclear materials in Africa, September 30, 2003[54]

Scooter has worked tirelessly on behalf of the American people and sacrificed much in the service of his country.

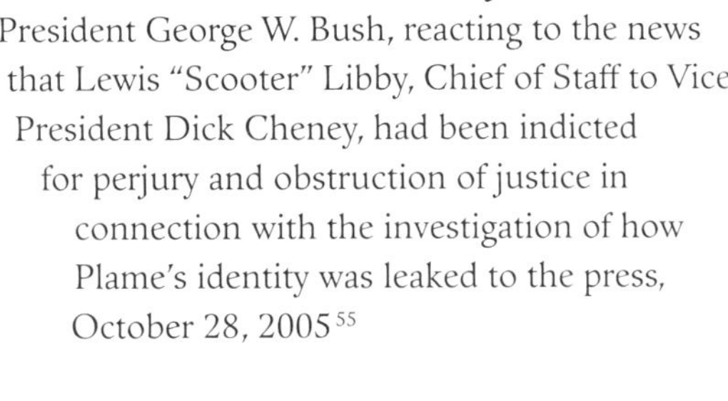

President George W. Bush, reacting to the news that Lewis "Scooter" Libby, Chief of Staff to Vice President Dick Cheney, had been indicted for perjury and obstruction of justice in connection with the investigation of how Plame's identity was leaked to the press, October 28, 2005[55]

IN FACT

On March 6, 2007, "Scooter" Libby was convicted on four counts of perjury and obstruction of justice in connection with the Valerie Plame leak probe, and on June 5, 2007, he was sentenced to thirty months in prison.

I have concluded that the prison sentence given to Mr. Libby is excessive. Therefore, I am commuting the portion of Mr. Libby's sentence that requires him to spend thirty months in prison.

President George W. Bush, July 2, 2007[56]

[See also "Unimpeachable Sources: The World According to Judith Miller," page 29.]

TORTURE: THE NEW PARADIGM

No president has done more for human rights than I have.

President George W. Bush, remark to New Yorker *writer Ken Auletta, quoted in* The New York Times, *January 20, 2004*[57]

OPTIONAL READING: THE GENEVA CONVENTION

An administration that had ample reading time for pundits like Robert Novak apparently had little time for reading such primary documents as the Geneva Convention. Here is a relevant excerpt:

JULY 16, 2006

"IRAQ'S BETTER."

☆ FRED BARNES, SENIOR EDITOR AT THE *THE WEEKLY STANDARD*[P44]

The following acts are and shall remain prohibited at any time and in any place whatsoever. . . .

(a) Violence to life and person, in particular murder of all kinds, mutilation, cruel treatment and torture

(b) Outrages upon personal dignity, in particular, humiliating and degrading treatment

(c) The passing of sentences and the carrying out of executions without previous judgment pronounced by a regularly constituted court affording all the judicial guarantees which are recognized as indispensable by civilized peoples.[58]

WELCOME TO GUANTÁNAMO!

The great weight of legal authority indicates that a federal district court could not properly exercise habeas jurisdiction over an alien detained at GBC [Guantánamo Bay, Cuba].

John C. Yoo and Patrick F. Philbin, Deputy Assistant Attorney Generals in the Office of Legal Counsel of the U.S. Department of Justice, memo opining that U.S. courts could not overrule as unconstitutional the indefinite detention of alleged Al Qaeda and Taliban personnel at Guantánamo, December 28, 2001[59]

IN FACT

With Yoo and Philbin's theory to guide them, the U.S. government began detaining prisoners at Guantánamo in 2002. These detainees were officially labeled "enemy combatants" to distinguish them from "prisoners of war," who, Yoo and his colleagues worried, might be covered under the fair trial and humane treatment rules established by the Geneva Convention.

Guantánamo has become the gulag of our times.

Irene Khan, Secretary General of Amnesty International, announcing her organization's 2005 annual report, which cited evidence, uncovered by the FBI and the Red Cross, of detainee abuse at the Guantánamo prison facility, May 25, 2005[60]

Guantánamo . . . is essentially a model facility. The contracts for the food, to ensure that our detainees have the proper Muslim-approved food, is $2.5 million annually, just to make sure they're fed right. We passed out 1,300 Korans in 13 different languages. We take extreme care to do that.

General Richard Myers, responding to charges by Amnesty International of human rights violations at Guantánamo, May 29, 2005[61]

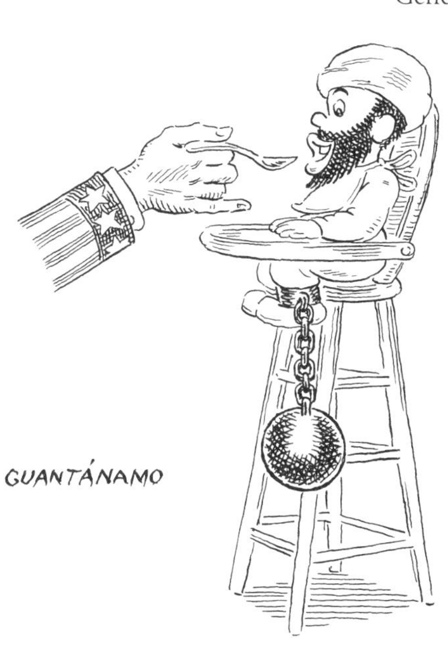

The inmates in Guantánamo have never . . . been treated better and they've never been more comfortable in their lives. . . . And the idea that somehow we are torturing people in Guantánamo is absolutely not true, unless you consider having to eat chicken three times a week is torture.

Representative Duncan Hunter (R-CA), Chairman of the House Armed Services Committee, at a Capitol Hill news conference, June 12, 2005[62]

JANUARY 23, 2006

"I THINK THAT WE'RE GOING TO KNOW AFTER SIX TO NINE MONTHS WHETHER THIS PROJECT HAS ANY CHANCE OF SUCCEEDING."

★ THOMAS FRIEDMAN, *NEW YORK TIMES* COLUMNIST[P45]

[Guantánamo] would make a beautiful resort.

Senator Jeff Sessions (R-AL), June 15, 2005[63]

I'm sitting here thinking, folks, that if this treatment that we are continuing to mete out to detainees—prisoners of war, terrorists-in-waiting at Gitmo—if the word of how they're being treated keeps getting out, we're going to have Al Qaeda people surrendering all over the world trying to get in the place.

Rush Limbaugh, commenting on reports from General Myers and others about excellent food and other amenities at Guantánamo, *The Rush Limbaugh Show*, June 16, 2005[64]

TORTURE AT GUANTÁNAMO?
"TAKE A LOOK FOR YOURSELF!"

The prisoners are well-treated in Guantánamo. There's total transparency. . . . And you're welcome to go. The press, of course, is welcome to go down to Guantánamo. . . . And for those of you . . . who have doubt, I'd suggest buying an airplane ticket and going down and look—take a look for yourself.

President George W. Bush, statement at a press appearance in Lyngby, Denmark, July 6, 2005[65]

IN FACT

Taking up President George Bush's challenge for reporters to visit the Guantánamo Bay military prison in Cuba, CNN took a camera crew the very next day, but they were denied access to portions of the base, and the video they were able to shoot was censored.[66]

IN FACT

On June 10, 2006, three detainees at the Guantánamo Bay camp committed suicide. Although the Defense Department has acknowledged forty-one incidents of "self-injurious behavior"—the Pentagon term for "suicide attempts"—at Guantánamo, the June 10 suicides were the first actual self-inflicted deaths reported at the facility.

[The triple suicide of three Guantánamo detainees] was not an act of desperation, but an act of asymmetric warfare committed against us.

U.S. Navy Rear Admiral Harry B. Harris Jr., camp commander of Guantánamo, June 11, 2006[67]

Postscript: Should Guantánamo Prison Be Shut Down?

We're looking at all alternatives and have been.

President George W. Bush, in a Fox News television interview, responding to Neil Cavuto's question, "Do you think [Guantánamo] should be shut down?," June 8, 2005[68]

I know of no one in the U.S. Government, in the executive branch, that is considering closing Guantánamo.

Donald H. Rumsfeld, U.S. Secretary of Defense, June 8, 2005[69]

MARCH 15, 2006

"THE NEXT SIX MONTHS IN IRAQ ARE GOING TO BE CRITICAL."

★ ASHRA QAZI, UN SECRETARY GENERAL'S SPECIAL REPRESENTATIVE FOR IRAQ[P46]

We need to shut down this Gitmo prison? Well, don't shut it down, we just need to start an advertising campaign. We need to call it, "Gitmo, the Muslim resort." Any resort that treated people like this would have ads all over *The New York Times* trying to get people to come down and visit for some R&R, for some rest and relaxation.

Rush Limbaugh, *The Rush Limbaugh Show*, June 14, 2005[70]

THE CASE FOR TORTURE

To be considered torture, techniques must produce lasting psychological damage or suffering "equivalent in intensity to the pain accompanying serious physical injury, such as organ failure, impairment of bodily function, or even death."

John Yoo, Deputy Assistant Attorney General in the Office of Legal Counsel of the U.S. Department of Justice, and Robert Delahunty, Justice Department Counsel, memorandum offering a newly flexible legal definition of torture, January 9, 2002[71]

Customary international law cannot bind the executive branch under the Constitution because it is not federal law.

John Yoo and Robert Delahunty, memo, January 9, 2002[72]

CIA lawyers believe that, to the extent that GPW's [the Geneva Convention on Prisoners of War] protections do not apply as a matter of law but those protections are applied as a matter of policy, it is desirable to circumscribe that policy so as to limit its application to the CIA.

Attachment to a memo from State Department Legal Advisor William H. Taft IV to White House Counsel Alberto Gonzales, February 2, 2002[73]

I accept the legal conclusion of the Department of Justice and determine that none of the provisions of Geneva apply to our conflict with al Qaeda in Afghanistan or elsewhere throughout the world because, among other reasons, al Qaeda is not a High Contracting Party to Geneva. . . .

I also accept the legal conclusion of the Department of Justice and determine that common Article 3 of Geneva does not apply to either al Qaeda or Taliban detainees, because, among other reasons, the relevant conflicts are international in scope and common Article 3 applies only to "armed conflict not of an international character."

Based on the facts supplied by the Department of Defense and the recommendation of the Department of Justice, I determine that the Taliban detainees are unlawful combatants and, therefore, do not qualify as prisoners of war under Article 4 of Geneva. I note that, because Geneva does not apply to our conflict with al Qaeda, al Qaeda detainees also do not qualify as prisoners of war.

I hereby reaffirm the order previously issued by the Secretary of Defense to the United States Armed Forces requiring that the detainees be treated humanely and, to the extent appropriate and consistent with military necessity, in a manner consistent with the principles of Geneva.

President George W. Bush, memorandum to the Vice President, the Secretaries of State and Defense, the Attorney General, the Director of Central Intelligence, the Chairman of the Joint Chiefs of Staff, and others, February 7, 2002[74]

MAY 11, 2006

"WELL, I THINK THAT WE'RE GOING TO FIND OUT . . . IN THE NEXT YEAR TO SIX MONTHS—PROBABLY SOONER—WHETHER A DECENT OUTCOME IS POSSIBLE THERE."

★ THOMAS FRIEDMAN, *NEW YORK TIMES* COLUMNIST[P47]

Any effort to apply [the law against torture] in a manner that interferes with the President's direction of such core war matters as the detention and interrogation of enemy combatants thus would be unconstitutional.

Jay Bybee, Assistant Attorney General, Office of Legal Counsel, U.S. Department of Justice, memo for Attorney General Alberto Gonzales, August 1, 2002[75]

If A kills B reasonably believing it to be necessary to save C and D, he is not guilty of murder even though, unknown to A, C and D could have been rescued without the necessity of killing B.

Jay Bybee, Assistant Attorney General, arguing that torture, or even murder, during the interrogation of a detainee may be legally justified if the interrogator believes, even incorrectly, that the "harm avoided" is greater than the "harm done," memo for Attorney General Alberto Gonzales, August 1, 2002[76]

The Geneva Convention does not apply to the war on terrorism.

John Yoo, former Deputy Assistant Attorney General and the principal legal architect of the Bush administration's "new paradigm" on the treatment of war prisoners, *Los Angeles Times*, June 11, 2004[77]

We must all be prepared to torture. Having established that, we can then begin to work together to codify rules of interrogation for the . . . very unpleasant but very real cases in which we are morally permitted—indeed morally compelled—to do terrible things.

Charles Krauthammer, *The Weekly Standard*, December 5, 2005[78]

[Congress has no power to] tie the President's hands in regard to torture as an interrogation technique. It's the core of the Commander-in-Chief function. They can't prevent the President from ordering torture.

John Yoo, former Deputy Assistant Attorney General, quoted in *The New Yorker*, February 14, 2005[79]

Death is worse than torture, but everyone except pacifists thinks there are circumstances in which war is justified. War means killing people. If we are entitled to kill people, we must be entitled to injure them. I don't see how it can be reasonable to have an absolute prohibition on torture when you don't have an absolute prohibition on killing.

John Yoo, former Deputy Assistant Attorney General, quoted in *The Daily Dish*, March 17, 2007[80]

Reasonable people will disagree about when torture is justified.

John C. Yoo, Former Deputy Assistant Attorney General, March 17, 2007[81]

One man's torture is another man's CIA-sponsored swim lesson.

Rachel Marsden, political columnist and television commentator, October 31, 2007[82]

Waterboarding is something of which every American should be proud.

Deroy Murdock, nationally syndicated columnist and Media Fellow with the Hoover Institution, November 7, 2007[83]

MAY 22, 2006

"WE WOULD SAY THAT THE NEXT SIX WEEKS, RATHER THAN MONTHS, WILL SHOW US WHERE THINGS ARE."

★ STRATEGIC FORECASTING, INC.[P48]

"RENDITION": ALL IN A DAY'S WORK

We don't kick the [expletive] out of them. We send them to other countries so they can kick the [expletive] out of them.

"Anonymous official" involved in "rendering" detainees for interrogation to overseas facilities where U.S. laws regarding humane treatment do not apply, quoted in the Washington Post, *December 26, 2002*[84]

If you don't violate someone's human rights some of the time, you probably aren't doing your job.

"Anonymous" U.S. official who has supervised the "rendition" of captured terrorists to overseas facilities, quoted in the Washington Post, *December 26, 2002*[85]

The United States does not transport, and has not transported, detainees from one country to another for the purpose of interrogation using torture.

Condoleezza Rice, U.S. Secretary of State, December 5, 2005[86]

Postscript: The President Calls the World to Action

The United States is committed to the worldwide elimination of torture and we are leading this fight by example. . . . I call on all governments to join with the United States and the community of law-abiding nations in prohibiting, investigating, and prosecuting all acts of torture and in undertaking to prevent other cruel and unusual punishment.

President George W. Bush, June 26, 2003[87]

THE COMFORTS OF ABU GHRAIB

We are treating the Iraqi prisoners extremely well. In fact I think they get good food and shelter and they're free from the horrible commanders they used to work for. I think most of them are much happier, frankly.

Paul Wolfowitz, U.S. Deputy Secretary of Defense, March 23, 2003[88]

When we moved some of the prisoners into . . . [the] renovated cells, they cried with joy, almost disbelieving the comfort and cleanliness they would live in. They even asked how much they had to pay to stay there.

Brigadier General Janis Karpinski, describing renovations at Abu Ghraib prison, which had been placed under her command the previous June, September 17, 2003[89]

[For many, the] living conditions are now better in prison than at home. At one point we were concerned they wouldn't want to leave.

Brigadier General Janis Karpinski, discussing the comforts of Abu Ghraib prison, December 14, 2003[90]

IN FACT

On April 28, 2004, the CBS television magazine *Sixty Minutes II* presented startling images of Americans exhibiting cruel, humiliating, and sadistic behavior toward Iraqi detainees in the Abu Ghraib prison in Baghdad. During the broadcast, it was revealed that at

MAY 23, 2006

"BY JULY 4 THERE EITHER WILL BE CLEAR SIGNS THAT THE SUNNIS ARE CONTROLLING THE INSURGENCY—OR THERE WON'T."

★ GEORGE FRIEDMAN, STRATEGIC FORECASTING, INC.[P49]

least one prisoner had died as a result of such treatment. It was soon learned that CBS News had withheld the photographs, and its accompanying feature story, for two weeks, but had decided to run it after learning that a detailed exposé of the incidents at Abu Ghraib by prize-winning investigative reporter Seymour Hersh would be published in the May 10 edition of *The New Yorker*.

Have you people noticed who the torturers are? Women! The babes! The babes are meting out the torture. . . . You know, if you look at—if you, really, if you look at these pictures, I mean, I don't know if it's just me, but it looks just like anything you'd see Madonna, or Britney Spears do on stage. . . . And get an NEA grant for something like this. I mean, this is something that you can see on stage at Lincoln Center from an NEA grant.

Rush Limbaugh, opining about recently released photographs showing U.S. military personnel mistreating Iraqi detainees at Abu Ghraib prison, *The Rush Limbaugh Show*, May 3, 2004[91]

LIMBAUGH

This is no different than what happens at the Skull and Bones initiation and we're going to ruin people's lives over it and we're going to hamper our military effort, and then we are going to really hammer them because they had a good time. You know, these people are being fired at every day. I'm talking about people having a good time, these people, you ever heard of emotional release? You ever heard of need to blow some steam off?

Rush Limbaugh, responding to a caller who compared the mistreatment of Iraqi detainees by U.S. military personnel at Abu Ghraib prison to "fraternity hazing," *The Rush Limbaugh Show*, May 4, 2004[92]

We're functioning in a—with peacetime restraints, with legal requirements—in a wartime situation, in the information age, where people are running around with digital cameras and taking these unbelievable photographs and then passing them off, against the law, to the media, to our surprise, when they had not even arrived in the Pentagon.

Donald H. Rumsfeld, U.S. Secretary of Defense, during a Senate Armed Services Committee hearing, May 12, 2004[93]

JUNE 1, 2006

"I KNOW IT'S THE CLICHÉ OF THE WAR. BUT WE'LL KNOW IN THE NEXT SIX MONTHS—AND THIS TIME, IT'LL BE THE LAST SIX MONTHS WE GET."

 ARMY COUNTERINSURGENCY SPECIALIST[P58]

I'm probably not the only one up at this table that is more outraged by the outrage than we are by the treatment. . . . [These detainees] are not there for traffic violations. If they're in cell block 1A or 1B, these prisoners—they're murderers, they're terrorists, they're insurgents. Many of them probably have American blood on their hands. And here we're so concerned about the treatment of those individuals.

Senator James Inhofe (R-OK), member of the Senate Armed Services Committee, during a hearing on the Abu Ghraib prison scandal, May 12, 2004[94]

I am also outraged that we have so many humanitarian do-gooders right now crawling all over these prisons looking for human rights violations while our troops, our heroes, are fighting and dying.

Senator James Inhofe, adding a final thought to his previous remarks, May 12, 2004[95]

The Christian in me says it's wrong, but the corrections officer in me says, "I love to make a grown man piss himself."

Specialist Charles Graner, Abu Ghraib prison guard, explaining his treatment of Iraqi detainees to Sergeant Joseph M. Darby, May 22, 2004[96]

AS A CHRISTIAN...

IN FACT

General Antonio Taguba, who had been asked by General Ricardo Sanchez in January 2004 to investigate allegations of inappropriate brutality at Abu Ghraib prison, issued a report two months later that found abuse of detainees to have been "systemic and illegal." There were, the report stated, "numerous incidents of sadistic, blatant, and wanton criminal abuses." Shortly after information—and photographs—of events at Abu Ghraib were leaked to the press, General John Abizaid, the commander of CENTOM, warned Taguba, "You and your report will be investigated." Soon thereafter, Taguba was asked to submit his resignation from the U.S. Armed Forces.

JUNE 7, 2006

"THE NEXT SIX MONTHS ARE GOING TO BE CRITICALLY IMPORTANT TO FUTURE DEVELOPMENTS IN IRAQ."

☆ SENATOR EVAN BAYH[PS1]

[The abusive list of "interrogation rules of engagement" used at the Abu Ghraib prison in Iraq] was drafted "at the company commander level." [I] had "no role in preparing or approving it."

Lieutenant General Ricardo Sanchez, May 20, 2004[97]

IN FACT

According to *The New York Times,* Sanchez, the top U.S. commander in Iraq, in a memo dated September 14, 2003, had "authorized prisoner interrogation tactics that were harsher than accepted Army practice, including the use of 'stress positions' (in which prisoners are placed in potentially painful positions to try to get them to talk) and guard dogs to exploit 'Arab fear of dogs.' "[98]

The idea that anyone would suggest that Donald Rumsfeld—and now Richard Myers!—should step down, in the midst of a global war, for the excesses and criminality of a handful of miscreant guards and their lax immediate superiors in the cauldron of Iraq is absurd and depressing all at once.

Victor Davis Hanson, *National Review Online,* May 14, 2004[99]

America will fund the construction of a modern, maximum security prison. . . . Then, with the approval of the Iraqi government, we will demolish the Abu Ghraib prison, as a fitting symbol of Iraq's new beginning.

President George W. Bush, remarks at the U.S. Army War College, May 24, 2004[100]

IN FACT

At 3,200 inmates, Abu Ghraib had already surpassed the 2,500 people it was designed to incarcerate. The military, a Pentagon spokesman announced in March 2005, will continue to operate the facility for "the foreseeable future."

Indeed, Mr. Bush couldn't have legally torn down the infamous prison even if he had wanted to, since a federal judge had officially designated it a crime scene and ordered that it remain standing until the end of all judicial action against Abu Ghraib defendants. Nor has the Iraqi government shown much interest in "approving" Mr. Bush's proposal: "Demolishing and rebuilding" it, said interim president Ghazi al-Yawir, "would be a waste of money."[101]

ALL HAIL THE VICEROY: JERRY BREMER AND THE CPA

The Coalition Provisional Authority (CPA) was established on April 21, 2003, by the Bush administration to serve as the transitional government of Iraq, and was dissolved, somewhat abruptly, on June 28, 2004.

Although he had never been to Iraq and spoke no Arabic, L. Paul "Jerry" Bremer III was appointed by President Bush to lead the CPA.

He's a man of enormous experience; a person who knows how to get things done; he's a can-do type person; he shares the same values as the American—most Americans share, and that is our deep desire to have an orderly country in Iraq that is free and at peace, where the average citizen has a chance to achieve his or her dreams.

President George W. Bush, May 6, 2003[102]

JUNE 7, 2006

"THE NEXT SIX MONTHS WILL BE CRITICAL."

★ ZALMAY KHALILZAD, U.S. AMBASSADOR TO IRAQ[PS2]

A REPRESENTATIVE ROSTER OF BREMER'S CPA STAFF

The Bush administration appointed Jim O'Beirne, whom Rajiv Chandrasekaran of the *Washington Post* described as "a Pentagon political appointee who screens prospective political appointees,"[103] to help Bremer fill out his CPA staff. Following is a brief list of some of the employees this human resources expert, the husband of *National Review* editor Kate O'Beirne, selected:

EXECUTIVE IN CHARGE OF REOPENING THE BAGHDAD STOCK EXCHANGE: JAY HALLEN

This twenty-four-year-old recent Yale graduate had no previous experience in finance, but *had* appeared in his campus adaptation of Dr. Seuss's *The Lorax,* a show that the *Yale Herald* deemed "sympathetic, teaching the audience that the concepts of absolute good and absolute evil are often far too simple for the complexities of the rest of the world."[104]

What they need to understand is that we're not reopening the old Baghdad stock market. We're building an entirely new one.

Jay Hallen, explaining, in the face of a crescendo of complaints from Iraqis, why their stock exchange, closed in March 2003 when the bombing of Baghdad began, had yet to be reopened eleven months later, quoted in the Wall Street Journal, *January 28, 2004*[105]

SENIOR ADVISOR TO THE IRAQI HEALTH CARE SYSTEM: JAMES HAVEMAN

James Haveman, a sixty-year-old social worker, launched an anti-smoking campaign and allocated funds for new community health centers rather than rehabilitate the emergency rooms and operating theaters at existing Iraqi hospitals, even though injuries from insurgent attacks were the country's single largest public health challenge.[106] When asked about slow progress in rebuilding Iraq's health system, he replied,

Logistics isn't easy folks; it's only been ten months.

James Haveman, quoted in Knight-Ridder Newspapers, March 3, 2004[107]

CHIEF ADVISOR FOR ECONOMIC POLICY: PETER MCPHERSON

When Peter McPherson, an old friend of Dick Cheney's and a passionate devotee of supply-side economics, was offered a position at the CPA, he arranged for a 130-day leave of absence from his job as president of Michigan State University and accepted.[108] Asked about the looting that occurred immediately after the U.S. invasion, he said,

I thought the privatization that occurs sort of naturally [with looting] . . . was just fine.

Peter McPherson, 2004[109]

(continued)

JUNE 9, 2006

"IF WE ARE RIGHT AND THIS IS THE TIPPING POINT, THEN THINGS JUST TIPPED TOWARD A POLITICAL SETTLEMENT. THIS WILL BECOME CLEARER OVER THE NEXT FEW DAYS."

 STRATEGIC FORECASTING, INC[P53].

CO-MANAGER OF IRAQ'S $13 BILLION BUDGET: SIMONE LEDEEN

Simone Ledeen, the daughter of the American Enterprise Institute's Freedom Scholar, Michael Ledeen, was one of six twentysomethings chosen to manage the Iraqi budget. Known among CPA staffers as the Brat Pack, all six received job offers as a result of sending their résumés to the conservative Heritage Foundation. None had any previous financial management experience, although Ledeen did list founding a cooking school among her accomplishments.[110]

Hillary Clinton is coming here tomorrow. For her sake I hope I don't see her. I might do something crazy like spit in her direction.

Simone Ledeen, commenting on Senator Hillary Clinton's scheduled arrival in Baghdad, November 27, 2003[111]

Many of us knew the right people to come. They were willing to come. We couldn't get them there.

Frank Willis, former Senior Advisor for the Coalition Provisional Authority, testimony before the Senate Democratic Policy Committee about "the lack of quality people" at the CPA, February 14, 2005[112]

RECONSTRUCTION, AMERICAN-STYLE

Individuals holding positions in the top three layers of management in every national government ministry, affiliated corporations and other government institutions (e.g., universities and hospitals) shall be interviewed for possible affiliation with the Ba'ath Party, and subject to investigation for criminal conduct and risk to security. Any such persons determined to be full members of the Ba'ath Party shall be removed from their employment.

L. Paul Bremer III, Director of the Coalition Provisional Authority, CPA Order #1, "de-Ba'athifying" Iraqi society, May 16, 2003[113]

IN FACT

Bremer's order, issued only ten days after his appointment as CPA Administrator, effectively cleansed vestiges of the Ba'athist regime from all aspects of Iraqi society.

The destruction of Saddam's tyranny . . . has been accomplished.

Douglas Feith, U.S. Undersecretary of Defense for Policy, Washington Foreign Press Center briefing, May 28, 2003[114]

Americans on the ground in Iraq reported other effects as well:

We had things running good on Wednesday, and by Saturday we had 400,000 new enemies.

A "former top advisor" for U.S. reconstruction efforts in Iraq, quoted in *Time,* June 20, 2004[115]

JUNE 11, 2006

"I THINK BETWEEN NOW AND CHRISTMAS IS THE CRUCIAL TIME."

★ GENERAL BARRY R. MCCAFFREY[P54]

We had a lot of directors general of hospitals who were very good, and, with de-Ba'athification, we lost them and their expertise overnight. . . . Nobody who was left knew anything.

Stephen Browning, former senior advisor to the Iraqi ministries of health, religious affairs, transportation and communications, quoted in *The New Yorker*, November 15, 2004[116]

The problem with the blanket ban is that you get rid of the infrastructure; I mean, after all, these guys ran the country, and you polarize them. So did these decisions contribute to the insurgency? Unequivocally, yes. And we have to ask ourselves: How well did we really know how to run Iraq? Zero.

An "American special-forces officer stationed in Baghdad," quoted in *The New Yorker*, November 15, 2004[117]

IN FACT

To "jump start" Iraqi reconstruction after de-Ba'athification, the Coalition Provisional Authority flew nearly $12 billion in shrink-wrapped $100 bills—literally 363 tons worth of cash—into Iraq for disbursement to Iraqi ministries and U.S. contractors. The final shipment, more than $2.4 billion delivered just before the CPA turned sovereignty over to the Iraqis, was the biggest transfer of cash in the history of the Federal Reserve.[118]

The funds, legally the property of the Iraqi people, consisted primarily of revenues realized from the sale of Iraqi oil and unspent money from the UN's Iraq "oil-for-food" program, and they had been entrusted to the United States by the United Nations for safekeeping after the fall of Saddam's regime.[119]

The officials who used to steal most of Iraq's resources, and misuse what little was left, have gone. All of Iraq's resources will now be spent on you, the Iraqi people, and on projects which directly benefit you.

L. Paul Bremer III, Director of the Coalition Provisional Authority, address to the Iraqi people, July 7, 2003[120]

As steward for the Iraqi people, the CPA will manage and spend Iraqi funds, which belong to the Iraqi people, for their benefit. . . . [T]hey shall be managed in a transparent manner that fully comports with the CPA's obligations under international law.

L. Paul Bremer III, Director of the Coalition Provisional Authority, memorandum outlining CPA obligations regarding Iraqi funds used for reconstruction, August 19, 2003[121]

IN FACT

In hearings beginning February 6, 2007, the House Committee on Oversight and Reform, citing, among others, the Special Inspector General for Iraq Reconstruction, provided examples of how, specifically, the CPA went about "managing these funds on behalf of the Iraqi people":

JUNE 16, 2006

"WE HAVE A WINDOW [OF OPPORTUNITY] OF FIVE MONTHS—MAYBE SEVEN AT THE MOST—TO EFFECT CHANGE. IF THE PEOPLE OF IRAQ DON'T SEE A DIFFERENCE IN THAT TIME, WE ARE GOING TO BE EXTREMELY CHALLENGED COME DECEMBER."

★ MAJOR GENERAL BILL CALDWELL[P55]

One contractor received a $2 million payment in a duffel bag stuffed with shrink-wrapped bundles of currency. Auditors discovered that the key to a vault was kept in an unsecured backpack. They also found that $774,300 in cash had been stolen from one division's vault. Cash payments were made from the back of a pickup truck, and cash was stored in unguarded sacks in Iraqi ministry offices. One official was given $6.75 million in cash, and was ordered to spend it in one week before the interim Iraqi government took control of Iraqi funds. A summary of the minutes from a May 2004 CPA meeting show a single disbursement of $500 million in security funding labeled merely "TBD," meaning "to be determined."

House Committee on Oversight and Government Reform, Majority Staff Report on "Cash Transfers to the Coalition Provisional Authority," February 6, 2007[122]

IN FACT

In addition, more than 7,600 of the 8,206 "guards" drawing paychecks courtesy of the CPA were found to be "ghost employees" who did not exist; Halliburton charged the CPA for 42,000 daily meals for soldiers, while in fact serving only 14,000 of them; and Bremer himself was reported to have had a "slush fund" in excess of $600 million for which there was no paperwork at all.[123]

I believe the CPA discharged its responsibilities to manage these Iraqi funds on behalf of the Iraqi people.

L. Paul Bremer III, former Director of the Coalition Provisional Authority, testimony before the House Committee on Oversight and Government Reform, February 6, 2007[124]

ADMIRAL DAVID OLIVER: I can't tell you whether or not the money went to the right things or didn't—nor do I actually think it's important.

BBC INTERVIEWER: But the fact is billions of dollars have disappeared without trace.

OLIVER: Of their [Iraqis'] money. Billions of dollars of their money, yeah I understand. . . . What difference does it make?

Excerpt of a BBC interview with Admiral David Oliver (retired), former CPA financial advisor, quoted in the *Guardian*, February 8, 2007[125]

Postscript: Money Players

You could spin them but not throw a spiral.

Frank Willis, CPA Advisor to the Iraqi Transportation Ministry, commenting on CPA staffers' practice of using packets of cash as "footballs" during horseplay in their Green Zone offices, quoted in *Vanity Fair*, October 2007[126]

JUNE 22, 2006

"THE NEXT SIX MONTHS ARE LIKELY TO BE CRITICAL IN DETERMINING WHETHER THE SITUATION IN IRAQ TURNS WORSE OR WHETHER WE MAY YET SALVAGE A MEASURE OF POLITICAL STABILITY."

 REPRESENTATIVE MARK UDALL[P56]

PERSPECTIVES ON CHAOS

More people get killed in New York every night than get killed in Baghdad. The fact of life is that there will never be such a thing as one hundred percent security—it doesn't exist.

L. Paul Bremer III, Director of the Coalition Provisional Authority, August 2003[127]

I keep reading stories about it's a country in chaos. This is simply not true. It is not a country in chaos, and Baghdad is not a city in chaos.

L. Paul Bremer III, Director of the Coalition Provisional Authority, August 27, 2003[128]

You know, the country is basically peaceful.

L. Paul Bremer III, Director of the Coalition Provisional Authority, interviewed by Jim Lehrer on *The NewsHour*, PBS, September 24, 2003[129]

On October 10, 2003, Bremer appeared on *Good Morning America*. During his interview, Charles Gibson noted that the previous day had been the "deadliest in Iraq in a month."

Well, you know, it's important to keep it in perspective, Charlie. We've had a really great six months, and there have been some bad days.... But look at how far we've come. Much further than anybody would've expected.... Life is basically quite normal here.

L. Paul Bremer III, Director of the Coalition Provisional Authority, October 10, 2003

IN FACT

On December 6, 2003, insurgents attempted to assassinate Paul Bremer by attacking his convoy while he was returning to the Green Zone from the Baghdad Airport. The back window of his vehicle was blown out, but Bremer escaped injury. The incident was not reported in the press until December 19.[130]

Off the record: Paris is burning. On the record: Security and stability are returning to Iraq.

Dan Senor, official civilian Coalition Provisional Authority spokesman in Iraq, discussing violence in Baghdad with a small group of reporters, April 2004[131]

If you go back and look at what has been accomplished, I would say that we have [done] almost everything we set out to accomplish at liberation. [President Bush and Prime Minister Blair] had a vision of an Iraq that was stable, pluralistic, democratic, at peace with itself—and we have accomplished most of that.

L. Paul Bremer III, Director of the Coalition Provisional Authority, interviewed just before his departure from Iraq, *Time* magazine, June 20, 2004[132]

Every benchmark . . . was achieved on time or ahead of schedule, including the transfer of sovereignty that ended his tenure.

President George W. Bush, awarding the Medal of Freedom, the nation's highest civilian honor, to L. Paul Bremer III, December 14, 2007[133]

IN FACT

As *The Washington Post* pointed out in its coverage of the medal ceremony, the President failed to add that Bremer's transfer of sovereignty to the Iraqis had been "hurriedly arranged two days early because of fears insurgents would attack the ceremonies."[134]

JUNE 26, 2006

"THE NEXT FIVE TO SIX MONTHS ARE CRITICAL FOR THIS GOVERNMENT."

 ZALMAY KHALILZAD, U.S. AMBASSADOR TO IRAQ[F57]

COMING REAL SOON NOW: THE NEW, DE-BA'ATHIFIED IRAQI SECURITY FORCES!

Our strategy can be summed up this way: As the Iraqis stand up, we will stand down.

President George W. Bush, nationally televised address to troops at Fort Bragg, North Carolina, June 28, 2005[135]

Immediately after taking the reins as CPA Director, Paul Bremer surprised many observers by signing an order decommissioning the entire Iraqi army.

We don't need them.

L. Paul Bremer III, explaining to an "anonymous senior CPA official" why it was not a problem to disband the Iraqi military, May 2003[136]

IN FACT

Bremer's move not only left tens of thousands of young, armed Iraqi men unemployed; it made it necessary to build an entirely new Iraqi military and police force from scratch. The Americans set about the task with great eagerness and optimism.

The original plan had been to train up 27 battalions over the course of two years. Based on our experience with the first battalion, we believe it's possible to do that—given sufficient resources and sufficient effort, to do that in just a year. We'll do that by focusing on leader training and use the pool of soldiers who already have had basic training to form effective units.

Walter Slocombe, Coalition Provisional Authority Special Advisor on Security and Defense, September 17, 2003[137]

Obviously they are not fully trained. They're not ready.

General John Abizaid, Commander, U.S. Central Command, after surviving an attack on a police station he was visiting in Fallujah, February 14, 2004

JULY 7, 2006

"THE SITUATION IN IRAQ IS A LOT BETTER, DIFFERENT THAN IT WAS A YEAR AGO."

★ SENATOR JOE LIEBERMAN[P58]

In terms of the timeline for [how long we will need] the presence of multinational forces to help us establish security and stability, I think it will be a question of months rather than years.

Ali Abdul-Amir Allawi, Defense Minister of Iraq, May 25, 2004[138]

The number of trained Iraqi forces that Allawi can rely on is somewhere over 120,000.

Condoleezza Rice, National Security Advisor, at her Senate confirmation hearings to become U.S. Secretary of State, January 1, 2005[139]

IN FACT

The *Los Angeles Times* reported on January 18, 2005, that the Pentagon listed "4,000 soldiers 'trained and on hand' " in Iraq.[140]

We fully recognize that Iraqi armed forces will not have an independent capability for some time, because they don't have an institutional base to support them. And so Level One [a rating for units that are capable of independent operations] is one battalion.

General George Casey, testifying before the Senate Armed Services Committee, September 29, 2005[141]

I'm encouraged by the increasing size and capability of the Iraqi security forces. Today they have more than 100 battalions operating throughout the country, and our commanders report that the Iraqi forces are serving with increasing effectiveness.

President George W. Bush, weekly radio address, October 1, 2005[142]

Right now there are . . . over 30 Iraqi battalions in the lead. And that is substantial progress from the way the world was a year ago.

President George W. Bush, October 4, 2005[143]

At the time of our Fallujah operations 11 months ago, there were only a few Iraqi army battalions in combat. Today there are more than 80 Iraqi army battalions fighting the insurgency alongside our forces.

President George W. Bush, televised address at a National Endowment for Democracy event, October 6, 2005[144]

The Iraqis are on the way to building a free and independent Iraq. Their military—two-thirds of their military is now ready, on their own, to lead the fight with some logistical backing from the U.S. or stand up on their own totally. That's progress.

Senator Joseph Lieberman (D-CT), during a Connecticut primary senatorial candidates' debate with Ned Lamont, July 7, 2006[145]

Iraqis can take over security in the next 12 to 18 months. The Iraqi security forces are progressing to a point where they can take on the security responsibilities for the country, with very little coalition support.

General George Casey, quoted in *USA Today*, August 29, 2006[146]

Our forces will be ready by June 2007.

Nuri al-Maliki, Prime Minister of Iraq, November 30, 2006[147]

JULY 7, 2006

"BY THE END OF THIS YEAR, WE WILL BEGIN TO DRAW DOWN SIGNIFICANT NUMBERS OF AMERICAN TROOPS."

★ SENATOR JOE LIEBERMAN[PS9]

IN FACT

A commission created by Congress reported on September 6, 2007, that "The ISF (Iraqi Security Forces) will be unable to fulfill their essential security responsibilities independently over the next 12–18 months. . . . Sectarian partisanship, bureaucratic inefficiency, the Ministry of Interior's reputation for corruption, a near universal rejection of the National Police as currently formed and administered, and a weak and ineffective Department of Border Enforcement continue to impede Iraq's overall progress toward security and stability."[148]

CONTRACTORS: "SKYDIVERS AND MOTORCYCLISTS"

"AN UPTICK IN LOCAL ENGAGEMENTS"

Western contractors are not targets. . . . The risks are akin to skydiving or riding a motorcycle.

Tom Foley, CPA's director of private sector development, at a Commerce Department Conference in Washington, urging U.S. security firms to become involved in Iraq, February 11, 2004[149]

You will want to be a part of this. Do not miss the boat.

Tom Foley, CPA's director of private sector development, concluding his Commerce Department pitch, February 11, 2004[150]

IN FACT

On March 31, 2004, scarcely a month after Foley spoke, four security contractors employed by Blackwater USA were ambushed by insurgents in Fallujah, after which an angry mob, chanting "Fallujah is the graveyard of Americans," set their vehicles on fire, dragged their charred and mutilated torsos through the streets, and suspended at least two of them from a bridge over the Euphrates River.[151]

Despite an uptick in local engagements, the overall Iraqi area of operations remains relatively stable with negligible impact on the coalition's ability to continue progress in governance, economic development, and restoration of essential services.

Brigadier General Mark Kimmit, chief military spokesperson for the Coalition Provisional Authority, at a news briefing hours after the Fallujah ambush, March 31, 2004[152]

The very fact that two vehicles traveled through Fallujah today and were attacked is a tragic event, but it is not indicative that there somehow is a barrier for any coalition vehicles to get through there. The coalition vehicles go through there every day without incident and without trouble.

Brigadier General Mark Kimmit, chief military spokesperson for the Coalition Provisional Authority, at the same news briefing, March 31, 2004[153]

JULY 8, 2006

"THERE'S GOING TO BE REALLY NO PROSPECT, IN MY VIEW, OF KEEPING ANY LARGE NUMBER OF AMERICAN FORCES [IN IRAQ]."

☆ SENATOR JOE BIDEN[P60]

I don't care about the people of Fallujah. You're not going to win their hearts and minds. They're going to kill you till the very end. They've proven that. So let's knock this place down. . . . [W]e know what the final solution should be.

Bill O'Reilly, *The O'Reilly Factor*, Fox News, March 31, 2004[154]

Those bodies lay in Fallujah from 10 in the morning until nightfall and the American military, 4,000 Marines nearby, did nothing. I think we need the name of the commander who made that decision. And I think he ought to be punished. . . . This is a sign of weakness. This is how we got 9/11.

Tucker Carlson, cohost of *Crossfire*, CNN, April 1, 2007[155]

There will be a price extracted, there will be a response, and it will be obvious to all.

Richard Armitage, U.S. Deputy Secretary of State, speaking to reporters at the State Department, April 1, 2004[156]

At this point we would advise against travel through the city of Fallujah, unless there's absolute necessity to do that, much like a travel warning put out from the State Department. We don't expect that travel warning to last that long.

Brigadier General Mark Kimmit, chief military spokesperson for the Coalition Provisional Authority, at a news briefing the day after the Fallujah ambush, April 1, 2004[157]

IN FACT

On April 4, 2004, the U.S. Marines commenced Operation Vigilant Resolve, a massive military response to the ambush of security contractors in Fallujah. In the course of the ensuing fighting, more than 600 Fallujan civilians were killed and much of the city was destroyed, but Coalition forces ultimately failed to capture the contractors' killers or to dislodge the insurgents.[158]

THE AMBUSH IN FALLUJAH: WHAT REALLY HAPPENED?

Those four Americans were there because they were hired to provide security to food caravans delivering life giving substances to native Iraqis. . . . They were there to do a job to save perishing people who have been intimidated and abused for most every moment of their lives. . . . [They] came for humanitarian reasons . . . to save a people.

Chaplain D. R. Staton, *Blackwater Tactical Weekly*, April 5, 2004[159]

IN FACT

It soon developed that the four men who were ambushed were not bringing food to Iraqis, but, rather, were escorting three empty trucks belonging to a European food caterer that managed dining halls on U.S. military bases.[160]

Why were they sent into the hottest zone in Iraq in unarmored, underpowered vehicles to protect a truck?

Daniel Browne, a Blackwater security contractor on assignment near Fallujah on the day of the ambush, in a portion of Blackwater's April 2004 internal investigation report not revealed publicly until it was obtained by the House Committee on Oversight and Government Reform[161]

AUGUST 30, 2006

"IRAQIS CAN TAKE OVER SECURITY IN THE NEXT 12 TO 18 MONTHS."

GENERAL GEORGE CASEY[P61]

IN FACT

On January 5, 2005, the families of the four security contractors killed in Fallujah filed a wrongful death lawsuit against Blackwater, alleging that, in order to save money, the company had made a series of decisions that unnecessarily jeopardized the contractors' lives. The suit claimed, among other things, that Blackwater's mission dispatcher boasted after the ambush that he had "saved two lives" by sending only four men instead of the six mandated for such assignments.[162]

Blackwater hopes that the honor and dignity of our fallen comrades are not diminished by the use of the legal process.

Chris Bertelli, official Blackwater spokesperson, responding, in an email statement, to the lawsuit brought by the families of the contractors slain in Fallujah, quoted in the *Raleigh News and Observer*, January 6, 2005[163]

IN FACT

Concerns for honor and dignity notwithstanding, Blackwater promply responded to the families of their "fallen comrades" by filing a $10 million countersuit of their own.[164]

Eyewitness accounts and investigative reports . . . portray a company that ignored multiple warnings about the dangers of traveling through Fallujah, cut essential personnel from the mission, and failed to supply its team with armored vehicles, machine guns, sufficient threat intelligence, or even maps of the area. Blackwater's own employees described its conduct as "flat out a sloppy . . . operation" and a "ship about to sink."

House Committee on Oversight and Government Reform, Majority Staff Report on "Blackwater's Actions in Fallujah," September 27, 2007[165]

Stronger weapons, armored vehicles, ammunition or maps would not have shielded these brave military veterans from the certain death that awaited them on that morning. Even if Blackwater had placed six men on the mission, the result would likely have been the same.

Blackwater USA, response to the House Committee on Oversight and Government Reform Majority Staff Report," October 23, 2007.[166]

"HUMANE DEMOCRACY" IN NISOUR SQUARE

If you're not willing to drink the Blackwater Kool-Aid and be committed to supporting humane democracy around the world, then there's probably a better place [to go work] because that's all we do.

Chris Taylor, Blackwater vice president for strategic initiatives, quoted in *The Weekly Standard,* December 18, 2006[167]

On Sunday, September 16, 2007, shots fired in Nisour Square, Baghdad, by Blackwater contractors killed seventeen Iraqi civilians and wounded twenty-four others.[168]

SEPTEMBER 22, 2006

"TIME IS SHORT, . . . THE NEXT THREE MONTHS ARE CRITICAL."

★ LEE HAMILTON, IRAQ STUDY GROUP CO-CHAIR[P62]

Blackwater's independent contractors acted lawfully and appropriately in response to a hostile attack in Baghdad on Sunday. . . . Blackwater regrets any loss of life, but this convoy was violently attacked by armed insurgents, not civilians, and our people did their job to defend human life.

Anne E. Tyrrell, Blackwater spokesperson, September 17, 2007[169]

The "civilians" reportedly fired upon by Blackwater professionals were in fact armed enemies, and Blackwater personnel returned defensive fire. Blackwater professionals heroically defended American lives in a war zone.

Anne E. Tyrrell, Blackwater spokesperson, in an email message, September 18, 2007[170]

We will not allow Iraqis to be killed in cold blood. There is a sense of tension and anger among all Iraqis, including the government, over this crime.

Nouri al-Maliki, Prime Minister of Iraq, speaking to reporters in his Baghdad office after an initial Iraqi probe indicated the Blackwater contractors had not been attacked before the Nisour Square shootings, September 19, 2007[171]

All I can say is in the incident reports I've seen, at least three of our armored vehicles were hit by small arms fire, incoming, and one of them damaged. . . . So there was definitely incoming small arms fire from insurgents.

Erik Prince, founder, chairman, and CEO of Blackwater, responding to reports that Blackwater guards had not been shot at before opening fire in Nisour Square, October 14, 2007[172]

Why had [Blackwater] opened fire? I do not know. No one—I repeat no one—had fired at them . . . there was no reason for them to shoot.

Hassan Jabar Salman, an Iraqi lawyer who was shot four times in the back during the Nisoor Square incident, quoted in *The Nation,* October 15, 2007[173]

IN FACT

According to *The New York Times,* FBI agents investigating the September 16 episode in which Blackwater security personnel shot and killed seventeen Iraqi civilians have concluded that "at least 14 of the shootings were unjustified and violated deadly-force rules in effect for security contractors in Iraq." The investigators, *The Times* reported, "found no evidence to support assertions by Blackwater employees that they were fired upon by Iraqi civilians."[174]

On January 13, 2008, the Associated Press reported that soon after the shootings, Blackwater had repainted and refurbished the trucks involved in the Nisour Square incident. "The repairs." the AP noted, "essentially destroyed evidence that Justice Department investigators hoped to examine . . . as they consider building a case against any of the 19 guards in the Sept. 16 convoy."[175]

[Any repairs] would have been done at the government's direction.

Anne E. Tyrrell, Blackwater spokesperson, quoted by the Associated Press, January 13, 2008[176]

OCTOBER 8, 2006

"THIS IS A DECISIVE PERIOD FOR EVERYONE AND EVERYONE KNOWS IT. THE NEXT SIX MONTHS WILL DETERMINE THE FUTURE OF IRAQ."

★ GENERAL GEORGE CASEY[P63]

SEE NO EVIL, HEAR NO EVIL

Contractors shall be immune from Iraqi legal process with respect to acts performed by them pursuant to the terms and conditions of a Contract or any sub-contract thereto.

This Order shall enter into force on the date of signature . . . and shall not terminate until the departure of the final element of the MNF from Iraq.

L. Paul Bremer III, Director of the Coalition Provisional Authority, CPA Order #17 (Revised), June 27, 2004[177]

In order for responsible federal contractors to accompany the U.S. Armed Forces on the battlefield, it is essential that their immunity from liability for casualties be federally protected.

Appellate brief filed by Blackwater, October 31, 2005[178]

The comprehensive regulatory scheme enacted by Congress and the President grant military contractors like Blackwater immunity from state-court litigation.

Blackwater petition to U.S. Supreme Court, contending that the company is "constitutionally immune" from lawsuits such as the one brought against it by the families of the four Blackwater contractors ambushed in Fallujah, quoted in *thenation.com,* October 25, 2006[179]

Blackwater employees and other civilian contractors cannot be tried in military courts and it is unclear what American criminal laws might cover criminal acts committed in a war zone.

The New York Times, October 29, 2007[180]

The State Department promised Blackwater USA bodyguards immunity from prosecution in its investigation of last month's deadly shooting of 17 Iraqi civilians, the Associated Press has learned. The immunity deal has delayed a criminal inquiry into the Sept. 16 killings and could undermine any effort to prosecute security contractors for their role in the incident that has infuriated the Iraqi government.

Associated Press, "Immunity Deal Hampers Blackwater Inquiry," October 29, 2007[181]

The State Department investigators from the agency's investigative arm, the Bureau of Diplomatic Security, offered the immunity grants even though they did not have the authority to do so.

The New York Times, citing anonymous government officials in a follow-up to the Associated Press's immunity deal scoop, October 29, 2007[182]

IN FACT

In the face of the criticism that accompanied its handling of the inquiry into the Blackwater shootings, the State Department yielded responsibility for coordinating its outsourced security convoys in Iraq to the Pentagon.

OCTOBER 26, 2006

"IF ANYONE IS RESPONSIBLE FOR THE POOR SECURITY SITUATION IN IRAQ IT IS THE COALITION."

★ NURI AL-MALIKI, PRIME MINISTER OF IRAQ[P64]

THE PRESIDENT ADDRESSES THE QUESTION OF CONTRACTOR ACCOUNTABILITY

On April 10, 2006, President George W. Bush made an address about the "Global War on Terror" at the Paul H. Nitze School of Advanced International Studies in Washington, D.C. Here is a partial transcript of the question-and-answer session that followed. . . .

Q: I'm a first-year student in South Asia studies. My question is in regards to private military contractors. Uniform Code of Military Justice does not apply to these contractors in Iraq. I asked your Secretary of Defense a couple months ago what law governs their actions.

THE PRESIDENT: I was going to ask him. Go ahead. (Laughter.) Help. (Laughter.)

Q: I was hoping your answer might be a little more specific. (Laughter.) Mr. Rumsfeld answered that Iraq has its own domestic laws which he assumed applied to those private military contractors. However, Iraq is clearly not currently capable of enforcing its laws, much less against—over our American military contractors. I would submit to you that in this case, this is one case that privatization is not a solution. And, Mr. President, how do you propose to bring private military contractors under a system of law?

THE PRESIDENT: I appreciate that very much. I wasn't kidding—(laughter.) I was going to—I pick up the phone and say, Mr. Secretary, I've got an interesting question. (Laughter.) This is what delegation—I don't mean to be dodging the question, although it's kind of convenient in this case, but never—(laughter). I really will—I'm going to call the Secretary and say you brought up a very valid question, and what are we doing about it? That's how I work. I'm—thanks. (Laughter.)[183]

[Secretary of Defense Gates believes this arrangement will give] commanders the knowledge of what is going on in the battlespace so they aren't blindsided by contractors running in and out of their battlespace and potentially causing problems.

Geoff Morrell, Defense Department Press Secretary, News Briefing, October 30, 2007[184]

IN FACT

Morrell failed to mention that the Pentagon had outsourced its own monitoring of private security teams in Iraq to the British firm Aegis Defence Systems, with whom it signed a $292 million contract in May 2004. In April 2005, the Inspector General for Iraq Reconstruction issued a report finding that the firm had performed deficiently in five areas covered by its contract, and that, as a result, "there is no assurance that Aegis is providing the best possible safety and security for government and reconstruction contractor personnel and facilities." Aegis, whose founder, Tim Spicer, was once investigated for arms smuggling, also attracted media attention when a video—accompanied by an Elvis Presley sound track—surfaced on the Internet that appeared to show some of its contract employees shooting up Iraqi civilian vehicles for sport.[185]

NOVEMBER 14, 2006

"MOST DEMOCRATS SHARE THE VIEW THAT WE SHOULD PRESSURE THE WHITE HOUSE TO COMMENCE THE PHASED REDEPLOYMENT OF U.S. TROOPS FROM IRAQ IN FOUR TO SIX MONTHS."

 SENATOR CARL LEVIN[P65]

POSTSCRIPT: THE COOKIE AND BUZZY SHOW

On November 14, 2007, the State Department's Inspector General, Howard J. "Cookie" Krongard, testified before the House Committee on Oversight and Government Reform in response to complaints from "seven current and former officials in his office" that he had improperly obstructed investigations into alleged illegal actions by State Department contractors, including Blackwater USA.

During the hearing, Krongard was confronted with evidence that his brother, Alvin "Buzzy" Krongard, was a member of Blackwater's advisory board, an obvious conflict of interest.

I can tell you very frankly, I am not aware of any financial interest or position he has with respect to Blackwater. It couldn't possibly have affected anything I've done, because I don't believe it. And when these ugly rumors started recently, I specifically asked him. I do not believe it is true that he is a member of the advisory board, as you stated.

Howard J. "Cookie" Krongard, State Department Inspector General, testimony before the House Oversight and Government Reform Committee, November 14, 2007[186]

IN FACT

During a break in the hearing, Krongard called his brother and, when the proceedings resumed, he announced his discovery that Buzzy not only was a Blackwater advisor, but that he had attended a board meeting just the day before.

I'm not my brother's keeper.

Howard J. "Cookie" Krongard, explaining, in response to a question from Representative Stephen Lynch, the unusual change in his testimony, November 14, 2007[187]

I had told my brother I was going on the advisory board. My brother says that is not the case. I stand by what I told my brother.

Alvin B. "Buzzy" Krongard, former CIA Executive Director and member of Blackwater's board of advisors, November 14, 2007[188]

IN FACT

On December 7, 2007, Howard J. "Cookie" Krongard announced his resignation, effective January 15, 2008, from his post as State Department Inspector General.

A CIVIL WAR? NOT BLOODY LIKELY!

I think the ethnic differences in Iraq are there but they're exaggerated.

Paul Wolfowitz, U.S. Deputy Secretary of Defense, March 5, 2003[189]

There's been a certain amount of pop sociology in America . . . that the Shia can't get along with the Sunni and the Shia in Iraq just want to establish some kind of Islamic fundamentalist regime. There's almost no evidence of that at all. Iraq's always been very secular.

William Kristol, interviewed on NPR, April 1, 2003[190]

NOVEMBER 14, 2006

"GENERAL ABIZAID HA[S] IT ABOUT RIGHT. . . . I THINK [ANOTHER FOUR TO SIX MONTHS] IS WHAT WE'RE LOOKING AT."

★ SENATOR JOHN CORNYN[P66]

There are hopeful signs that Iraqis of differing religious, ethnic and political persuasions can work together. . . . [There is] a broad Iraqi consensus favoring the idea of pluralism.

William Kristol, *The Weekly Standard*, March 22, 2004[191]

The terrorists in Iraq failed to incite an Iraqi civil war.

President George W. Bush, June 28, 2005[192]

Why do they [Arabs] hate each other? Why do Sunnis kill Shiites? How do they tell the difference? They all look the same to me.

Senator Trent Lott (R-MS), speaking shortly before a scheduled meeting with President Bush and Vice President Cheney, September 28, 2006[193]

Do I care if the Sunnis and Shiites kill each other in Iraq? No. I don't care. Let's get our people out of there. Let them kill each other. Maybe they'll all kill each other, and then we can have a decent country in Iraq.

Bill O'Reilly, American political commentator, December 5, 2006[194]

Within Iraq, the sectarian militias are engaged in civil war or so close to it as to make little practical difference. The conflict between Shias and Sunnis goes back 1,400 years. . . . The civil war in Iraq threatens to usher in a cycle of domestic upheavals and a war between Shia and Sunni states, with a high potential of drawing in countries from outside the region.

Henry Kissinger, former U.S. Secretary of State, January 19, 2007[195]

Some call this civil war; others call it emergency—I call it pure evil.

President George W. Bush, remarks on the situation in Iraq to the National Cattlemen's Beef Association, March 28, 2007[196]

MISSION ACCOMPLISHED REVISITED

Well, the mission of those forces that he went to greet had been accomplished.

Condoleezza Rice, National Security Advisor, explaining why the "Mission Accomplished" banner displayed during the President's speech aboard the USS *Lincoln* was not "premature," September 28, 2003[197]

The mission accomplished sign, of course, was put up by the members of the U.S.S. Abraham Lincoln, saying that their mission was accomplished. . . . I know it was attributed somehow to some ingenious advance man from my staff. They weren't that ingenious, by the way.

President George W. Bush, October 28, 2003[198]

The mission accomplished banner was suggested by those on the ship. . . . The mission for those people on board the ship was accomplished.

Scott McClellan, Deputy Press Secretary, October 29, 2003[199]

IN FACT

The "Mission Accomplished" banner was, in fact, made by Scott Sforza, a former ABC producer on the White House PR team. There is no reason to believe that the marines suggested, or were in any other way involved in, its creation.

NOVEMBER 26, 2006

"MY GUESS IS [THE] NEXT FOUR TO SIX MONTHS ARE CRUCIAL."

GENERAL BARRY MCCAFFREY[F67]

VOLUME V

CLOSING

THE END

THE RING

GAME?

If there is ever going to be an end game in Iraq, we are now in it.

Stratfor (Strategic Forecasting, Inc.), the "world's leading private intelligence firm," "The Beginning of the End Game," March 17, 2006[1]

SHOULD WE STAY OR SHOULD WE GO?
THE NEW YORK TIMES ANSWERS "YES!"

It is time for the United States to leave Iraq, without any more delay than the Pentagon needs to organize an orderly exit.

Editorial, The New York Times, *July 8, 2007*[2]

The United States cannot walk away from the new international terrorist front it created in Iraq. It will need to keep sufficient forces and staging points in the region to strike effectively against terrorist sanctuaries there or a Qaeda bid to hijack control of a strife-torn Iraq.

Editorial, The New York Times, *August 13, 2007*[3]

MEASURING THE IRAQ WAR IN "FRIEDMAN UNITS"

"*New York Times* foreign affairs columnist Tom Friedman is considered by many of his media colleagues to be one of the wisest observers of international affairs," noted Fairness and Accuracy in Reporting (FAIR), the national media watchdog group, in an article posted on its website on May 16, 2006.

In particular, FAIR noted how expertly Friedman had managed, during a May 11, 2006, appearance on MSNBC's *Hardball*, to boil down the complexities of the situation in Iraq into a single "make-or-break deadline."[4] The following, selectively culled from FAIR's volumious Friedman archives, is a representative sampling:

The next six months in Iraq—which will determine the prospects for democracy-building there—are the most important six months in U.S. foreign policy in a long, long time.

Thomas Friedman, *The New York Times*, November 30, 2003[5]

What I absolutely don't understand is just at the moment when we finally have a UN-approved Iraqi-caretaker government made up of—I know a lot of these guys—reasonably decent people and more than reasonably decent people, everyone wants to declare it's over. I don't get it. It might be over in a week, it might be over in a month, it might be over in six months, but what's the rush? Can we let this play out, please?

Thomas Friedman, interviewed on NPR's *Fresh Air*, June 3, 2004[6]

What we're gonna find out, Bob, in the next six to nine months is whether we have liberated a country or uncorked a civil war.

Thomas Friedman, interviewed by Bob Schieffer on CBS's *Face the Nation*, October 3, 2004[7]

Improv time is over. This is crunch time. Iraq will be won or lost in the next few months. But it won't be won with high rhetoric. It will be won on the ground in a war over the last mile.

Thomas Friedman, *The New York Times*, November 28, 2004[8]

I think we're in the end game now. . . . I think we're in a six-month window here where it's going to become very clear.

Thomas Friedman, on NBC's *Meet the Press*, September 25, 2005[9]

Maybe the cynical Europeans were right. Maybe this neighborhood is just beyond transformation. That will become clear in the next few months as we see just what kind of minority the Sunnis in Iraq intend to be. If they come around, a decent outcome in Iraq is still possible, and we should stay to help build it. If they won't, then we are wasting our time.

Thomas Friedman, *The New York Times*, September 28, 2005[10]

We've teed up this situation for Iraqis, and I think the next six months really are going to determine whether this country is going to collapse into three parts or more or whether it's going to come together.

Thomas Friedman, on CBS's *Face the Nation*, December 18, 2005[11]

I think that we're going to know after six to nine months whether this project has any chance of succeeding.

Thomas Friedman, interviewed on *The Oprah Winfrey Show*, January 23, 2006[12]

I think we're in the end game there, in the next three to six months, Bob. We've got for the first time an Iraqi government elected on the basis of an Iraqi constitution. Either they're going to produce the kind of inclusive consensual government that we aspire to in the near term, in which case America will stick with it, or they're not, in which case I think the bottom's going to fall out.

Thomas Friedman, interviewed by Bob Schieffer on *CBS News*, January 31, 2006[13]

I think we are in the end game. The next six to nine months are going to tell whether we can produce a decent outcome in Iraq.

Thomas Friedman, on NBC's *Today*, March 2, 2006[14]

Can Iraqis get this government together? If they do, I think the American public will continue to want to support the effort there to try to produce a decent, stable Iraq. But if they don't, then I think the bottom is going to fall out of public support here for the whole Iraq endeavor. So one way or another, I think we're in the end game in the sense it's going to be decided in the next weeks or months whether there's an Iraq there worth investing in. And that is something only Iraqis can tell us.

Thomas Friedman, on CNN's *Late Edition with Wolf Blitzer*, April 23, 2006[15]

Well, I think that we're going to find out, Chris, in the next year to six months—probably sooner—whether a decent outcome is possible there, and I think we're going to have to just let this play out.

Thomas Friedman, interviewed by Chris Matthews on MSNBC's *Hardball*, May 11, 2006[16]

DECEMBER 17, 2006

"WE'VE GOT TO TURN THE CORNER ON THIS THING, AND WE'VE GOT TO DO IT, I WOULD SAY, IN THE NEXT SIX MONTHS."

★ SENATOR JOHN THUNE[P68]

As a tribute to Thomas Friedman's prognostications, the blogger Atrios (Duncan Black) has coined the phrase "Friedman Unit (F.U.)" defined as any period of six months extending into the future.[17]

TURNING POINTS

This month will be a political turning point for Iraq. . . . We will see the beginnings of the process of creating Iraqi self-government after more than three decades of horrendous tyranny.

Douglas J. Feith, U.S. Undersecretary of Defense for Policy, July 9, 2003[18]

We've reached another great turning point—and the resolve we show will shape the next stage of the world democratic movement.

President George W. Bush, December 6, 2003[19]

A turning point will come two weeks from today.

President George W. Bush, June 16, 2004[20]

WHAT WAR IS GOOD FOR: DESPITE THE NEGATIVE REACTION BY MUCH OF THE MEDIA, U.S. MARINES DID A GOOD JOB IN FALLUJAH, A BATTLE THAT MIGHT PROVE A TURNING POINT.

Headline of editorial by Max Boot, *Montreal Gazette*, December 9, 2004

The Iraqi election of 2005 . . . will turn out to have been a genuine turning point . . . [the] key moment in vindicating the Bush Doctrine as the right response to 9/11. And now there is the prospect of further and accelerating progress.

William Kristol, *The Weekly Standard*, March 7, 2005[21]

On January 30th in Iraq, the world witnessed an important moment in the global struggle against tyranny, a moment that historians might one day call a major turning point.

Donald H. Rumsfeld, U.S. Secretary of Defense, February 2, 2005[22]

There's still a lot of difficult work to be done in Iraq, but thanks to the courage of the Iraqi people, the year 2005 will be recorded as *a turning point* **in the history of Iraq, the history of the Middle East, and the history of freedom.**

President George W. Bush, December 12, 2005[23]

DECEMBER 20, 2006

"IT SEEMS VERY LIKELY THAT 2007 WILL BE MAKE OR BREAK TIME IN IRAQ."

☆ NINA KAMP AND MICHAEL O'HANLON, BROOKINGS INSTITUTION[P69]

And while the level of violence has continued, I do believe that when we look back on this period of time, 2005 will have been the turning point when, in fact, we made sufficient progress both on the political front and the security front so that we'll see that as the watershed year.

Vice President Dick Cheney, interviewed on ABC News, December 18, 2005

This is a—we believe this is a turning point for the Iraqi citizens, and it's a new chapter in our partnership.

President George W. Bush, May 1, 2006[24]

There have been setbacks and missteps—like Abu Ghraib—that were felt immediately and have been difficult to overcome. Yet we have now reached a turning point in the struggle between freedom and terror.

President George W. Bush, May 22, 2006[25]

I think—tide turning—see, as I remember—I was raised in the desert, but tides kind of—it's easy to see a tide turn—did I say those words?

President George W. Bush, June 14, 2006[26]

A MODEST PROPOSAL

I think all foreigners should stop interfering in the internal affairs of Iraq.

Paul Wolfowitz, U.S. Deputy Secretary of Defense, July 22, 2003[27]

VIGILANCE, THE PRICE OF LIBERTY

SOME DARE CALL IT TREASON: AMERICA'S FIFTH COLUMN

The blood of hundreds of thousands of . . . Americans is on the hands of the antiwar activists.

David Horowitz, founder, The David Horowitz Freedom Center, September 28, 2001[28]

We expect every American to support our military, and if they can't do that, to shut up. Americans, and indeed our allies, who actively work against our military once the war is underway will be considered enemies of the state by me. Just fair warning to you, Barbra Streisand, and others who see the world as you do.

Bill O'Reilly, American political commentator, Fox News Channel, February 26, 2003[29]

JANUARY 12, 2007

"AT SIX MONTHS WE'LL KNOW AND THEN WE HAVE TO DO SOMETHING DRAMATIC."

★ SECRETARY OF STATE CONDOLEEZZA RICE[P70]

The American public knows how important this war is and is not as casualty sensitive as the weenies in the American press are.

Fred Barnes, Executive Editor, *The Weekly Standard*, Fox News Channel, March 23, 2003[30]

Over the next couple of weeks when we find the chemical weapons this guy was amassing, the fact that this war was attacked by the left and so the right was so vindicated, I think, really means that the left is going to have to hang its head for three or four more years.

Dick Morris, Fox News Channel, April 9, 2003[31]

Every step of the way, they were lecturing us on how it wasn't well thought out . . . we didn't have enough troops there, it was going to be a quagmire. All of these thousands, according to naysayers, of troops are going to die. . . . They've . . . made fools of themselves.

Sean Hannity, *Hannity & Colmes*, April 10, 2003[32]

[Saddam Hussein's] gruesome qualities matter less to the Left than the fact of his confronting and defying the United States. In its view, anyone who does that can't be too bad—never mind that he brutalizes his subjects and invades his neighbors. The Left takes to the streets to assure his survival, indifferent both to the fate of Iraqis and even to their own safety. . . .

In sum: 9/11 and the prospect of war against Saddam Hussein have exposed the Left's political self-delusion, intellectual bankruptcy and moral turpitude.

Daniel Pipes, *New York Post*, March 19, 2003[33]

IN FACT

On April 1, 2003, less than two weeks after Pipes's column appeared, President George W. Bush nominated him to serve on the board of directors of the U.S. Institute of Peace (USIP), an official government institution established in 1986 by the U.S. Congress to promote the "prevention, management, and peaceful resolution of international conflicts." Opposition in the Senate kept the nomination from coming to a floor vote, but, on August 22, President Bush recess-appointed Pipes to the USIP board.

Whether they are defending the Soviet Union or bleating for Saddam Hussein, liberals are always against America. They are either traitors or idiots, and on the matter of America's self-preservation, the difference is irrelevant.

Ann Coulter, *Treason: Liberal Treachery from the Cold War to the War on Terrorism*, June 2003[34]

Conservatives saw the savagery of 9/11 and the attacks and prepared for war. Liberals saw the savagery of the 9/11 attacks and wanted to prepare indictments and offer therapy and understanding to our attackers.

Karl Rove, Deputy Chief of Staff to President George W. Bush, June 22, 2005[35]

JANUARY 23, 2007

"I THINK IT WILL BE RATHER CLEAR IN THE NEXT 60 TO 90 DAYS AS TO WHETHER THIS PLAN IS GOING TO WORK."

★ REPRESENTATIVE JOHN BOEHNER[P71]

When our soldiers hear politicians in Washington question the mission they are risking their lives to accomplish, it hurts their morale. In a time of war, we have a responsibility to show that whatever our political differences at home, our nation is united and determined to prevail.

President George W. Bush, January 10, 2006[36]

I ask all Americans to hold their elected leaders to account, and demand a debate that brings credit to our democracy—not comfort to our adversaries.

President George W. Bush, January 10, 2006[37]

I listen to my Democrat friends, and I wonder if they're more interested in protecting terrorists than in protecting the American people.

Representative John Boehner (R-OH), House Majority Leader, September 12, 2006[38]

IN FACT

When asked if he really meant to accuse his Democratic colleagues of treason, Boehner stressed the fact that he'd only *wondered* if they were more interested in protecting terrorists than in protecting the American people.

If you can find any evidence disproving that Democrats want us to lose this war, and hate the troops, I would be interested to hear it.

Ann Coulter, journalist, appearance on *Fox News*, September 10, 2007[39]

This war of ideas . . . is no less bloody than the one being fought by our troops in the Middle East . . . nothing less than a kind of civil war.

Norman Podhoretz, in his book *World War IV*, referring to the dispute between the opponents of Bush's war and its defenders, September, 2007[40]

FEAR ITSELF: THE BUSH ADMINISTRATION REASSURES AMERICA

Your government will stand at the ready 24 hours a day, seven days a week, to stop terrorism during the holiday season and beyond. . . . Continue with your holiday plans.

Tom Ridge, U.S. Secretary of Homeland Security, announcing that his department was raising the National Threat Level from yellow to orange, just in time for Christmas, because of "a substantial increase in the volume of threat-related intelligence reports," December 21, 2003[41]

Terrorists will hit the United States hard . . . either on the fourth of July or during the political conventions or on election day. . . . Be aware of your surroundings, remain vigilant. . . . Unfortunately, we currently do not know what form the threat may take . . . and that is why we must locate these seven individuals.

John Ashcroft, U.S. Attorney General, remarks offered while holding up the photos of seven wanted terrorists, May 27, 2004[42]

IN FACT

These attacks never occurred. It soon developed that the photos were of people who were not in the country at the time and whose images had already been used on previous occasions for the purpose of warning the public.

FEBRUARY 4, 2007

"WE CAN KNOW FAIRLY WELL IN A FEW MONTHS."

★ SENATOR JOHN MCCAIN[P72]

My gut feeling is that the United States face[s] an increased risk of attack this summer.

Michael Chertoff, U.S. Secretary of Homeland Security, July 11, 2007[43]

CHERTOFF'S GUT

IN FACT

On July 13, 2007, Chertoff emphasized, "We don't have any specific information about an imminent or near-term attack on the homeland."[44]

THINGS WE MUSTN'T DO (SO THE TERRORISTS WON'T WIN)

> *I want to talk about three issues facing America. The first are homeland security.*
>
> President George W. Bush, April 15, 2002[45]

If we give in to fear, if we aren't able to do these simple and ordinary things, the terrorists have won the war.

Frank Pierson, President of the Academy of Motion Picture Arts and Sciences, justifying his decision not to postpone the 74th Academy Awards, October 15, 2001[46]

We can't let the terrorists win. This is a time when more than ever people need the kind of escapism bands like ours provide.

Christopher Ready, saxophonist for the Frank Scott Bunnell High School Marching Band, explaining why a school board initiative in the interests of safety, to prevent his Stratford, Connecticut, band from appearing at the Rose Bowl Festival in Pasadena, California, would have been a victory for Islamofascism, quoted in *The New York Times,* November 4, 2001[47]

FEBRUARY 24, 2007

"THE LOGICAL THING IS TO WAIT FOUR TO SIX MONTHS."

★ MICHAEL O'HANLON, SENIOR FELLOW, FOREIGN POLICY STUDIES, BROOKINGS INSTITUTION[P73]

To me, the terrorists have certainly succeeded if so few of you participate in a companywide effort to "get together."

Martha Stewart, memo decrying the tepid response to her suggestion that, in lieu of a big company Christmas party, individual staffers invite ten Stewart employees each to small soirées in their own homes, quoted in the *Los Angeles Times*, November 27, 2001[48]

The kind of debate that we've had in the United States, suggestions, for example, that we should withdraw U.S. forces from Iraq, simply . . . validates the strategy of the terrorists.

Vice President Dick Cheney, September 10, 2006[49]

The Democrat approach in Iraq comes down to this: the terrorists win and America loses.

President George W. Bush, October 30, 2006[50]

If the standard of success is no car bombings or suicide bombings, we have just handed those who commit suicide bombings a huge victory.

President George W. Bush, interviewed on PBS, April 24, 2007[51]

POSTSCRIPT: THE HUNT FOR OSAMA BIN LADEN

I don't know where he [Osama bin Laden] is. You know, I just don't spend that much time on him . . . I truly am not that concerned about him.

President George W. Bush, March 13, 2002[52]

Gosh, I just don't think I ever said I'm not worried about Osama bin Laden. It's kind of one of those exaggerations. Of course we're worried about Osama bin Laden. We're on the hunt after Osama bin Laden. We're using every asset at our disposal to get Osama bin Laden."

President George W. Bush, October 13, 2004[53]

As for catching Osama, it's irrelevant. Things are going swimmingly in Afghanistan.

Ann Coulter, appearing on *Hannity & Colmes*, August 24, 2006[54]

When guest cohost Kirsten Powers challenged her on this claim, Coulter, after fruitlessly attempting to interrupt her, blurted, "OK, well, good night! It was nice being here," and stormed off the set.[55]

COULTER- SWIMMINGLY

MAY 4, 2007

"AS THE WAR DEVELOPS IN THE NEXT TWO CRUCIAL MONTHS, THE POLITICAL SOLIDARITY MAY CHANGE."

REPRESENTATIVE JACK KINGSTON[P74]

VOLUME VI

TRIUMPH OR

AMERICA LOOKS BACK AT

TRAGEDY?

FIVE YEARS OF CONFLICT

WHY WE FIGHT

One of the great goals of this nation's war [against terror] is to restore public confidence in the airline industry.

President George W. Bush, visiting with airline employees at O'Hare Airport, September 27, 2001[1]

© Paul J. Richard/AFP/Getty Images

IN FACT

According to *Foreign Policy* magazine, the administration followed up the President's O'Hare appearance by quickly launching a "pro-consumption publicity blitz" (in the words of the *Boston Globe)* on behalf of the U.S. travel industry. One of the highlights: Bush himself starred in a campaign by the Travel Industry Association designed, as one industry executive put it, "to link travel to patriotic duty."[2]

Our mission is clear in Iraq. Should we have to go in, our mission is very clear: disarmament.

President George W. Bush, March 6, 2003[3]

Our forces have been given a clear mission: to end a regime that threatened its neighbors and the world with weapons of mass destruction and to free a people that had suffered far too long.

President George W. Bush, April 14, 2003[4]

Our mission is clear . . . [in Iraq], and that is to train the Iraqis so they can do the fighting . . . [and] make sure they can stand up to defend their freedoms, which they want to do.

President George W. Bush, June 2, 2005[5]

The principal task of our military is to find and defeat the terrorists.

President George W. Bush, June 28, 2005[6]

American forces are . . . in Iraq not as a favor to its government or as a reward for its conduct. They are there as an expression of the American national interest to prevent the Iranian combination of imperialism and fundamentalist ideology from dominating a region on which the energy supplies of the industrial democracies depend.

Henry Kissinger, former U.S. Secretary of State, January 19, 2007[7]

If the president wants to go to war, our job is to find the intelligence to allow him to do so.

Alan Foley, Director, CIA Weapons, Intelligence, Nonproliferation and Arms Control Center, quoted in *The Italian Letter*, April 2007[8]

[See also "A Burning Question: What's Oil Got to Do with It?", page 49.]

PLANTING THE SEEDS OF FREEDOM (THE DEVIL IS IN THE DETAILS)

HISTORY'S JUDGMENT

History will record . . . that the plan for Operation Iraqi Freedom was a good plan—and that the execution of that plan by our young men and women in uniform was unequalled in excellence by anything in the annals of war.

General Tommy Franks, former Commander of the United States Central Command (CENTCOM) and the leader of Coalition forces during the invasion of Iraq, in his memoir, *American Soldier*, August 2004[9]

IN FACT

Thomas E. Ricks, the two-time Pulitzer Prize–winning military correspondent, presented a slightly different view in his 2006 book *Fiasco.* "It now seems more likely," he wrote, "that history's judgment will be that the U.S. invasion of Iraq in the spring of 2003 was based on perhaps the worst war plan in American history."[10]

JULY 15, 2007

"I THINK THE ODDS ARE FINALLY BETTER THAN 50-50 THAT WE WILL PREVAIL."

 WILLIAM KRISTOL, EDITOR OF *THE WEEKLY STANDARD*[P75]

"RESOLVE, CONSTANCY AND UNITY OF PURPOSE"

For these policies [in Iraq] to succeed, we will need to proceed with resolve, constancy and unity of purpose. If confirmed, I will do my utmost to serve the administration and the American people to these ends.

John Negroponte, during his confirmation hearings for U.S. ambassador to Iraq, April 27, 2004[11]

I've got to get out of there. . . . I want to get out of Baghdad as soon as possible.

John Negroponte, quoted in *The New York Times* by a "senior administration official who asked not to be named because he did not want to publicly question Mr. Negroponte's enthusiasm for his service in Iraq," February 18, 2005[12]

IN FACT

John Negroponte was named ambassador to Iraq on June 23, 2004. He was replaced by Zalmay Khalilzad on June 21, 2005.

PROFILES IN COMPASSIONATE CONSERVATISM

I'm honored to shake the hand of a brave Iraqi citizen who had his hand cut off by Saddam Hussein.

President George W. Bush, remarks after meeting with Iraqis receiving medical care in the United States, May 25, 2004[13]

As you know, you go to war with the Army you have. They're not the Army you might want or wish to have at a later time.

Donald Rumsfeld, U.S. Secretary of Defense, at a "Town Hall Meeting" in the Kuwaiti desert, answering a soldier who asked why the Pentagon wasn't equipping military vehicles in Iraq with adequate protective armor, December 8, 2004[14]

IN FACT

Although *The New York Times* and *The Washington Post* reported immediately after this exchange that the soldier's question had been prompted by an American reporter, the soldier made a public statement one week afterward, saying that he had decided to ask it entirely on his own. He added, "If it costs me my career to save another soldier, I'll give it."[15]

JULY 30, 2007

"WE ARE FINALLY GETTING SOMEWHERE IN IRAQ. . . . IN WAR, SOMETIMES IT'S IMPORTANT TO PICK THE RIGHT ADVERSARY, AND IN IRAQ WE SEEM TO HAVE DONE SO."

★ MICHAEL O'HANLON AND KENNETH M. POLLACK[P76]

As you can possibly see, I have an injury myself—not here at the hospital, but in combat with a cedar. I eventually won. The cedar gave me a little scratch. As a matter of fact, the Colonel asked if I needed first aid when she first saw me. I was able to avoid any major surgical operations here, but thanks for your compassion, Colonel.

President George W. Bush, remarks during a New Year's Day visit to wounded veterans from the Amputee Care Center of Brooke Army Medical Center, San Antonio, Texas, January 1, 2006[16]

RUMSFELD'S PERFORMANCE: THE DECIDER DECIDES

The president believes Secretary Rumsfeld is doing a very fine job during a challenging period in our nation's history. The secretary has led the Department of Defense during two wars, wars that resulted in the liberation of 25 million people in Afghanistan and 25 million people in Iraq.

Scott McClellan, White House Press Secretary, April 13, 2006[17]

I'm the decider, and I decide what is best. And what's best is for Don Rumsfeld to remain as the secretary of defense.

President George W. Bush, responding to questions about calls for Rumsfeld's resignation from six retired generals, April 18, 2006[18]

THE DECIDER

He leads in a way that the good Lord tells him is best for our country.

General Peter Pace, Chairman of the U.S. Joint Chiefs of Staff, praising Secretary of Defense Donald Rumsfeld at a ceremony at U.S. Southern Command Headquarters, Miami, Florida, October 19, 2006[19]

The timing is right for new leadership at the Pentagon.

President George W. Bush, announcing his decision to accept the resignation of Donald Rumsfeld as U.S. Secretary of Defense, November 6, 2006[20]

This man knows how to lead, and he did. And the country is better off for it.

President George W. Bush, describing Donald Rumsfeld at Rumsfeld's retirement ceremony outside the Pentagon, December 15, 2006[21]

The record speaks for itself: Don Rumsfeld is the finest secretary of defense this nation has ever had.

Vice President Dick Cheney, describing Donald Rumsfeld at Rumsfeld's retirement ceremony outside the Pentagon, December 15, 2006[22]

AUGUST 5, 2007

"GIVE IT SIX MORE MONTHS OR SO, MAYBE NINE MORE MONTHS."

☆ MICHAEL O'HANLON, SENIOR FELLOW, FOREIGN POLICY STUDIES, BROOKINGS INSTITUTION[P77]

THE DECIDER THINKS AGAIN . . . AND AGAIN

One of the interesting things people ask me, now that we're asking questions, is, can you ever win the war on terror? Of course, you can.

President George W. Bush, April 13, 2004[23]

I don't think you can win.

President George W. Bush, August 30, 2004[24]

Make no mistake about it, we are winning and we will win.

President George W. Bush, August 31, 2004[25]

NOTHING FAILS LIKE SUCCESS!

In part, our problem arises from our very success and the intrinsic power of the U.S. military. We can take out rogue regimes within a matter of days or weeks without inflicting the level of pain, injury, and humiliation on enemy forces that traditionally rids opponents of any lingering doubts about the end of the old order and the onset of the new. In short, *we win so quickly that some of the losers inevitably do not quite concede that they were really defeated.*

Victor Davis Hanson, Senior Fellow at the Hoover Institution, 2003[26]

Had we had to do it over again . . . we would look at the consequences of catastrophic success, being so successful so fast that an enemy that should have surrendered or been done in escaped and lived to fight another day.

President George W. Bush, blaming failure in Iraq on success, August 29, 2004[27]

WHO, ME?

I didn't advocate invasion.

Donald H. Rumsfeld, U.S. Secretary of Defense, November 20, 2005[28]

Huge mistakes were made, and I want to be very clear on this: They were not made by neoconservatives, who had almost no voice in what happened, and certainly almost no voice in what happened after the downfall of the regime in Baghdad. I'm getting damn tired of being described as an architect of the war. I was in favor of bringing down Saddam. Nobody said, "Go design the campaign to do that." I had no responsibility for that.

Richard Perle, former Chairman of the Pentagon's Defense Policy Board, November 3, 2006[29]

I just presumed that what I considered to be the most competent national security team since Truman was indeed going to be competent. They turned out to be among the most incompetent teams in the post-war era. Not only did each of them, individually, have enormous flaws, but together they were deadly, dysfunctional.

Kenneth Adelman, Defense Policy Board member until 2005, November 3, 2006[30]

I do not feel "remorseful," since I had and have no involvement with our Iraq policy. I opposed the military invasion of Iraq before it took place.

Michael Ledeen, Freedom Scholar at the American Enterprise Institute, *National Review Online*, November 4, 2006[31]

AUGUST 13, 2007

"PLAY THIS OUT FOR THE NEXT SIX MONTHS."

☆ WILLIAM KRISTOL, EDITOR OF *THE WEELKY STANDARD*[P78]

IN FACT

Ledeen's statement in *The Wall Street Journal* on September 4, 2002, that "Saddam Hussein is a terrible evil, and President Bush is entirely right in vowing to end his reign of terror" is only one of his countless calls for regime change, by way of military invasion, in Iraq.[32]

I HAD MY FINGERS CROSSED WHEN I SAID IT . . .

The only prudent and realistic course of action left to the United States is to mount a full-scale invasion of Iraq to smash the Iraqi armed forces, depose Saddam's regime, and rid the country of weapons of mass destruction.

Kenneth M. Pollack, former Director for Persian Gulf Affairs, U.S. National Security Council, The Threatening Storm: The Case for Invading Iraq, *September, 2002*[33]

Kenneth Pollack, the Clinton National Security Council expert whose argument for invading Iraq is surely the most influential book of this season, has provided intellectual cover for every liberal finding himself inclining toward war but uneasy about Mr. Bush.

Bill Keller, The New York Times, *February 8, 2003*[34]

I don't like to characterize myself as a supporter of the invasion.

Kenneth M. Pollack, interviewed by Michael Massing in the Columbia Journalism Review, *November–December 2007*[35]

THE NEW CRUSADERS

We should invade their countries, kill their leaders and convert them to Christianity.

Ann Coulter, *National Review Online,* September 13, 2001[36]

This crusade, this war on terrorism is going to take a while. And the American people must be patient. I'm going to be patient.

President George W. Bush, September 16, 2001[37]

I couldn't imagine somebody like Osama bin Laden understanding the joy of Hanukkah.

President George W. Bush, at a White House menorah-lighting ceremony, December 10, 2001[38]

I cannot speak strongly enough about how we must collectively get after those who kill in the name of—in the name of some kind of false religion.

President George W. Bush, speaking with reporters in the Oval Office during a meeting with King Abdullah of Jordan, August 2, 2002[39]

There is no escaping the unfortunate fact that Muslim government employees in law enforcement, the military and the diplomatic corps need to be watched for connections to terrorism, as do Muslim chaplains in prison and the armed forces.

Daniel Pipes, *New York Post,* January 24, 2003[40]

MAY 2, 2007

"THE WAR WILL BE WON OR LOST, LIKE IT OR NOT, FAIRLY OR UNJUSTLY, IN THE NEXT SIX MONTHS IN BAGHDAD."

★ VICTOR DAVIS HANSON, *NATIONAL REVIEW ONLINE* COLUMNIST[P79]

A faceless enemy [of terrorists] drive taxi cabs in the daytime and kill at night.

Senator Conrad Burns (R-MT), speaking at an "ice cream social" in Belgrade, Montana, August 30, 2005[41]

Sir, prove to me that you are not working with our enemies.

Glenn Beck, *CNN Headline News* host, interviewing Representative Keith Ellison (D-MN), the first Muslim elected to the U.S. Congress, November 14, 2006[42]

The Muslim Representative from Minnesota [Keith Ellison] was elected by the voters of that district and if American citizens don't wake up and adopt the Virgil Goode position on immigration there will likely be many more Muslims elected to office. . . . In the next century we will have many more Muslims in the United States if we do not adopt the strict immigration policies that I believe are necessary to preserve the values and beliefs traditional to the United States of America.

Representative Virgil H. Goode Jr. (R-VA), letter to constituents, December 7, 2006[43]

IN FACT

Keith Ellison's family has been in North America since 1742, thirty-four years before the United States declared its independence.

GOD IS ON OUR SIDE

God told me to strike at Al Qaida and I struck them, and then He instructed me to strike at Saddam, which I did.

Remark attributed to President George W. Bush, who, according to the Tel Aviv newspaper *Ha'aretz*, shared it with Prime Minister Mahmoud Abbas and other Palestinian leaders while at a meeting in Aqaba, Jordan, June 4, 2003[44]

I know my God is bigger than his.

General William G. Boykin, U.S. Deputy Undersecretary of Defense for Intelligence, explaining how he was able to confront a Muslim warlord in Somalia, October 16, 2003[45]

God is pro-war.

Rev. Jerry Falwell, title of commentary posted on *World Net Daily*, January 31, 2004[46]

I trust God speaks through me. Without that, I couldn't do my job.

President George W. Bush, speaking (presumably by and for himself) to an Amish group during a campaign stop at Lapp Electric Service in Smokestown, Pennsylvania, quoted by *Mennonite Weekly Review* columnist Jack Brubaker, July 2004[47]

POSTSCRIPT: GOD IS ON THEIR SIDE, TOO

God is on our side, and Satan is on the side of the United States.

Saddam Hussein, President of Iraq, August 29, 1990[48]

God, praise and glory be to Him, ordered us to carry out Jihad . . . against the Jews and Americans.

Osama bin Laden, May 1998[49]

SEPTEMBER 24, 2007

"I'M AFRAID WE'VE RUN OUT OF SIX MONTHS."

 THOMAS FRIEDMAN, *NEW YORK TIMES* COLUMNIST[F80]

Oh Allah, destroy the kingdom of Bush as you destroyed the kingdom of Caesar.

Abu Musab al-Zarqawi, alleged leader of al-Tawhid wal-Jihad, later known as "Al Qaeda in Iraq," audiotape, February 2004[50]

AND GOD KNOWS WE WERE RIGHT

If the instigation for jihad . . . in order to liberate Al-Aksa Mosque and the Holy Kaaba is considered a crime, let history be a witness that I am a criminal.

Osama bin Laden, January 11, 1999[51]

I'm ready to meet my Maker and answer for those who have died or been horribly maimed as a result of my decisions.

Tony Blair, Prime Minister of Great Britain, May 5, 2003[52]

PAX AMERICANA

The answer to terrorism? Colonialism.

Paul Johnson, historian, October 6, 2001[53]

Afghanistan and other troubled lands today cry out for the sort of enlightened foreign administration once provided by self-confident Englishmen in jodhpurs and pith helmets.

Max Boot, Senior Fellow for National Security Studies, Council of Foreign Relations, October 15, 2001[54]

Every ten years or so, the United States needs to pick up some small crappy little country and throw it against the wall, just to show the world we mean business.

Michael Ledeen, Freedom Scholar at the American Enterprise Institute Scholar, ca. 1992, as paraphrased by Jonah Goldberg in *National Review Online*, April 23, 2002[55]

We need a little bit of logistical support, but we don't need the moral support of anyone, because we're on the side of the angels in this.

Peter Beinart, editor of *The New Republic*, interviewed on *Bill Moyers Journal*, PBS, April 29, 2002[56]

It is precisely because American foreign policy is infused with an unusually high degree of morality that other nations find they have less to fear from its otherwise daunting power.

William Kristol, *Weekly Standard* editor, and Robert Kagan, American scholar and political commentator, quoted by Francis Fukuyama in *The New York Times*, February 19, 2006[57]

SEPTEMBER 6, 2007

"WE'RE KICKING ASS."

PRESIDENT GEORGE W. BUSH[P81]

Call it a "forceful response," "decisive action"—whatever. Those are all nice euphemisms for killing people. And the world is a better place because America saw the necessity of putting steel beneath the velvet of those euphemisms.

Jonah Goldberg, columnist for the *National Review*, January 29, 2003[58]

Wherever the English nations have banded together in common cause, the world has been the better for it. Now the English nations are banding together again, to strip one of the world's greatest menaces of his power.

John Ibbitson, columnist for the Toronto *Globe and Mail*, January 25, 2003[59]

More than 125,000 American troops occupy Mesopotamia. They are backed up by the resources of the world's richest economy. In a contest for control of Iraq, America can outspend and outmuscle any competing faction.

Max Boot, *USA Today*, May 6, 2003[60]

Beyond Iraq, the U.S. will win the War on Terror because it's what Americans do: we win military conflicts.

Larry Schweikart, American historian and author, July 10, 2006[61]

IN CLOSING: A MESSAGE OF UNITY AND HOPE FROM PRESIDENT GEORGE W. BUSH

Free societies are hopeful societies. And free societies will be allies against these hateful few who have no conscience, who kill at the whim of a hat.

President George W. Bush, "Victory 2004" luncheon, September 17, 2004[62]

SEPTEMBER 12, 2007

"THE NEXT SIX MONTHS ARE GOING TO BE CRITICAL."

★ SENATOR JOHN MCCAIN[P82]

EPILOGUE

Finally, an Expert Who Was Right

With some embarrassment, we at the Institute of Expertology confess that it took a rival institute, the American Enterprise Institute, to uncover an expert—the first, as we explain in our introduction, that we have ever encountered—who both the experts and the expertologists can agree was right.

In an interview with the AEI, this expert was uncanny in his analysis of what might have happened if, after the First Gulf War, American forces had decided to invade the heart of Iraq, move into Baghdad, and unseat Saddam Hussein. His warnings, had they been heeded, would have radically changed the course of Operation Iraqi Freedom, if, indeed, Operation Iraqi Freedom had even been launched at all.

Here is the AEI interview, reproduced in its entirety:

Q: Do you think the U.S., or U.N. forces, should have moved into Baghdad?

A: No.

Q: Why not?

A: Because if we'd gone to Baghdad we would have been all alone. There wouldn't have been anybody else with us.

There would have been a U.S. occupation of Iraq.

None of the Arab forces that were willing to fight with us in Kuwait were willing to invade Iraq.

Once you got to Iraq and took it over, took down Saddam Hussein's government, then what are you going to put in its place?

That's a very volatile part of the world, and if you take down the central government of Iraq, you could very easily end up seeing pieces of Iraq fly off: part of it, the Syrians would like to have to the west, part of it—eastern Iraq—the Iranians would like to claim, they fought over it for eight years. In the north you've got the Kurds, and if the Kurds spin loose and join with the Kurds in Turkey, then you threaten the territorial integrity of Turkey.

It's a quagmire if you go that far and try to take over Iraq.

The other thing was casualties. Everyone was impressed with the fact we were able to do our job [during the First Gulf War] with as few casualties as we had. But for the 146 Americans killed in action, and for their families—it wasn't a cheap war. And the question for the president, in terms of whether or not we went on to Baghdad, took additional casualties in an effort to get Saddam Hussein, was how many additional dead Americans is Saddam worth?

Our judgment was, not very many, and I think we got it right.

And who, we are confident you're wondering, was this expert, and where is he now, when America could have benefited so greatly from his extraordinary foresight?

The answer is Richard Bruce "Dick" Cheney, who, when the interview with the American Enterprise Institute took place in 1994, was the former U.S. Secretary of Defense. In the intervening years, he left government for a stint as chairman and CEO of Halliburton (from whom he still receives deferred compensation), and then returned to the public sector as Vice President of the United States.

In closing, the Institute of Expertology would like to congratulate Mr. Cheney for his stunning, and totally unexpected, achievement and to recommend to our readers that they study his continuing words and deeds with acuity and care as he continues his unique and remarkable career.

ACKNOWLEDGMENTS

First and foremost we want to thank the thousands of experts who have gone on the record on how we won (or will shortly win) the war in Iraq. This compendium would not have been possible without them. Next we want to thank Eugene Ashton-Gonzalez and Susannah Vila for their heroic work as researchers, and to congratulate them on their election as vice presidents of the Institute of Expertology (see page 267). Also, we wish to acknowledge the headhunter who discovered them, Lindy Hess, who has been elected an honorary member of the Institute. Of course, this wouldn't be an acknowledgments page if we didn't acknowledge our debt to the world champion quote collector, Bill Effros, whose book and website, *Quote without Comment,* as well as his always friendly advice, proved invaluable. And we wish to express our gratitude to our fellow scholars Richard R. Lingeman and Dilip Hiro for reading earlier drafts of the manuscript. Any errors in this book may, of course, be attributed to their failure to catch them, but they have our gratitude nevertheless. We also thank Robert Grossman, the Institute's Artist-in-Residence, for his accurate renderings of the experts. We are grateful to Mary Schilling and Victoria Chiaro for their efforts to keep this study on track. We thank Eric Alterman, Peter Rothberg, and our colleagues at *The Nation* and at Sirius Thinking,

Ltd., for their understanding and assistance. We are grateful to Joe Duax and Peter C. Baker for lending us their deadline scholarship. Not to mention our friends in cyberspace, who answered our research queries with expert sightings across the globe. We thank Binky Urban for her expert negotiating skill, or rather, we should say, for making sure that the Institute of Expertology received its due.

And we are, of course, in the debt of the many writers and filmmakers whose books, documentaries, and articles got there before we did and thereby facilitated our scholarly research. Among them: Rajiv Chandrasekaran for *Imperial Life in the Emerald City*; Scott Ritter for *Iraq Confidential*; Michael Isikoff and David Corn for *Hubris*; Sheldon Rampton and John Stauber for *The Best War Ever* and *Weapons of Mass Deception*; Thomas E. Ricks for *Fiasco*; Bob Woodward for *Plan of Attack, State of Denial*, and *Bush at War*; Lloyd C. Gardner and Marilyn B. Young for *Iraq and the Lessons of Vietnam*; George Packer for *The Assassin's Gate*; Jeremy Scahill for *Blackwater*; Charles Ferguson for his documentary *No End in Sight*; Norman Solomon for "War Made Easy"; Eugene Jarecki for "Why We Fight"; Rick MacArthur for "The Lies We Bought" in *Columbia Journalism Review*; Michael Massing for his pieces on Iraq in *The New York Review of Books*; all the reporters at Fairness and Accuracy in Reporting (especially Peter Hart and Jim Naureckas), Media Matters for America, and the Center for American Progress; Danny Schechter at Media Channel; and many more bloggers and Internet watchdogs.

Of course, we would be remiss if we did not thank Fox News for reporting what it knows best. Additionally, the sages at the Project for a New American Century and the American Enterprise Institute have proved invaluable.

A big high five to Winston Churchill for giving us the organizing principle for our book.

The work of many members of our government also helped, notably that of Representative Henry A. Waxman and his colleagues on the House Committee on Oversight and Government Reform, including the "Iraq on the Record" report that Representative Waxman commissioned. The White House, the Department of Defense, and the Coalition Provisional Authority are also to be commended for keeping such comprehensive and exact records of their press conferences.

And finally, we thank Katherine and Annie for their forbearance.

NOTES

PROLOGUE

1. "U.S. Envoy Visits Iraq to Talk of New Ties," *Christian Science Monitor*, December 21, 1983, page 2.
2. Micah L. Sifry and Christopher Cerf, *The Iraq War Reader: History, Documents, Opinions* (New York: Touchstone Books, 2003), page 45.
3. Micah L. Sifry and Christopher Cerf, *The Gulf War Reader: History, Documents, Opinions* (New York: Three Rivers Press, 1991), page 121.
4. Ibid., page 120.
5. Micah L. Sifry and Christopher Cerf, *The Iraq War Reader: History, Documents, Opinions* (New York: Touchstone Books, 2003), page 45.
6. "Interview with Scott Ritter and Ken Adelman," *Fox on the Record with Greta Van Susteren*, Fox News Network, transcript, February 13, 2002.
7. Dana Milbank, "Upbeat Tone Ended with War," *The Washington Post*, March 29, 2003, retrieved from http://www.washingtonpost.com/ac2/wp-dyn/A44801-2003Mar28?language=printer, November 4, 2007.
8. Michael Ledeen, "The War on Terror Won't End in Baghdad," *The Wall Street Journal*, September 4, 2002, retrieved from http://www.aei.org/publications/filter.all,pubID.14216/pub_detail.asp, December 1, 2007.
9. David Von Drehle, "Debate over Iraq Focuses on Outcome," *The Washington Post*, October 7, 2002.
10. "How Should We Use Our Power? A Debate on Iraq," The Common-

wealth Club, January 28, 2003, retrieved from http://www.commonwealth club.org/archive/03/03-01hitchensdanner-qa.html, December 1, 2007.

11. "Iraq Seminar with Richard Perle and Kanan Makiya," March 17, 2003, retrieved from http://www.bendorassociates.com/article/6641, December 1, 2007.
12. "Deputy Secretary of Defense Interview with Nolan Finley of the *Detroit News*," February 23, 2003, retrieved from http://www.defenselink.mil/tran scripts/transcript.aspx?transcriptid=1989, December 1, 2007.
13. Richard Perle, "Take Out Saddam—It's the Only Way," *News of the World*, retrieved from http://www.aei.org/publications/pubID.16100,filter.all/pub _detail.asp, December 1, 2007.
14. Susan Page, "Confronting Iraq," *USA Today*, April 1, 2003, retrieved from http://www.usatoday.com/educate/war28-article.htm, December 1, 2007.
15. Dick Cheney, *Meet the Press*, MSNBC, March 16, 2003.
16. "Senator John McCain Discusses the Beginning of the War in Iraq," NBC News *Today*, NBC, March 20, 2003, transcript.
17. Richard W. Stevenson, "President's Political Thorn Grows Only More Stubborn," June 17, 2004, retrieved from http://query.nytimes.com/gst/full page.html?res=9A03E3D61F30F934A25755C0A9629C8B63, October 26, 2007.

VOLUME I: THE GATHERING STORM

1. Elisabeth Bumiller, "Traces of Terror: The Strategy; Bush Aides Set Strategy to Sell Policy on Iraq," *The New York Times*, September 7, 2002, retrieved from http://query.nytimes.com/gst/fullpage.html?res=9C07E6D7103EF9 34A3575AC0A9649C8B63, November 11, 2007.
2. "Vice President Speaks at VFW 103rd National Convention," official White House press release, retrieved from www.whitehouse.gov/news/ releases/2002/08/20020826.html, October 10, 2007.
3. "Press Briefing by Ari Fleischer," official White House press briefing, retrieved from http://www.whitehouse.gov/news/releases/2002/09/200209 06-3.html, November 4, 2007.
4. "Rumsfeld Speaks to Armed Services Committee," CNN transcript, retrieved from http://transcripts.cnn.com/TRANSCRIPTS/0209/18/se.01 .html, November 4, 2007.
5. "Executive Summary," *The Iraq Dossier*, retrieved from http://www.number 10.gov.uk/output/Page281.asp, November 4, 2007.

6. Jim Garamone, "Rumsfeld Answers Questions on Iraqi Threat," American Forces Press Service, September 27, 2002, retrieved from http://www.defenselink.mil/news/newsarticle.aspx?id=43410, November 4, 2007.
7. "Interview with Colin Powell," *The Oprah Winfrey Show*, ABC, October 22, 2002.
8. "Press Briefing by Ari Fleischer," official White House press briefing, retrieved from http://www.whitehouse.gov/news/releases/2002/12/20021205–7.h tml, November 4, 2007.
9. Bob Woodward, *Plan of Attack* (New York, Simon & Schuster, 2004).
10. "U.S. Secretary of State Colin Powell Addresses the U.N. Security Council," official White House press release, February 5, 2003, retrieved from http://www.whitehouse.gov/news/releases/2003/02/20030205–1.html, November 4, 2007.
11. Richard Cohen, "A Winning Hand for Powell," *The Washington Post*, February 6, 2003, retrieved from http://www.washingtonpost.com/ac2/wp-dyn/A32571-2003Feb5?language-printer, November 4, 2007.
12. Jim Hoagland, "An Old Trooper's Smoking Gun," *Washington Post*, February 6, 2003, page A37.
13. Cal Thomas, "Colin Powell's Slam Dunk," *Townhall.com,* February 6, 2003, retrieved from http://www.townhall.com/columnists/CalThomas/2003/02/06/colin_powells_slam_dunk, November 4, 2007.
14. "Interview with Bill O'Reilly," *Good Morning America*, ABC March 18, 2003.
15. "Interview with Condoleezza Rice," *Late Edition with Wolf Blitzer*, CNN, transcript, September 8, 2002, retrieved from http://transcripts.cnn.com/TRANSCRIPTS/0209/08/le.00.html, November 4, 2007.
16. "President's Remarks at the United Nations General Assembly," official White House transcript, September 12, 2002, retrieved from http://www.whitehouse.gov/news/releases/2002/09/20020912-1.html, November 4, 2007.
17. "President Bush Outlines Iraqi Threat," official White House transcript, October 7, 2002, retrieved from http://www.whitehouse.gov/news/releases/2002/10/20021007–8.html, November 4, 2007.
18. "President Delivers 'State of the Union,' " official White House transcript, January 28, 2003, retrieved from http://www.whitehouse.gov/news/releases/2003/01/20030128-19.html, November 4, 2007.
19. Ibid.

20. "Interview with Vice President Dick Cheney," *Meet the Press*, NBC, March 16, 2003, transcript, retrieved from http://www.mtholyoke.edu/acad/intrel/bush/cheneymeetthepress.htm, November 4, 2007.
21. "U.S. Department of Defense News Briefing—Secretary Rumsfeld and Gen. Myers," June 24, 2003, official news transcript, retrieved from www.defenselink.mil/transcripts/transcript.aspx?transcriptid-2760, December 7, 2007.
22. Press conference, Kuwait City, June 11, 2002, retrieved from http://www.globalsecurity.org/wmd/library/news/iraq/2002/iraq-020611-usia01.html, November 4, 2007.
23. Colin Powell's UN presentation, CNN, February 5, 2003, transcript, retrieved from http://www.cnn.com/2003/US/02/05/sprj.irq.powell.transcript.06/index.html, November 4, 2007.
24. George W. Bush, "All the World Can Rise to This Moment," statement from the White House, February 6, 2003, retrieved from http://www.whitehouse.gov/news/releases/2003/02/20030206-17.html, October 22, 2007.
25. "Report on the U.S. Intelligence Community's Prewar Intelligence Assessments on Iraq, Select Committee on Intelligence," United States Senate, ordered reported on July 7, 2004, page 221, retrieved from http://www.globalsecurity.org/intell/library/congress/2004_rpt/iraq-wmd-intell_chapter6-e.html, November 28, 2007.
26. Powell's UN presentation, CNN, February 5, 2003, transcript, retrieved from http://www.cnn.com/2003/US/02/05/sprj.irq.powell.transcript.06/index.html, November 4, 2007.
27. "Text of Donald Rumsfeld remarks," March 12, 2003, news transcript, retrieved from http://news.bbc.co.uk/2/hi/americas/2842943.stm, November 4, 2007.
28. Joby Warrick, "Lacking Biolabs, Trailers Carried Case for War," *The Washington Post*, April 12, 2006, p. A01, retrieved from http://www.washingtonpost.com/wp-dyn/content/article/2006/04/11/AR2006041101888.html, November 28, 2007.
29. "Press Conference at the French American Press Club," May 22, 2003, transcript, retrieved from http://www.state.gov/secretary/former/powell/remarks/2003/20909.htm, November 4, 2007.
30. "Interview with Donald Rumsfeld," WNYW-TV, New York City (Fox News affiliate), May 27, 2003.

31. "This Week with George Stephanopoulos," ABC, transcript, June 8, 2003.
32. "Interview on CNN's Late Edition with Wolf Blitzer," State Department transcript, June 8, 2003, retrieved from http://www.state.gov/secretary/former/powell/remarks/2003/21320.htm, November 4, 2007.
33. U.S. Department of State press briefing, July 10, 2003, retrieved from http://www.fas.org/irp/news/2003/07/dos071003.html, November 4, 2007.
34. David Kay on the "Interim Progress Report on the Activities of the Iraq Survey Group," testimony before the House Permanent Select Committee on Intelligence, the House Committee on Appropriations, Subcommittee on Defense, and the Senate Select Committee on Intelligence, October 2, 2003.
35. *The Constitution in Crisis*, Investigative Status Report of the House Judiciary Committee Democratic Staff, December 20, 2005, pages 141–42.
36. "Press Briefing by Ari Fleischer," official White House press briefing, retrieved from http://www.whitehouse.gov/news/releases/2001/10/20011004-12.html, November 4, 2007.
37. David Rose and Ed Vulliamy, "U.S. Hawks Accuse Iraq over Anthrax: Five More Test Positive in Florida," *The Observer* (London), October 14, 2001, page 1.
38. "Ex–U.N. Weapons Inspector: Possible Iraq-Anthrax Link," *CNN.com*, October 15, 2001, retrieved from http://archives.cnn.com/2001/HEALTH/conditions/10/15/anthrax.butler/, November 4, 2007.
39. "Interview on CNN's Late Edition with Wolf Blitzer," State Department transcript, October 21, 2001, retrieved from http://www.state.gov/secretary/former/powell/remarks/2001/5470.htm, November 4, 2007.
40. Richard Cohen, "Public Enemy No. 2; If This Is the 'War' President Bush Says It Is, Then We Cannot Stop with bin Laden and al Qaeda," *The Washington Post*, October 18, 2001, page A39.
41. Daniel McGrory, "Hijacker 'Given Anthrax Flask by Iraqi Agent'," *The Times* (London), October 27, 2001.
42. Jarret Wolfstein, "Mylroie: Evidence Shows Saddam Is Behind Anthrax Attacks," *NewsMax*, retrieved from http://archive.newsmax.com/archives/articles/2001/11/8/181505.shtml, October 26, 2007.
43. Ibid.
44. Robert L. Bartley, "Anthrax: The Elephant in the Room," *The Wall Street Journal*, October 29, 2001, retrieved from http://www.anthraxinvestigation.com/wsj.html, November 4, 2007.

45. William Kristol, "The Wrong Strategy," *The Washington Post*, October 30, 2001, retrieved from http://www.washingtonpost.com/ac2/wp-dyn?page name=article&contentId=A9030-2001Oct29¬Found-true, November 4, 2007.
46. "Congress Debates Action on Iraq," *CNN Inside Politics*, September 18, 2002, transcript, retrieved from http://transcripts.cnn.com/TRAN SCRIPTS/0209/18/ip.00.html, November 18, 2002.
47. "Gore Assails Bush's Iraq Policy," *washingtonpost.com*, September 23, 2002, retrieved from http://www.washingtonpost.com/wp-srv/politics/transcripts/gore_text092302.html, October 24, 2007.
48. "The Washington Post's Reckless Reporting on WMD Claims," official White House press release, *whitehouse.gov*, April 12, 2006, retrieved from http://www.whitehouse.gov/news/releases/2006/04/20060412-8.html, October 24, 2007.
49. "Setting the Record Straight: Sen. Levin on Iraq," official White House press release, November 14, 2005, retrieved from http://www.whitehouse .gov/news/releases/2005/11/20051114-1.html, November 4, 2007.
50. "Statement Regarding the Possible War with Iraq," press release, October 10, 2002, retrieved from http://www.house.gov/waxman/news_files/news_statements_res_iraq_10_10_02.htm, November 4, 2007.
51. "Floor Speech of Senator Hillary Rodham Clinton on S.J. Res. 45, a Resolution to Authorize the Use of United States Armed Forces against Iraq," retrieved from www.clinton.senate.gov/speeches/iraq_1011002 .html, October 10, 2007.
52. Speech, *johnkerry.com*, January 23, 2003, retrieved from http://web.archive.org/web/20040204225854/www.johnkerry.com/pressroom/speeches/spc_2003_0123.html, October 24, 2007.
53. "Interview with Senator Evan Bayh," *The O'Reilly Factor*, Fox News, March 17, 2003, retrieved from src.senate.gov/public/_files/graphics/IraqPacket20 .pdf, November 4, 2007.
54. "Anthrax Scare: Discussion with Former U.N. Chief Weapons Inspector Richard Butler," CNN, transcript, October 17, 2001, retrieved from http://transcripts.cnn.com/TRANSCRIPTS/0110/17/se.15.html, November 4, 2007.
55. Joe Lieberman, "After bin Laden, We Must Target Saddam," *Wall Street Journal*, October 29, 2001, retrieved from http://www.anthraxinvestigation .com/wsj.html, November 4, 2007.

56. "Laurie Mylroie: Is Iraq Involved with U.S. Terror Attacks?," CNN, October 29, 2001, retrieved from http://archives.cnn.com/2001/COMMUNITY/10/29/mylroie/, November 4, 2007.
57. "President Bush Outlines Iraqi Threat," www.whitehouse.gov/news/releases/2002/10/20021007-8.html, retrieved October 2, 2003.
58. "President Calls for Strengthened and Reformed Medicare Program," official White House press release, January 29, 2003, retrieved from http://www.whitehouse.gov/news/releases/2003/01/20030129-4.html, November 4, 2007.
59. Transcript of Powell's UN presentation, CNN, February 5, 2003, retrieved from http://www.cnn.com/2003/US/02/05/sprj.irq.powell.transcript.06/index.html, November 4, 2007.
60. "Secretary Rumsfeld Address to the Munich Conference on European Security Policy," February 8, 2003, U.S. Department of Defense news transcript, retrieved from http://www.defenselink.mil/transcripts/transcript.aspx?transcriptid=1918, November 4, 2007.
61. "Wolfowitz Interview with Nolan Finley of the *Detroit News*," March 5, 2003, U.S. Department of Defense news transcript, retrieved from http://www.defenselink.mil/transcripts/transcript.aspx?transcriptid=1989, November 4, 2007.
62. "In Their Own Words: Who Said What When?," web article posted by *Frontline*, WGBH Television, *www.pbs.org/wgbh*, retrieved October 2, 2007.
63. Richard Cheney, "Cheney Stands by Bush's Iraq Policies," *Rocky Mountain News*, January 10, 2004, retrieved from http://www.rockymountainnews.com, January 13, 2008.
64. "Transcript: President Bush, Part 2: Couric's Interview with President Bush," *www.cbsnews.com*, September 6, 2006, page 1.
65. James Risen, "The Struggle for Iraq: Intelligence; Hussein Warned Iraqis to Beware Outside Fighters, Document Says," *The New York Times*, January 14, 2004.
66. U.S. Department of Defense news briefing, official transcript, February 13, 2003. Rumsfeld's uncharacteristically poetic response earned him the "Foot in Mouth" Prize, awarded annually by Great Britain's Plain English Campaign for the most baffling statement by a public figure. "We think we know what he means," said campaign spokesman John Lister. "But we don't know if we really know." ("UK Plain English Campaign cites Donald Rumsfeld for 'foot in mouth' prize," Associated Press Worldstream, December 2, 2003.)

67. William Safire, "Prague Connection," *The New York Times*, November 12, 2001, retrieved from http://query.nytimes.com/gst/fullpage.html?res=9F05E3D61238F931A25752C1A9679C8B63, November 4, 2007.
68. "The Vice President Appears on NBC's *Meet the Press*," official White House transcript, December 9, 2001, retrieved from http://www.whitehouse.gov/vicepresident/news-speeches/speeches/vp20011209.html, November 4, 2007.
69. Robert Kagan and William Kristol, "What to Do about Iraq?" *The Weekly Standard*, January 21, 2002, retrieved from http://www.carnegieendowment.org/publications/index.cfm?fa=view&id=940&prog=zgp&proj=zusr, November 4, 2007.
70. Mark Hosenball, "9/11: A Special White House Slide Show," *Newsweek*, January 9, 2006, retrieved from www.msnbc.msn.com, October 1, 2007.
71. Michael Isikoff and David Corn, *Hubris* (New York: Three Rivers Press, 2007), page 103.
72. "Saddam's Ultimate Solution," *Wide Angle*, PBS, television host interview transcript, July 11, 2002, retrieved from http://www.pbs.org/wnet/wideangle/printable/transcript_saddam.html, October 14, 2007.
73. "Rumsfeld Speaks to Armed Services Committee," CNN, transcript, retrieved from http://transcripts.cnn.com/TRANSCRIPTS/0209/18/se.01.html, November 4, 2007.
74. "President Bush Discusses Iraq with Congressional Leaders—Remarks by the President on Iraq," official White House press release, September 26, 2002, retrieved from http://www.globalsecurity.org/wmd/library/news/iraq/2002/iraq-020926-usia01.htm, October 13, 2007.
75. "Showdown: Iraq—The Weapons Report," CNN, January 26, 2003, retrieved from http://transcripts.cnn.com/TRANSCRIPTS/0301/26/le.00.html, November 4, 2007.
76. "Press Briefing by Scott McClellan," official White House press briefing, retrieved from http://www.whitehouse.gov/news/releases/2004/01/20040127-6.html, November 4, 2007.
77. "Interview with President George W. Bush," *Meet the Press*, NBC, February 8, 2004, retrieved from http://www.msnbc.msn.com/id/4179618/, November 4, 2007.
78. The Iraqi National Congress (INC) was formed after the first Persian Gulf War—with the help of the U.S. government, and in particular an

American public relations specialist named John Rendon—for the purpose of fomenting the overthrow of Saddam Hussein's government. In this role, Miller's own paper, *The New York Times*, wrote in 2004, Chalabi "became a favorite of hard-liners within the Bush administration and a paid broker of information from Iraqi exiles."

79. Judith Miller and Michael Gordon, "Threats and Responses: The Iraqis; U.S. Says Hussein Intensifies Quest for A-Bomb Parts," *The New York Times*, September 8, 2002.
80. Ibid.
81. Judith Miller and Michael Gordon, "Threats and Responses: Baghdad's Arsenal; White House Lists Iraq Steps to Build Banned Weapons," *The New York Times*, September 13, 2002.
82. Judith Miller, "Threats and Responses: Germ Weapons; C.I.A. Hunts Iraq Tie to Soviet Smallpox," *The New York Times*, December 2, 2002.
83. Judith Miller, "A Nation Challenged: Secret Sites; Iraqi Tells of Renovations at Sites for Chemical and Nuclear Arms," *The New York Times*, December 20, 2001.
84. Jonathan S. Landay, "White House Released Claims of Defector Deemed Unreliable by CIA," Knight-Ridder newspapers, May 18, 2004.
85. Judith Miller, "Threats and Responses: Chemical Weapons; Iraq Said to Try to Buy Antidote Against Nerve Gas," *The New York Times*, November 12, 2002.
86. Judith Miller, "Aftereffects: Prohibited Weapons; Illicit Arms Kept till Eve of War, an Iraqi Scientist Is Said to Assert," *The New York Times*, April 21, 2003.
87. "War and Its Discontents," *The Connection*, WBUR Radio archived program, February 3, 2004, retrieved from http://www.theconnection.org/shows/2004/02/20040203_b_main.asp, November 29, 2007.
88. "Interview with Judith Miller," *Frontline*, PBS, July 13, 2005, retrieved from http://www.pbs.org/wgbh/pages/frontline/newswar/interviews/miller.html, November 4, 2007.
89. Marc Fisher, "Potomac Confidential: Washington's Hour of Talk Power," *The Washington Post*, January 25, 2007, retrieved from http://www.washingtonpost.com/wp-dyn/content/discussion/2007/01/19/DI2007011901246_pf.html, December 1, 2007.
90. Judith Miller, "A Personal Account: My Four Hours Testifying in the Federal Grand Jury Room," *The New York Times*, October 16, 2005.

91. Susan Schmidt and Jim VandeHei, "N.Y. Times Reporter Released from Jail," *The Washington Post*, September 30, 2005.
92. "Saddam's Ultimate Solution," *Wide Angle*, PBS, July 11, 2002, retrieved from http://www.pbs.org/wnet/wideangle/printable/transcript_saddam.html, November 28, 2007.
93. "Should the U.S. Attack Iraq? Should Women Be Allowed to Join Augusta National Golf Club?," *Talkback Live*, CNN, September 19, 2002, transcript.
94. *Imus in the Morning*, syndicated radio show synopsis, Video Monitoring Services of America, February 23, 2003.
95. Jonah Goldberg, "Where's the French Anti-Defamation League?" *National Review Online*, April 6, 2001, retrieved from http://www.nationalreview.com/goldberg/goldbergprint040601.html, November 10, 2007.
96. Jonah Goldberg, "The European 'Miracle,'" *National Review Online*, July 31, 2002, retrieved from http://article.nationalreview.com/?=MWNjYzJhNzk2MTc1YjIxMTIxOTM5NWI3YjYxMTQ5N2Q=, November 4, 2007.
97. Sean Loughlin, "House Cafeterias Change Names for 'French' Fries and 'French' Toast," *CNN.com*, Wednesday, March 12, 2003, retrieved from http://www.cnn.com/2003/ALLPOLITICS/03/11/sprj.irq.fries/, November 4, 2007.
98. Ibid.
99. Steve Dunleavy, column, *New York Post*, February 10, 2003, quoted in Gary Younge and Jon Henley, "Wimps, Weasels and Monkeys—the U.S. Media View of 'Perfidious France,'" *The Guardian* (London), February 11, 2003, retrieved from http://www.guardian.co.uk/france/story/0,11882,893202,00.html, November 10, 2007.
100. "Reaction to U.N. Report," *Larry King Live*, with guest host Tucker Carlson, CNN, February 14, 2003, transcript.
101. William Kristol, "The Imminent War," *The Weekly Standard*, March 17, 2003, retrieved from http://www.weeklystandard.com/Content/Public/Articles/000/000/002/341lxxol.asp, November 4, 2007.
102. "U.S. Policy toward Iraq: Hearing before the U.S. House Committee on International Relations," 107th Congress, 2nd Session, transcript, September 19, 2002, retrieved from http://commdocs.house.gov/committees/intlrel/hfa81814.000/hfa81814_0f.htm, November 4, 2007.
103. "President Outlines Priorities," official White House transcript, November 7, 2002, retrieved from http://www.whitehouse.gov/news/releases/2002/11/20021107-2.html, December 1, 2007.

104. "Remarks by the President at Bill Signing of the Dot Kids Implementation and Efficiency Act of 2002," December 4, 2002, retrieved from http://www.whitehouse.gov/news/releases/2002/12/20021204-1.html, December 1, 2007.
105. "Analysis of Military Buildup in Iraq," *CNN Saturday Morning News*, December 21, 2002, retrieved from http://transcripts.cnn.com/TRANSCRIPTS/0212/21/smn.01.html, December 1, 2007.
106. "President Discusses Iraq and North Korea with Reporters," official White House press release, December 31, 2002, retrieved from http://www.whitehouse.gov/news/releases/2002/12/20021231-1.html, November 4, 2007.
107. "President Bush: This Is a Defining Moment for the U.N. Security Council, Remarks by the President to the Press Pool," official White House press release, February 7, 2003, retrieved from http://www.whitehouse.gov/news/releases/2003/02/20030207-3.html, December 1, 2007.
108. "President Bush Discusses Iraq in National Press Conference," official White House press release, March 6, 2003, retrieved from http://www.whitehouse.gov/news/releases/2003/03/20030306-8.html, December 1, 2007.
109. "War on Terror: President's Radio Address," official White House transcript, March 8, 2003, retrieved from http://www.whitehouse.gov/news/releases/2003/03/20030308-1.html, November 4, 2007.
110. "DoD News Briefing: Secretary Rumsfeld and Gen. Myers," March 20, 2003, retrieved from http://merln.ndu.edu/merln/pfiraq/archive/dod/RumsfieldMyers20mar03.pdf, November 10, 2007.
111. "Downing Street Memo," retrieved from http://www.downingstreetmemo.com/memos.html, November 10, 2007.

VOLUME II: THEIR FINEST HOUR

1. Ken Adelman, "Cakewalk in Iraq," *The Washington Post*, February 13, 2002, page A27.
2. Richard Perle, "Saddam's Ultimate Solution," *Wide Angle*, PBS, July 11, 2002, retrieved from http://www.pbs.org/wnet/wideangle/printable/transcript_saddam.html, October 14, 2007.
3. Kenneth Adelman, "Desert Storm II Would Be a Walk in the Park," *The Times* (London), August 29, 2002.

4. Kathryn Jean Lopez, "Closing In: A Conversation with Lawrence Kaplan and Bill Kristol on Iraq," *National Review Online*, February 24, 2003, retrieved from http://www.nationalreview.com/interrogatory/interrogatory022403.asp, October 31, 2007.
5. Richard Perle, "Saddam's Ultimate Solution," *Wide Angle*, PBS, July 11, 2002, retrieved from http://www.pbs.org/wnet/wideangle/printable/transcript_saddam.html, October 14, 2007.
6. "The Day After: Planning for a Post-Saddam Iraq," American Enterprise Institute for Public Policy Research, October 3, 2002, conference transcript.
7. Eric Shinseki, testimony, "Hearing of the Senate Armed Services Committee; Subject: The Fiscal Year 2004 Defense Budget," Federal News Service, February 25, 2003.
8. "Secretary Rumsfeld Media Availability with Afghan President Karzai," February 27, 2003, retrieved from http://www.defenselink.mil/transcripts/transcript.aspx?transcriptid=1957, December 1, 2007.
9. "U.S. Representative Jim Nussle (R-IA) Holds Hearing on FY 2004 Defense Budget Request," Federal News Service, February 27, 2003.
10. Ibid.
11. "Remarks to the Nation by President George W. Bush Regarding the Situation in Iraq," Federal News Service, June 28, 2005.
12. Rich Lowry, "Retired Brass Look Backward," *Seattle Post-Intelligencer*, April 19, 2006, page B7.
13. Alan Cooperman, "Bush Predicted No Iraq Casualties, Robertson Says," *The Washington Post*, October 21, 2004; page A09.
14. Joyce Marcel, "Her Beautiful Mind," *commondreams.com,* April 29, 2004, retrieved from http://www.commondreams.org/views04/0429-11.htm, November 11, 2007.
15. "Iraq: What Lies Ahead," American Enterprise Institute forum, March 25, 2003, transcript, retrieved from http://www.aei.org/events/eventID.242/transcript.asp, November 17, 2007.
16. I. Lewis Libby, and Paul Wolfowitz, "U.S. Defense Planning Guidance for Fiscal Years 1994–1999," February 18, 1992.
17. Project for a New American Century, "Wolfowitz Statement on U.S. Policy toward Iraq," March 18, 2007, retrieved from http://www.newamericancentury.org/iraqsep1898.htm, November 3, 2007.
18. Ibid.

19. Dan Morgan and David B. Ottaway, "In Iraqi War Scenario, Oil Is Key Issue; U.S. Drillers Eye Huge Petroleum Pool," *The Washington Post*, September 15, 2002, page A01.
20. Donald Lambro, "Regimen to Sustain Recovery," *The Washington Times*, September 19, 2002, page A19.
21. Bill O'Reilly, "Impact Interview with Osama Siblani," *The O'Reilly Factor*, Fox News, January 14, 2003.
22. "Secretary Rumsfeld Interview with Al Jazeera TV," official U.S. Department of Defense transcript, retrieved from http://www.defenselink.mil/transcripts/transcripts.aspx?transcriptid=1946, November 3, 2007.
23. *Hardball with Chris Matthews*, MSNBC, April 19, 2006.
24. Alan Greenspan, *The Age of Turbulence: Adventures in a New World* (New York: Penguin Press, 2007).
25. Richard Perle, "Saddam's Ultimate Solution," *Wide Angle*, PBS, July 11, 2002, retrieved from http://www.pbs.org/wnet/wideangle/printable/transcript_saddam.html, October 14, 2007.
26. Donald Lambro, "Economic Effect of War Seen as Small; Lindsey Says Benefits of Ousting Saddam Outweigh Cost," *Washington Times*, September 16, 2002, page A14.
27. Kenneth M. Pollack, *The Threatening Storm: The Case for Invading Iraq* (New York: Random House, 2002), quoted in Michael Massing, "The War Expert: Wrong, Wrong, Wrong Again. But the Media Still Want Ken Pollack," *Columbia Journalism Review*, November–December 2007, retrieved from http://www.cjr.org/on_the_contrary/the_war_expert.php?page=all, December 2, 2007.
28. "What They Said Before the War," *New York Daily News*, March 7, 2005, page 19.
29. "Rumsfeld Urges Congress to Support Supplemental Funding Request," official transcript of the Secretary's prepared testimony before the Senate and House Appropriations Committees, March 27, 2003, distributed by the Office of International Information Programs, U.S. Department of State, retrieved from http://www.globalsecurity.org/military/library/news/2003/03/mil-030327-usia02.htm, October 28, 2007.
30. "U.S. Representative Jerry Lewis (R-CA) Holds Hearing on FY 2004 Appropriations," FDCH political transcripts, March 27, 2003.
31. "Nightline Project Iraq," *Nightline*, ABC, April 23, 2003, retrieved from http://www.fas.org/sgp/temp/natsios042303.html, January 13, 2008.

32. "Bush Appoints Former 'Big Dig' Manager as Special Envoy to Darfur," *thinkprogress.org*, September 19, 2006, retrieved from http://thinkprogress.org/2006/09/19/natsios-darfur/, November 10, 2007.
33. Mike Allen and Jonathan Weisman, "Officials Argue for Fast U.S. Exit from Iraq," *The Washington Post*, April 21, 2003, page A01.
34. "Press Briefing by Ari Fleischer, February 18, 2003," retrieved from http://www.globalsecurity.org/military/library/news/2003/02/mil-030218-wh01.htm, December 1, 2007.
35. Glenn Kessler and Jim VandeHei, "Misleading Assertions Cover Iraq War and Voting Records," *The Washington Post*, October 6, 2004, page A15, retrieved from http://www.washingtonpost.com/wp-dyn/articles/A10244-2004Oct5.html, November 5, 2007.
36. Ibid.
37. "Saddam's Ultimate Solution," *Wide Angle*, PBS, transcript, July 11, 2002, retrieved from http://www.pbs.org/wnet/wideangle/printable/transcript_saddam.html, October 14, 2007.
38. "What They Said Before the War," *New York Daily News*, March 7, 2005, page 19.
39. "The Final Word Is Hooray!" Fairness and Accuracy in Reporting Media Advisory, March 15, 2006, retrieved from http://www.fair.org/index.php?page=2842, December 1, 2007.
40. Susan Page, "Prewar Predictions Coming Back to Bite," *USA Today*, March 31, 2003, retrieved from http://www.usatoday.com/news/world/iraq/2003-03-31-then-and-now-usat_x.htm, December 1, 2007.
41. "The Final Word Is Hooray!" Fairness and Accuracy in Reporting Media Advisory, March 15, 2006, retrieved from http://www.fair.org/index.php?page=2842, December 1, 2007.
42. *The News with Brian Williams*, CNBC, February 18, 2003.
43. David Frum, "The 'Rush' to War, and the Day After Never," *National Review*, February 24, 2003, retrieved from http://www.davidfrum.com/archive.asp?YEAR=2003&ID=151, November 29, 2007.
44. "Clinton Airs Views on Iraq, Affirmative Action," *The Tavis Smiley Show*, PBS, March 6, 2003, retrieved from http://www.npr.org/templates/story/story.php?storyId=1184052, December 1, 2007.
45. Quoted in Hendrik Hertzberg, "Cakewalk," *The New Yorker*, April 14, 2003, retrieved from http://www.newyorker.com/archive/2003/04/14/030414ta_talk_hertzberg, December 1, 2007.

46. Susan Page, "Prewar Predictions Coming Back to Bite," *USA Today*, March 31, 2003, retrieved from http://www.usatoday.com/news/world/iraq/2003-03-31-then-and-now-usat_x.htm, November 29, 2007.
47. Ibid.
48. Richard Perle, "Thank God for the Death of the UN," *The Guardian* (London), March 21, 2003, retrieved from http://www.guardian.co.uk/Iraq/Story/0,,918812.00.html, October 14, 2007.
49. *Hardball with Chris Matthews*, MSNBC, August 19, 2002.
50. David Frum, "The 'Rush' to War, and the Day After Never," *National Review*, February 24, 2003, retrieved from http://www.davidfrum.com/archive.asp?YEAR=2003&ID=151, November 29, 2007.

VOLUME III: THE GRAND ALLIANCE

1. "President Bush, President Havel Discuss Iraq, NATO," Office of the Press Secretary, November 20, 2002, retrieved from http://www.whitehouse.gov/news/releases/2002/11/20021120-1.html, October 9, 2007.
2. "DoD News Briefing—Secretary Rumsfeld and Gen. Myers," March 20, 2003, retrieved from http://www.defenselink.mil/transcripts/transcript.aspx?transcriptid=2072, October 10, 2007.
3. "Who Are the Current Coalition Members?," Office of the Press Secretary, March 27, 2003, retrieved from http://www.whitehouse.gov/infocus/iraq/news/20030327-10.html, October 29, 2007.
4. Ivo H. Daalder, "The Coalition That Isn't," *Brookings Daily War Report*, The Brookings Institution, March 24, 2003; Glenn Kessler, "United States Puts a Spin on Coalition Numbers," *The Washington Post*, March 21, 2003, page A29; Ian MacLeod, "The 'Coalition of the Willing': 3 of 45 Have Sent Combat Troops to War; Many of the Others Will Expect Payback," *Ottawa Citizen*, March 26, 2003, page A04.
5. "Address by the President to the Nation on the Way Forward in Iraq," Office of the Press Secretary, September 13, 2007, retrieved from http://www.whitehouse.gov/news/releases/2007/09/20070913-2.html., November 29, 2007.
6. "Coalition Troops Encircle Baghdad," *CNN News*, April 7, 2003, retrieved from http://www.cnn.com/2003/WORLD/meast/04/06/sprj.irq.war.main/index.html, December 1, 2007.
7. Center for Individual Freedom, "The Collected Quotations of 'Baghdad

Bob,' " April 10, 2003, retrieved from http://www.cfif.org/htdocs/freedom line/current/in_our_opinion/baghdad_bob.htm, December 1, 2007.

8. Maria Puente, "Saddam's Spokesman Staying on Message," *USA Today*, April 7, 2003, retrieved from http://www.usatoday.com/news/world/iraq/2003-04-07-iraq-information-minister_x.htm, December 1, 2007.
9. "Baghdad Offensive Under Way," *CNN News*, April 7, 2003, retrieved from http://transcripts.cnn.com/TRANSCRIPTS/0304/07/bn.04.html, December 1, 2007.
10. Nadim Ladki, "Reality Does Not Deter Spokesman: Iraqi Minister," *National Post* (Toronto), April 8, 2003, page A03.
11. Susan Schmidt and Vernon Loeb, "Lynch Kept Firing Until She Ran Out of Ammo," *Washington Post*, April 3, 2003, retrieved from http://www.postgazette.com/nation/20030403rescuenatp3.asp, December 1, 2007.
12. " 'General' Heaps Praise on Rescued POW Lynch," Associated Press, April 3, 2003, retrieved from http://espn.go.com/ncb/news/2003/0403/1533742.html, August 8, 2007.
13. Ibid.
14. Sgt. Joseph R. Chenelly, USMC, "Iraqi Family Risks It All to Save American POW," American Forces Press Service, April 4, 2003, retrieved from http://www.globalsecurity.org/wmd/library/news/iraq/2003/iraq-030404-afps04.htm, April 4, 2003.
15. David D. Kirkpatrick, "Jessica Lynch Criticizes U.S. Accounts of Her Ordeal," *The New York Times*, November 7, 2003.
16. Jamie McIntyre, "Pentagon calls BBC's Lynch Allegations 'Ridiculous,' " *CNN.com,* May 19, 2003, updated June 17, 2003, retrieved from http://www.cnn.com/2003/US/05/19/sprj.irq.bbc.lynch.dod/index.html, October 21, 2007.
17. Mona Charen, "Pax Americana," *Creators Syndicate*, March 21, 2003, retrieved from http://www.jewishworldreview.com/cols/charen032103.asp, December 1, 2007.
18. "The Final Word Is Hooray!" Fairness and Accuracy in Reporting Media Advisory, March 15, 2006, retrieved from http://www.fair.org/index.php?page=2842, December 7, 2007.
19. David Carr, "Dilemma's Definition: The Left and Iraq," *The New York Times*, April 16, 2003, page E1.
20. "Iraq and the Media: A Critical Timeline," Fairness and Accuracy in

Reporting, March 19, 2007, retrieved from http://www.fair.org/index.php?page=3062, November 20, 2007.

21. "The Final Word Is Hooray!" Fairness and Accuracy in Reporting Media Advisory, March 15, 2006, retrieved from http://www.fair.org/index.php?page=2842, December 1, 2007.
22. Ibid.
23. William Kristol, "The Era of American Weakness and Doubt in Response to Terrorism Is Over," *The Weekly Standard*, April 28, 2003, retrieved from http://www.weeklystandard.com/Content/Public/Articles/000/000/002/564ueebn.asp, December 1, 2007.
24. Richard Perle, "Relax, Celebrate Victory," *USA Today*, May 1, 2003, retrieved from http://www.usatoday.com/news/opinion/editorials/2003-05-01-oppo se_x.htm, December 1, 2007.
25. "Garner: Americans Should Beat Chests with Pride," Reuters, April 30, 2003, retrieved from http://www.commondreams.org/headlines03/0430-12.htm, December 1, 2007.
26. "The Final Word Is Hooray!" Fairness and Accuracy in Reporting Media Advisory, March 15, 2006, retrieved from http://www.fair.org/index.php?page=2842, December 1, 2007.
27. "President Bush Announces Major Combat Operations Have Ended," Office of the Press Secretary, May 1, 2003, retrieved from http://www.whitehouse.gov/news/releases/2003/05/20030501-15.html, December 1, 2007.
28. "The Architects of War: Where Are They Now?," September 22, 2003, retrieved from http://thinkprogress.org/the-architects-where-are-they-now/, December 1, 2007.
29. Bill Sammon, "Bush Likens Saddam's Fall to End of Berlin Wall," *The Washington Times*, April 13, 2005, page A3.
30. David Zucchino, "Army Stage-Managed Fall of Hussein Statue," *Los Angeles Times*, July 3, 2004, retrieved from http://www.commondreams.org/headlines04/0703-02.htm, November 29, 2007.
31. Bill O'Reilly, *The O'Reilly Factor*, Fox News, March 26, 2003.

VOLUME IV: THE HINGE OF FATE

1. Fred Kaplan, "War-Gamed: Why the Army Shouldn't Be So Surprised by Saddam's Moves," *Slate*, March 28, 2003, retrieved from http://www.slate.com/id/2080814/, November 1, 2007.

2. "Mayhem, Merriment in Baghdad Streets," Cox News Service, April 10, 2003.
3. "Press Briefing with Ari Fleischer," official White House Press transcript, April 10, 2003, retrieved from http://www.whitehouse.gov/news/releases/2003/04/20030410-6.html, October 29, 2007.
4. "DoD News Briefing—Secretary Rumsfeld and Gen. Myers," official Department of Defense transcript, April 11, 2003, retrieved from http://www.defenselink.mil/transcripts/transcript.aspx?transcriptid=2367,October 29, 2007.
5. Ibid.
6. Chalmers Johnson, *Nemesis: The Last Days of the American Republic* (New York: Metropolitan Books, 2006), page 47.
7. "DoD News Briefing—Secretary Rumsfeld and Gen. Myers," official Department of Defense transcript, April 11, 2003, retrieved from http://www.defenselink.mil/transcripts/transcript.aspx?transcriptid=2367,October 29, 2007.
8. "CENTCOM Briefing, Aired April 15, 2003," CNN, transcript, retrieved from http://edition.cnn.com/TRANSCRIPTS/0304/15/sec.01.html, October 29, 2007.
9. Ann Coulter, "Liberals Meet Unexpected Resistance," Universal Press Syndicate, May 1, 2003, retrieved from http://www.frontpagemag.com/Articles/Read.aspx?GUID=7B2EAC92-8DF4-4BB9-8906-F3A6F5FBEA5A, December 1, 2007.
10. "DoD News Briefing—Mr. Di Rita and Mr. Slocombe," September 17, 2003, retrieved from http://www.defenselink.mil/transcripts/transcript.aspx?transcriptid=3164, October 29, 2007.
11. "Pockets of Iraqi Resistance Still in Baghdad," *American Morning with Paula Zahn*, CNN, transcript, April 8, 2003.
12. Quoted in Howard Kurtz, "Hillary's New Friends," *The Washington Post*, May 2, 2007, retrieved from http://www.washingtonpost.com/wp-dyn/content/blog/2007/05/02/BL2007050200485_pf.html, December 1, 2007.
13. "Rumsfeld Blames Iraq Problems on 'Pockets of Dead-enders,' " Associated Press, June 18, 2003, retrieved from http://www.usatoday.com/news/world/iraq/2003-06-18-rumsfeld_x .htm, October 30, 2007.
14. "Maj. Gen. Odierno Videoteleconference from Baghdad," official Defense Department transcript, June 18, 2003, retrieved from http://www.global

security.org/wmd/library/news/iraq/2003/06/iraq-030618-dod02.htm, October 14, 2007.

15. Peter Slevin and Vernon Loeb, "Bremer: Iraq Effort to Cost Tens of Billions," *The Washington Post*, August 27, 2003, page A01, retrieved from http://www.washingtonpost.com/ac2/wp-dyn/A50396-2003Aug26?language=printer, December 1, 2007.
16. "Iraq Needs Tens of Billions," *BBC News*, August 27, 2003, retrieved from http://news.bbc.co.uk/2/hi/middle_east/3183979.stm, December 1, 2007.
17. Liane Hansen, "The State of Affairs in Iraq," *Weekend Edition*, NPR September 28, 2003, retrieved from http://www.brookings.edu/interviews/2003/0928iraq_ohanlon.aspx, December 1, 2007.
18. Rajiv Chandrasekaran, *Imperial Life in the Emerald City* (New York: Knopf, 2007), page 179.
19. "All-Star Panel Discusses the Latest Deadly Bombing in Iraq and Democratic Candidates and Voters," *Special Report with Brit Hume*, Fox News, October 27, 2003.
20. Michael O'Hanlon and Stephen J. Solarz, "Iraq's Timely Vote," *The Washington Times*, February 17, 2004, retrieved from http://www.brookings.edu/opinions/2004/0217iraq_ohanlon.aspx, December 1, 2007.
21. James Risen, "The Struggle for Iraq: Intelligence; Account of Broad Shiite Revolt Contradicts White House Stand," *The New York Times*, April 8, 2004, retrieved from http://query.nytimes.com/gst/fullpage.html?res=9A04E5D61438F93BA3 5757C0A9629C8B63, December 1, 2007.
22. "Iraq Insurgency in 'Last Throes,' Cheney says," *CNN News*, June 20, 2005, retrieved from http://www.cnn.com/2005/US/05/30/cheney.iraq/, December 1, 2007.
23. "U.S. Forces in Iraq on the Attack," *American Morning*, CNN, November 14, 2005, retrieved from http://transcripts.cnn.com/TRANSCRIPTS/0311/14/ltm.19.html, December 1, 2007.
24. "Iraq Battling More Than 200,000 Insurgents," Agence France-Presse, January 3, 2005, retrieved from http://www.commondreams.org/headlines05/0103-06.htm, November 29, 2005.
25. Paul Wein, "Rep. King Discusses Homeland Security, Meets with Jewish Leaders at Breakfast," Herald Community Newspapers, February 9, 2006, retrieved from http://www.liherald.com/site/news.cfm?newsid=16096256&BRD=1601&PAG=461&dept_id=62803&rfi=8, December 1, 2007.

26. Interview by Diane Sawyer and Robin Roberts, "Will Bush's New Plan Work? Rudy's View on Troop Surge," *Good Morning America*, CBS, January 11, 2007.
27. NewsHounds, January 18, 2007, retrieved from http://www.newshounds.us/2007/01/18/clueless_ann_coulter_says_iraq_is_like_california_you_have_the_crips_and_the_bloods_in_baghdad.php, December 1, 2007.
28. "McCain Discusses Iraq Market Visit," *CBS News*, April 8, 2007, retrieved from http://www.cbsnews.com/stories/2007/04/04/60minutes/main2648779.shtml, December 1, 2007.
29. "McCain Lauds Security During Baghdad Visit," *CNN News*, April 2, 2007, retrieved from http://www.cnn.com/2007/WORLD/meast/04/01/iraq.main/index.html, December 1, 2007.
30. Sudarsan Raghavan, "Sum of Death Statistics: A Perilous Iraq," *The Washington Post*, April 4, 2007, page A09, retrieved from http://www.washingtonpost.com/wp-dyn/content/article/2007/04;sh03/AR2007040301948_pf.html, December 1, 2007.
31. "McCain Touts Crackdown During Baghdad Visit," *NBC Nightly News*, April 1, 2007, transcript, retrieved from http://www.msnbc.msn.com/id/17901573/, November 6, 2007.
32. Kirk Semple, "McCain Wrong on Iraq Security, Merchants Say," *New York Times*, April 3, 2007, retrieved from http://www.nytimes.com/2007/04/03/world/middleeast/03mccain.html?_r=1&th&emc=th&oref=slogin, November 6, 2007.
33. Ryan Dilley, "Battle for Hearts and Minds at Umm Qasr," *BBC News Online*, March 26, 2003, retrieved from http://www.bbc.co.uk/pressoffice/pressreleases/stories/2005/10_october/06/bush.shtml, October 30, 2007.
34. Philip Hoare, "My Week," *The Independent* (London), March 30, 2003, retrieved from http://findarticles.com/p/articles/mi_qn4159/is_20030330/ai_n12737121, October 30, 2007.
35. Tommy R. Franks, "Briefing on Military Operations in Iraq," United States Central Command, March 22, 2003, retrieved from http://www.gulfinvestigations.net/document351.html, December 1, 2007.
36. "Secretary Rumsfeld Remarks on ABC 'This Week' with George Stephanopoulos," Department of Defense news transcript, March 30, 2003, retrieved from http://www.defenselink.mil/transcripts/transcript.aspx?transcriptid=2185, December 1, 2007.
37. "President Bush Meets with Prime Minister Blair in Northern Ireland,"

Office of the Press Secretary, April 8, 2003, retrieved from http://www.whitehouse.gov/news/releases/2003/04/20030408.html, December 1, 2007.

38. "Press Briefing with Ari Fleischer," Office of the Press Secretary, April 10, 2003, transcript, retrieved from http://www.whitehouse.gov/news/releases/2003/04/20030410-6.html#8, October 21, 2007.
39. Judith Miller, "A Nation at War: Arms Inspection; U.S. Inspectors Find No Forbidden Weapons at Iraqi Arms Plant," *The New York Times*, April 16, 2003, retrieved from http://query.nytimes.com/gst/fullpage.html?res=9806EED71E3BF935A25757C0A9659C8B63&sec=&spon=&pagewanted=all, December 1, 2007.
40. "Interview of the President by TVP, Poland," Office of the Press Secretary, May 29, 2003, retrieved from http://www.whitehouse.gov/g8/interview5.html, December 1, 2007.
41. *Meet the Press*, MSNBC, September 14, 2003, retrieved from http://www.msnbc.msn.com/id/3080244/, December 1, 2007.
42. "Interview on 'The World' with Lisa Mullins," BBC World Services, January 14, 2004, retrieved from http://www.state.gov/secretary/former/powell/remarks/28168.htm, December 1, 2007.
43. Juan Williams, "Cheney: U.S. to Continue Search for Iraqi WMD," NPR, January 22, 2004, retrieved from http://www.npr.org/templates/story/story.php?storyId=1610113, December 6, 2007.
44. Thomas Friedman, "The Meaning of a Skull," *The New York Times*, April 17, 2007, retrieved from http://query.nytimes.com/gst/fullpage.html?res=9B00EFDD153DF934A15757C0A9659C8B63&sec=&spon=&pagewanted=print, October 31, 2007.
45. Frank Rich, "Why Dick Cheney Cracked Up," *The New York Times*, February 4, 2007, retrieved from http://www.commondreams.org/views07/0204-22.htm, December 1, 2007.
46. "Wolfowitz: WMD Secondary Issue in Iraq," Associated Press, July 22, 2003, retrieved from http://www.usatoday.com/news/world/iraq/2003-07-22-wolfowitz-ir aq_x.htm, October 31, 2007.
47. Joseph C. Wilson IV, "What I Did Not Find in Africa," *The New York Times*, July 6, 2003, retrieved from http://www.nytimes.com/2003/07/06/opinion/06WILS.html?ex=1372824000&en=6c6aeb1ce960dec0&ei=5007, December 1, 2007.
48. *Meet the Press*, NBC, July 6, 2003, quoted in Walter Pincus and Mike Allen,

"Probe Focuses on Month before Leak to Reporters," *The Washington Post*, October 12, 2003, retrieved from http://www.washingtonpost.com/ac2/wp-dyn/A13696-2003Oct11?language=printer, December 1, 2007.

49. "Press Gaggle with Ari Fleischer," Office of the Press Secretary, July 12, 2003, retrieved from http://www.whitehouse.gov/news/releases/2003/07/20030712-11.html, December 1, 2007.
50. "Rumsfeld Says U.S. Forces Will Stay in Iraq Despite Difficulties," interview on *This Week*, ABC, July 13, 2003, retrieved from http://www.globalsecurity.org/wmd/library/news/iraq/2003/07/iraq-030713-usia01.htm, December 1, 2007.
51. "Bush: CIA Intelligence 'Darn Good,' " CBS/Associated Press, July 14, 2003, retrieved from http://www.cbsnews.com/stories/2003/07/15/iraq/main563260.shtml, December 1, 2007.
52. Dana Bash, "Bush: U.S. Had 'Darn Good Intelligence' on Iraq," *CNN News*, July 15, 2003, retrieved from http://www.cnn.com/2003/ALLPOLITICS/07/14/white.house.intel=, December 1, 2007.
53. David E. Sanger, "After the War: The President; In Speech, Bush Reiterates Threat Hussein Posed, but Makes No Mention of Weapons Search," *The New York Times*, June 17, 2003, retrieved from http://query.nytimes.com/gst/fullpage.html?res=9D07E6D71238F934A25755C0A9659C8B63, November 29, 2009.
54. "Bush Commutes Libby Sentence, Saying 30 Months 'Is Excessive,' " *New York Times*, July 3, 2007, page A01, retrieved from http://www.nytimes.com/2007/07/03/washington/03libby.html?hpl, December 1, 2007.
55. "President Bush's Statement," *New York Times*, October 28, 2005, retrieved from http://www.nytimes.com/2005/10/28/politics/28bush-text.html, November 29, 2007.
56. "Bush Commutes Libby Sentence, Saying 30 Months 'Is Excessive,' " *The New York Times*, July 3, 2007, page A01, retrieved from http://www. nytimes.com/2007/07/03/washington/03libby.html?hp, December 1, 2007.
57. Quoted in Paul Krugman, "Going for Broke," *The New York Times*, January 20, 2004, retrieved from http://query.nytimes.com/gst/fullpage.html?res=9400E0DC1539F933A15752C0A9629C8B63, November 29, 2007.
58. David Swanson, "Geneva Convention? We Thought You Said Geneva Chocolate," *Truthout*, July 12, 2006, retrieved from http://www.truthout.org/cgi-bin/artman/exec/view.cgi/62/21087, December 1, 2007.

59. Patrick F. Philbin and John C. Yoo, "Memorandum for William J. Haynes, II, General Counsel, Department of Defense Regarding Possible Habeas Jurisdiction over Aliens Held in Guantanamo Bay, Cuba," U.S. Department of Justice Office of Legal Counsel, December 28, 2001, retrieved from http://www2.gwu.edu/~nsarchiv/NSAEBB/NSAEBB127/01.12.28.pdf, December 1, 2007.
60. "Amnesty International Report 2005 Speech by Irene Khan at Foreign Press Association," Amnesty International, May 25, 2005, transcript, retrieved from http://web.amnesty.org/library/Index/ENGPOL100142005, November 30, 2007.
61. "General Richard Myers on Fox News Sunday," *Fox News*, May 29, 2005, retrieved from http://www.foxnews.com/story/0,2933,158014,00.html, December 1, 2007.
62. Otto Kreisher and Toby Eckert, "Hunter Says Menus from Guantanamo a Proof of Good Care," Copley News Service, June 14, 2005, retrieved from http://www.signonsandiego.com/uniontrib/20050614/news_1n14gitmo.html, November 11, 2007.
63. Senator Jeff Sessions, remarks at a Senate Judiciary Committee hearing, June 15, 2005, *commondreams.org*, June 16, 2005, retrieved from http://www.commondreams.org/views05/0616-28.htm, November 11, 2007.
64. "Limbaugh Touted 'Club G'itmo, the Muslim Resort,' " *mediamatters.org*, June 17, 2005, retrieved from http://mediamatters.org/items/200506170004, November 11, 2005.
65. "President and Danish Prime Minister Rasmussen Discuss G8, Africa," White House Press Office, official transcript, July 6, 2005, retrieved from http://www.whitehouse.gov/news/releases/2005/07/20050706-3.html, October 14, 2007
66. UPI, July 7, 2005, retrieved from http://news.webindia123.com/news/index.html, October 14, 2007.
67. Sara Baxter, "Three Die in Guantanamo Suicide Pact," *The Times* (London), June 11, 2006, retrieved from http://www.timesonline.co.uk/article/0,,2089-2220935,00.html, December 1, 2007.
68. "President Bush on 'Your World,' " *Fox News*, June 8, 2005, transcript, retrieved from http://www.foxnews.com/story/0,2933,158960,00.html, November 11, 2007.
69. Thom Shanker, "Rumsfeld Says Guantanamo Isn't Being Considered

for Closing," *The New York Times*, June 9, 2005, retrieved from http://www.nytimes.com/2005/06/09/international/europe/09rumsfeld.html, December 1, 2007.

70. "Limbaugh Touted 'Club G'itmo, the Muslim Resort,' " *mediamatters.org*, June 17, 2005, retrieved from http://mediamatters.org/items/200506170004, November 11, 2005.
71. John Yoo and Robert Delahunty, "Application of Treaties and Laws to al Qaeda and Taliban Detainees," January 9, 2002, retrieved from http://www.pegc.us/archive/DOJ/20020109_yoomemo.pdf, December 1, 2007.
72. Ibid.
73. William H. Taft IV, "Comments on Your Paper on the Geneva Convention," memorandum to White House Counsel Alberto Gonzales, February 2, 2002, retrieved from http://www.gwu.edu/~nsarchiv/NSAEBB/NSAEBB127/, December 1, 2007.
74. "Order Signed by President Bush Outlining Treatment of Al-Qaeda and Taliban Detainees," February 7, 2002, retrieved from http://lawofwar.org/Bush_torture_memo.htm, December 1, 2007.
75. Memorandum for Alberto R. Gonzales, Counsel to the President, August 1, 2002, Office of Legal Counsel, retrieved from www.washingtonpost.com/wp-srv/nation/documents/dojinterrogationmemo20020801.pdf.
76. Ibid.
77. John Yoo, "With 'All Necessary and Appropriate Force,' " *Los Angeles Times*, June 11, 2004, retrieved from http://www.discourse.net/archives/2004/06/yoo_unrepentant.html, December 1, 2007
78. Charles Krauthammer, "The Truth about Torture," *The Weekly Standard*, December 5, 2005, retrieved from http://www.weeklystandard.com/Content/Public/Articles/000/000 /006/400rhqav.asp, December 1, 2007.
79. Jane Mayer, "Outsourcing Torture," *The New Yorker*, February 14, 2005, retrieved from http://www.newyorker.com/archive/2005/02/14/050214fa_fact6, December 1, 2007.
80. Andrew Sullivan, "The Daily Dish," *theatlantic.com*, March 17, 2007, retrieved from http://andrewsullivan.theatlantic.com/the_daily_dish/2007/03; shquote_for_the_d_20.html, November 30, 2007.
81. Ibid.
82. *The Situation Room*, CNN, October 31, 2007, transcript, retrieved from

http://transcripts.cnn.com/TRANSCRIPTS/0710/31/sitroom.03.html, November 9, 2007.

83. Deroy Murdock, "Waterboarding Has Its Benefits," *National Review Online*, November 5, 2007, retrieved from http://article.nationalreview.com/?q=ZjNkYmU2NWV1OWE4MTU5MjhiOGNmMWUwMjdjZjU2ZjA, November 9, 2007.
84. Dana Priest and Barton Gellman, "U.S. Decries Abuse but Defends Interrogations; Stress and Duress Tactics Used on Terrorism Suspects Held in Secret Overseas Facilities," *The Washington Post*, December 26, 2002, retrieved from http://www.washingtonpost.com/wp-dyn/content/article/2006/06;sh09/AR2006060901356_2.html, November 30, 2007.
85. Ibid.
86. "Rice Says United States Does Not Torture Terrorists," December 5, 2005, retrieved from http://usinfo.state.gov/dhr/Archive/2005/Dec/05-436751.html, November 30, 2007.
87. Statement by the President, Office of the Press Secretary, June 26, 2003, retrieved from http://www.whitehouse.gov/news/releases/2003/06/20030626-3.ht ml, December 1, 2007.
88. "Deputy Secretary of Defense Paul Wolfowitz Interview with WSVN-TV," Department of Defense news transcript, March 23, 2003, retrieved from http://www.defenselink.mil/transcripts/transcript/aspx?transcriptid=2113, December 1, 2007.
89. Tarek Al-Issawi, "Walls of Abu Ghraib Prison Remain Witness to Fear of Inmates," Associated Press, September 17, 2003.
90. Susan Taylor Martin, "Her Job: Lock Up Iraq's Bad Guys," *St. Petersburg Times*, December 14, 2003, page 1A.
91. "Limbaugh on Torture of Iraqis: U.S. Guards Were 'Having a Good Time,' 'Blow[ing] Some Steam Off,' " *mediamatters.org*, May 4, 2004, retrieved from http://mediamatters.org/items/200405050003, December 1, 2007.
92. Dick Meyer "Rush: MPs Just Blowing Off Some Steam," *CBS News*, May 4, 2004, retrieved from http://www.cbsnews.com/stories/2004/05/06/opinion/meyer/m ain616021.shtml, December 1, 2007.
93. "Rumsfeld Testifies before Senate Armed Services Committee," *Washington Post*, May 7, 2004, http://www.washingtonpost.com/ac2/wp-dyn/A8575-2004May7?language=printer, December 1, 2007.

94. "GOP Senator Labels Abused Prisoners 'Terrorists,' " *CNN.com,* May 12, 2007, retrieved from http://www.cnn.com/2004/ALLPOLITICS/05/11/inhofe.abuse/, October 14, 2007.
95. Ibid.
96. Quoted in Scott Higham and Joe Stephens, "Punishment and Amusement," *The Washington Post,* May 22, 2004, page A01, retrieved from http://www.washingtonpost.com/wp-dyn/articles/A46523-2004May21.html. December 1, 2007.
97. John Diamond, "Sanchez Says He Never Saw Rules for Interrogation," *USA Today*, May 20, 2004, retrieved from http://www.usatoday.com/news/world/iraq/2004-05-20-interrogation-rules_x.htm?POE-NEWISVA, December 1, 2007.
98. *The New York Times,* March 30, 2005, retrieved from http://www.nytimes.com/2005/03/30/international/middleeast/30abuse.html, November 6, 2007.
99. Victor Davis Hanson, "American Cannibalism," *National Review Online*, May 14, 2004, retrieved from http://www.nationalreview.com/hanson/hanson200405140838.asp, December 1, 2007.
100. "President Outlines Steps to Help Iraq Achieve Democracy and Freedom," Office of the Press Secretary, May 24, 2004, official White House transcript, retrieved from http://www.whitehouse.gov/news/releases/2004/05/20040524-10.html, November 6, 2007.
101. "Judge: Abu Ghraib a Crime Scene," *CNN.com,* June 21, 2004, retrieved from http://www.cnn.com/2004/WORLD/meast/06/21/iraq.abuse.trial;/index.html, November 30, 2007.
102. Official White House transcript, "President Names Envoy to Iraq," Office of the Press Secretary, May 6, 2003, retrieved from http://www.whitehouse.gov/news/releases/2003/05/20030506-3.html, November 8, 2007.
103. Rajiv Chandrasekaran, "Ties to GOP Trumped Know-How Among Staff Sent to Rebuild Iraq," *The Washington Post*, September 17, 2006, page A01.
104. Ibid.
105. Yochi J. Dreazen, "How a 24-Year-Old Got a Job Rebuilding Iraq's Stock Market," *Wall Street Journal*, January 28, 2004, page A01.
106. Rajiv Chandrasekaran, "Ties to GOP Trumped Know-How Among Staff Sent to Rebuild Iraqi," *The Washington Post*, September 17, 2006, page A01.

107. Ken Dilanian, "Iraqi Hospitals Remain Bleak Without US Aid," Knight-Ridder newspapers, March 3, 2004, retrieved from http://www.commondreams.org/headlines04/0303-11.htm, December 6, 2007.
108. Rajiv Chandrasekaran, "Ties to GOP Trumped Know-How Among Staff Sent to Rebuild Iraqi," *The Washington Post*, September 17, 2006, page A01.
109. Rajiv Chandrasekaran, *Imperial Life in the Emerald City* (New York: Alfred A. Knopf, 2006), p. 120.
110. Ibid., p. 94.
111. Ariana Eunjung Cha, "In Iraq, the Job Opportunity of a Lifetime: Managing a $13 Billion Budget with No Experience," *The Washington Post*, May 23, 2004, page A01, retrieved from http://www.washingtonpost.com/wp-dyn/articles/A48543-2004May22.html, November 20, 2007.
112. "An Oversight Hearing on Waste, Fraud and Abuse in U.S. Government Contracting in Iraq," Senate Democratic Policy Committee, transcript, February 14, 2005.
113. Coalition Provisional Authority Order Number 1: De-Ba'athification of Iraqi Society, May 16, 2003, retrieved from http://www.iraqcoalition.org/regulations/20030516_CPAORD_1_De-Ba_athification_of_Iraqi_Society_.pdf, November 25, 2007.
114. "Briefing with Douglas Feith, Defense Undersecretary for Policy, Subject: On Iraq Reconstruction," distributed by the Bureau of International Information Programs, U.S. Department of State, May 28, 2003, transcript, retrieved from http://www.globalsecurity.org/wmd/library/news/iraq/2003/05/iraq-030528-usia01.htm, November 23, 2007.
115. Bill Powell and Bobby Ghosh, "Paul Bremer's Rough Ride," *Time*, June 20, 2004, retrieved from http://www.time.com/time/magazine/article/0.9171.655426-1.00.html, November 17, 2007.
116. Jon Lee Anderson, "Letter from Iraq: Out on the Street," *The New Yorker*, November 15, 2004, retrieved from http://www.newyorker.com/archive/2004/11/15/041115fa_fact?printable=true, November 23, 2007.
117. Ibid.
118. David Pallister, "How the US Sent $12Bn in Cash to Iraq. And Watched It Vanish," *Guardian*, February 8, 2007, retrieved from http://www.guardian.co.uk/Iraq/Story/0,,2008189,00.html, November 11, 2007.
119. "Audit: U.S. Lost Track of $9 Billion in Iraq Funds," *CNN.com*, January 31, 2005, retrieved from http://edition.cnn.com/2005/WORLD/meast/01/30/iraq.audit/, December 2, 2007.

120. "Text of Ambassador Bremer's Address to the Iraqi People: Budget and Banknotes," Bureau of International Information Programs, U.S. Department of State, July 7, 2003, transcript, retrieved from http://usinfo.state.gov/xarchives/display.html?p=washfile-english&y=2003&m=July&x=20030707124156namrevlisv7.943362e-02, November 21, 2007.
121. Coalition Provisional Authority, "Memorandum No. 4: Contract and Grant Procedures Applicable to Vested and Seized Iraqi Property and the Development Fund for Iraq," August 19, 2003.
122. "Cash Transfers to the Coalition Provisional Authority," U.S. House of Representatives, Committee on Oversight and Government Reform, Majority Staff Memorandum, February 6, 2007, retrieved from http://oversight.house.gov/documents/20070206130101-80952.pdf, December 2, 2007.
123. "Audit: U.S. Lost Track of $9 Billion in Iraq Funds," *CNN.com,* January 31, 2005, retrieved from http://edition.cnn.com/2005/WORLD/meast/01/30/iraq.audit/, December 2, 2007; "Rebuilding Iraq: U.S. Mismanagement of Iraqi Funds," U.S. House of Representatives Committee on Oversight and Government Reform, Minority Staff, Special Investigations Division, June 2005, retrieved from http://oversight.house.gov/documents/20050621114229-22109.pdf, December 2, 2007; Ed Harriman, "Where Has All the Money Gone?", *London Review of Books*, July 7, 2005, retrieved from http://www.lrb.co.uk/v27/n13/harr04_.html, December 2, 2007; "Cash Transfers to the Coalition Provisional Authority," U.S. House of Representatives, Committee on Oversight and Government Reform, Majority Staff Memorandum, February 6, 2007, retrieved from http://oversight.house.gov/documents/20070206130101-80952.pdf, December 2, 2007.
124. "Bremer's Opening Statement," *The Washington Post*, February 6, 2007, retrieved from http://www.washingtonpost.com/wp-dyn/content/article/2007/02; sh06/AR2007020601070.html, December 6, 2007.
125. "Special Flights Brought in Tonnes of Banknotes Which Disappeared into the War Zone," *The Guardian*, retrieved from http://www.guardian.co.uk/Iraq/Story/0,,2008189,00.html, November 11, 2007.
126. Donald L. Barlett and James B. Steele, "Billions over Baghdad," *Vanity Fair*, October 2007, retrieved from http://www.vanityfair.com/politics/features/2007/10/iraq_billions200710?currentPage=1, November 22, 2007.
127. Jon Lee Anderson, "Letter from Iraq: Out on the Street," *The New Yorker*,

November 15, 2004, retrieved from http://www.newyorker.com/archive/2004/11/15/041115fa_fact?printable=true, November 23, 2007.

128. Peter Slevin and Vernon Loeb, "Bremer: Iraq Effort to Cost Tens of Billions," *The Washington Post*, August 27, 2003, page A01, retrieved from http://www.washingtonpost.com/ac2/wp-dyn/A50396-2003Aug26?language=printer, November 23, 2007.
129. "Newsmaker: Paul Bremer," *The NewsHour with Jim Lehrer*, PBS, September 24, 2003, transcript, retrieved from http://www.pbs.org/newshour/bb/middle_east/july-dec03/bremer_9-24.html, November 23, 2007.
130. "Paul Bremer Saying Assassination Attempt on His Life Made," *American Morning*, CNN, December 19, 2003, transcript, retrieved from http://transcripts.cnn.com/TRANSCRIPTS/0312/19/ltm.14.html, November 20, 2007.
131. Quoted in Rajiv Chandrasekaran, *Imperial Life in the Emerald City*, (New York: Alfred A. Knopf, 2006), p. 146.
132. Bill Powell and Bobby Ghosh, "Paul Bremer's Rough Ride," *Time*, June 20, 2004, retrieved from http://www.time.com/time/magazine/article/0,9171,655426-1.00.html, November 17, 2007.
133. Ann Gerhart, "Bush Gives Medal of Freedom to 'Pivotal' Iraq Figures," *The Washington Post*, December 14, 2004, page C01, retrieved from http://www.washingtonpost.com/wp-dyn/articles/A63623-2004Dec14.html, November 24, 2007.
134. Ibid.
135. "President Addresses Nation, Discusses Iraq, War on Terror," June 28, 2005, retrieved from http://www.whitehouse.gov/news/releases/2005/06/20050628-7.html, December 1, 2007.
136. Quoted in Bill Powell and Bobby Ghosh, "Paul Bremer's Rough Ride," *Time*, June 20, 2004, retrieved from http://www.time.com/time/magazine/article/0,9171,655426-1,00.html, November 17, 2007.
137. "DoD News Briefing—Mr. Di Rita and Mr. Slocombe," Department of Defense news transcript, September 17, 2003, retrieved from http://www.defenselink.mil/transcripts/transcript.aspx?transcriptid=3164, December 1, 2007.
138. "Blair: Iraq Veto over Troops," *CNN News*, May 25, 2004, retrieved from http://www.cnn.com/2004/WORLD/europe/05/25/uk.iraq.blair/index.html, December 1, 2007.
139. "Confirmation Hearing of Condoleezza Rice," *The New York Times*, January

18, 2005, retrieved from http://www.nytimes.com/2005/01/18/politics/18TEXT-RICE.html?pagewanted=all&position=December 1, 2007.

140. http://www.latimes.com/news/nationworld/iraq/la-fgmilitary18jan18.0.2773590.story?coll=la-home-headlines.

141. Jim Macdonald, "How Many Battalions Does the Pope Have?," retrieved from http://nielsenhayden.com/makinglight/archives/006909.html, November 11, 2007.

142. "President's Radio Address," White House Radio, Office of the Press Secretary, October 1, 2005, official transcript, retrieved from http://www.whitehouse.gov/news/releases/2005/10/20051001.html, November 11, 2007.

143. "President Holds Press Conference," Office of the Press Secretary, October 4, 2005, retrieved from http://www.whitehouse.gov/news/releases/2005/10/20051004-1.html, January 13, 2008.

144. "Bush: Islamic Radicalism Doomed to Fail," *CNN.com,* October 6, 2005, transcript, retrieved from http://www.cnn.com/2005/POLITICS/10/06/bush.transcript/, November 11, 2007.

145. "Lieberman, Lamont Spar in Connecticut Primary Debate," *The Washington Post,* July 7, 2006, transcript, retrieved from http://www.washingtonpost.com/wp-dyn/content/article/2006/07/07/AR2006070700029.html, December 1, 2007.

146. "Top U.S. General: Iraqis Can Take Over Security within 18 Months," Associated Press, August 30, 2006, retrieved from http://www.usatoday.com/news/world/iraq/2006-08-30-iraq-security_x.htm, January 13, 2008.

147. "Iraqi PM: 'Our Forces Will Be Ready by June '07,' " MSNBC, November 30, 2006, retrieved from http://www.msnbc.msn.com/id/15946832/, January 13, 2008.

148. General James L. Jones, U.S. Marine Corps (Retired), Chairman, *The Report of the Independent Commission on the Security Forces of Iraq*, September 6, 2007, retrieved from http://www.fcnl.org/pdfs/iraq/jonescommissionreport.pdf, November 30, 2007.

149. Cited in Naomi Klein, "Baghdad Year Zero," *Harper's Magazine*, September 2004, retrieved from http://www.harpers.org/archive/2004/09/0080197, November 28, 2007.

150. Ibid.

151. "Military Officials: Empty Streets, Media Point to Planned Iraq Attack,"

CNN.com, April 3, 2004, retrieved from http://www.cnn.com/2004/WORLD/meast/04/02/iraq.main/index.html, December 2, 2007.

152. Kimmitt-Senor Briefing, Coalition Provisional Authority, March 31, 2004, retrieved from http://www.iraqcoalition.org/transcripts/20040331_Mar31_KimmittSenor.html, December 2, 2007.
153. Ibid.
154. Quoted in Jeremy Scahill, *Blackwater: The Rise of the World's Most Powerful Mercenary Army,* (New York: Nation Books, 2007), p. 107.
155. *Crossfire,* CNN, April 1, 2007, transcript, retrieved from http://www.alfrankenweb.com/crossfiregordon.html, November 27, 2007.
156. Agence France-Presse, "US retaliation for Fallujah Ambush 'Will Be Obvious to All'—Armitage," April 2, 2004, retrieved from Lexis-Nexis, November 27, 2007.
157. Kimmitt-Senor Briefing, Coalition Provisional Authority, April 1, 2004, retrieved from http://www.iraqcoalition.org/transcripts/20040401_Apr1_KimmittSenor.html, November 27, 2007.
158. Iraq Coalition Casualty Count, *Fatalities by Month: April 2004,* retrieved from www.icasualties.org, September 25, 2007; Jonathan F. Keiler, *Who Won the Battle of Fallujah?,* The Naval Institute: Proceedings, January 2005; The Iraq Body Count, *No Longer Unknowable: Fallujah's April Civilian Toll Is 600,* October 26, 2004, retrieved from http://www.iraqbodycount.org/analysis/reference/press-releases/9/, November 26, 2007.
159. Chaplain D. R. Staton, "Chaplain's Corner," *Blackwater Tactical Weekly,* April 5, 2004, retrieved from http://www.blackwaterusa.com/btw2004/articles/0405chaplain.html, November 24, 2007.
160. Jay Price and Joseph Neff, "Families Sue over Fallujah Ambush," *News and Observer,* January 7, 2005, retrieved from http://www.newsobserver.com/nation_world/bridge/story/219750. html, November 26, 2007.
161. House Committee on Oversight and Government Reform, Majority Staff, "Private Military Contractors in Iraq: An Examination of Blackwater's Actions in Fallujah," September 27, 2007, retrieved from http://oversight.house.gov/documents/20070927104643.pdf, November 26, 2007.
162. Jay Price and Joseph Neff, "Families Sue over Fallujah Ambush," *News and Observer,* January 7, 2005, retrieved from http://www.newsobserver.com/nation_world/bridge/story/219750.html, November 26, 2007.
163. Jay Price and Joseph Neff, "Families Sue Over Fallujah Ambush," *News and*

Observer, January 6, 2005, retrieved from http://www.newsobserver.com/511/story/219750.html, December 2, 2007.

164. "Iraqi Reconstruction: Reliance on Private Military Contractors and Status Report," hearing before the Committee on Oversight and Government Reform of the U.S. House of Representatives, first session, February 7, 2007, official transcript, pages 90, 177, retrieved from http://www.fas.org/irp/congress/2007_hr/iraq020707.pdf, December 2, 2007.
165. House Committee on Oversight and Government Reform, Majority Staff, "Private Military Contractors in Iraq: An Examination of Blackwater's Actions in Fallujah," September 27, 2007, retrieved from http://oversight.house.gov/documents/20070927104643.pdf, November 26, 2007.
166. "Blackwater's Response to 'Majority Staff Report' on 'Private Military Contractors in Iraq: An Examination of Blackwater's Actions in Fallujah,'" October 23, 2007, retrieved from http://www.blackwaterusa.com/press_releases/Blackwater%20Response%20to%20Majority%20Staff%20Report.pdf, November 26, 2007.
167. Mark Hemingway, "Warriors for Hire," *The Weekly Standard,* December 18, 2006, retrieved from http://www.weeklystandard.com/Content/Public/Articles/000/ 000/013/062fxarf.asp, January 13, 2008.
168. Jeremy Scahill, "Blackwater's Brothers," *thenation.com,* November 15, 2007, retrieved from http://www.thenation.com/doc/20071203/scahill, January 13, 2008.
169. Robert H. Reid, "Iraq moves to expel U.S. security firm," Associated Press, September 18, 2007, retrieved from http://www.philly.com/inquirer/special/iraq/20070918_Iraq_ moves_to_expel_U_S_security_firm.html, November 21, 2007.
170. Jeremy Scahill, "Making a Killing," *The Nation,* October 15, 2007, page 21, retrieved from http://www.thenation.com/doc/20071015/scahill, January 13, 2008.
171. Megan Greenwell, "Maliki Denounces Blackwater 'Crime,'" *The Washington Post,* September 20, 2007, p. A18, retrieved from http://www.washingtonpost.com/wpdyn/content/article/2007/09/19/AR2007091902151.html, November 27, 2007.
172. Erik Prince, interviewed on *Late Edition with Wolf Blitzer,* CNN, October 14, 2007, retrieved from http://transcripts.cnn.com/TRANSCRIPTS/0710/14/le.01.html, January 13, 2008.
173. Jeremy Scahill, "Making a Killing," *The Nation,* October 15, 2007, page 21,

retrieved from http://www.thenation.com/doc/20071015/scahill, January 13, 2008.

174. David Johnston and John M. Broder, "F.B.I. Says Guards Killed 14 Iraqis Without Cause," *The New York Times,* November 14, 2007, retrieved from http://www.nytimes.com/2007/11/14/world/middleeast/14blackwater.html?_r=1&scp=11&sq=Blackwater+shootings&oref=slogin, January 12, 2008.

175. "FBI Finds Blackwater Trucks Patched," Associated Press, January 13, 2008, retrieved from http://www.nytimes.com/aponline/us/AP-Blackwater-Prosecutions.html?sq=Blackwater%20shootings&scp=1&pagewanted=print, January 13, 2008.

176. Ibid.

177. Coalition Provisional Authority, Official website, Regulations, retrieved from http://www.cpa-iraq.org/regulations/20040627_CPAORD_17_Status_of_Coalition_Rev_with_Annex_A.pdf, November 17, 2007.

178. Quoted in Jeremy Scahill, *Blackwater: The Rise of the World's Most Powerful Mercenary Army* (New York: Nation Books, 2007), page 233.

179. Jeremy Scahill and Garrett Ordower, "From Whitewater to Blackwater," *thenation.com*, October 25, 2006, retrieved from http://www.thenation.com/doc/20061113/whitewater_to_blackwater, November 25, 2007.

180. David Johnston, "Immunity Deals Offered to Blackwater Guards," *The New York Times,* October 29, 2007, retrieved from http://www.nytimes.com/2007/10/29/washington/30cndblackwater.html?_r=1&hp&oref=slogin, November 26, 2007.

181. Lara Jakes Jordan, "Immunity Deal Hampers Blackwater Inquiry," Associated Press, October 29, 2007, retrieved from http://ap.google.com/article/ALeqM5g8j2u56IMqRcZhCnXxakvpIEJ3-OD8SJ6JCG1, November 27, 2007.

182. David Johnston, "Immunity Deals Offered to Blackwater Guards," *The New York Times,* October 29, 2007, retrieved from http://www.nytimes.com/2007/10/29/washington/30cndblackwater.html?_r=1&hp&oref=slogin, November 26, 2007. The *Times* failed to note another important fact: the State Department investigators are employed by the very same agency—the Bureau of Diplomatic Security—responsible for the mission that led to the Iraqi shootings. In other words (as R. J. Hillhouse has pointed out on her blog, *The Spy Who Billed Me*), they granted immunity to their own contractors.

183. "President Bush Discusses Global War on Terror," the Paul H. Nitze

School of Advanced International Studies, the Johns Hopkins University, Washington, D.C., official White House transcript, Office of the Press Secretary, April 10, 2006, retrieved from http://www.whitehouse.gov/news/releases/2006/04/20060410-1.html, November 25, 2007.

184. "DoD News Briefing with Press Secretary Morrell from the Pentagon Briefing Room, Arlington, VA," official U.S. Department of Defense transcript, retrieved from http://www.defenselink.mil/transcripts/transcript.aspx?transcriptid=4075, November 27, 2007.

185. "Who Are the Contractors," WGBH web pages, retrieved from http://www.pbs.org/wgbh/pages/frontline/shows/warriors/contractors/companies.html, December 2, 2007.

186. "Krongard Confirms 'Ugly Rumor': Brother Attended Blackwater Advisory Board Meeting Yesterday," *thinkprogress.org,* November 14, 2007, retrieved from http://thinkprogress.org/2007/11/14/krongard-blacwater-brother/, December 2, 2007.

187. Spencer Ackerman, "Krongard Recuses Himself from Blackwater Investigations," *TPM Muckraker*, November 14, 2007, retrieved from http://www.tpmmuckraker.com/archives/004706.php, December 2, 2007.

188. Spencer Ackerman, exclusive interview with Alvin B. "Buzzy" Krongard, *TPM Muckraker*, November 14, 2007, retrieved from http://www.tpmmuckraker.com/archives/004711.php, December 2, 2007. At the end of his interview, Buzzy Krongard asked Ackerman, "Am I my brother's keeper?"—an echo of his brother Cookie's testimony before the House Committee on Oversight and Government Reform earlier in the day.

189. "Wolfowitz Interview with Nolan Finley of the *Detroit News*," Department of Defense news transcript, March 5, 2003.

190. *Fresh Air*, NPR, April 1, 2003, retrieved from http://www.npr.org/templates/story/story.php?storyId=1215563, December 1, 2007.

191. William Kristol, "Iraq One Year Later," *The Weekly Standard*, March 22, 2004, retrieved from http://www.weeklystandard.com/Content/Public/Articles/000/000/003/852lnwyn.asp, November 3, 2007.

192. "President Addresses Nation, Discusses Iraq, War on Terror," Office of the Press Secretary, June 28, 2005, retrieved from http://www.whitehouse.gov/news/releases/2005/06/20050628-7.html, December 1, 2007.

193. "Lott: Bush Barely Mentioned Iraq in Meeting with Senate Republicans," CNN, September 28, 2006, retrieved from http://www.cnn.com/POLI

TICS/blogs/politicalticker/2006/09/lott-bush-barely-mentioned-iraq-in .html, December 1, 2007.

194. *The Radio Factor* with Bill O'Reilly, December 5, 2006, retrieved from http://mediamatters.org/items/200612060006, December 1, 2007.
195. Henry A. Kissinger, "The New Iraq Strategy," *Khaleej Times*, January 19, 2007, retrieved from http://www.khaleejtimes.com/DisplayArticleNew.asp?section=opinion&xfile=data/opinion/2007/january/opinion_january62.xml, December 1, 2007.
196. "President Bush Discusses Economy, War on Terror During Remarks to the Cattlemen's Beef Association; Holiday Inn on the Hill," Office of the Press Secretary, March 28, 2007, retrieved from http://www.whitehouse.gov/news/releases/2007/03/20070328-2.html, December 1, 2007.
197. *Meet the Press*, MSNBC, September 28, 2003, retrieved from http://www.msnbc.com/news/973028.asp?cpl=1, December 1, 2007.
198. "President Holds Press Conference," Office of the Press Secretary, October 28, 2003, retrieved from http://www.whitehouse.gov/news/releases/2003/10/20031028-2.html, December 1, 2007.
199. Press Briefing by Scott McClellan, Office of the Press Secretary, October 29, 2003, retrieved from http://www.whitehouse.gov/news/releases/2003/10/20031029-2.html, December 1, 2007.

VOLUME V: CLOSING THE RING

1. Stratfor (Strategic Forecasting, Inc.), quoted in "Situation Report on the Expedition to Iraq, Part I of a New Series," *Fabius Maximus's Blog*, November 12, 2006, retrieved from http://www.d-n-i.net/fcs/fabius_iraq_series_2006_part_I.htm, November 30, 2007.
2. "The Road Home," editorial, *The New York Times*, July 8, 2007, retrieved from http://www.nytimes.com/2007/07/08/opinion/08sun1.html, November 30, 2007.
3. "The Wrong Way out of Iraq," *The New York Times*, August 13, 2007, retrieved from http://www.nytimes.com/2007/08/13/opinion/13mon1.html, November 30, 2007.
4. Fairness and Accuracy in Reporting (FAIR), "Tom Friedman's Flexible Deadlines: Iraq's 'Decisive' Six Months Have Lasted Two and a Half Years," May 16, 2006, retrieved from http://www.fair.org/index.php?page=2884, October 14, 2007.
5. Thomas Friedman, "The Chant Not Heard," *The New York Times*, Novem-

ber 20, 2003, retrieved from http://query.nytimes.com/gst/fullpage.html?res=9F05E2D7123AF933A05752C1A9659C8B63&n=Top/Opinion/Editorials%20and%20Op-Ed/Op-Ed/Columnists/Thomas%20L%20Friedman, December 1, 2007.

6. Thomas Friedman, interview on *Fresh Air,* NPR, June 3, 2004, quoted in "Tom Friedman's Flexible Deadlines," Fairness and Accuracy in Reporting Media Advisory, May 16, 2006, retrieved from http://www.fair.org/index.php?page=2884, January 13, 2008.
7. Thomas Friedman, interview on *Face the Nation,* CBS, October 3, 2004, transcript retrieved from http://www.cbsnews.com/htdocs/pdf/face_100304.pdf, January 13, 2008.
8. Thomas Friedman, "The Last Mile," *The New York Times,* November 28, 2004, retrieved from http://www.nytimes.com/2004/11/28/opinion/28friedman.html?_r=1&n=Top/Opinion/Editorials%20and%20Op-Ed/Op-Ed/Columnists/Thomas%20L%20Friedman&oref=slogin, December 1, 2007.
9. Thomas Friedman, appearance on *Meet the Press,* NBC, September 25, 2005, MSNBC transcript, retrieved from http://www.msnbc.msn.com/id/9438988/, January 13, 2008.
10. Thomas Friedman, "The End Game in Iraq," *The New York Times,* September 28, 2005, retrieved from http://select.nytimes.com/2005/09/28/opinion/28friedman.html?n=Top/Opinion/Editorials%20and%20Op-Ed/Op-Ed/Columnists/Thomas%20L%20Friedman, December 1, 2007.
11. Thomas Friedman, interview on *Face the Nation,* CBS, December 18, 2005, transcript retrieved from http://www.cbsnews.com/htdocs/pdf/face_121805.pdf, January 13, 2008.
12. Thomas Friedman, interview on *The Oprah Winfrey Show,* quoted in "Tom Friedman's Flexible Deadlines," Fairness and Accuracy in Reporting Media Advisory, May 16, 2006, retrieved from http://www.fair.org/index.php?page=2884, January 13, 2008.
13. Thomas Friedman, interviewed by Bob Schieffer on *CBS News,* January 31, 2006, quoted in "Tom Friedman's Flexible Deadlines," Fairness and Accuracy in Reporting Media Advisory, May 16, 2006, retrieved from http://www.fair.org/index.php?page=2884, January 13, 2008.
14. Thomas Friedman, appearance on *The Today Show,* NBC, March 2, 2006, quoted in "Tom Friedman's Flexible Deadlines," Fairness and Accuracy in

Reporting Media Advisory, May 16, 2006, retrieved from http://www.fair.org/index.php?page=2884, January 13, 2008.

15. Thomas Friedman, appearance on *Late Edition with Wolf Blitzer,* CNN, April 23, 2006, transcript, retrieved from http://transcripts.cnn.com/TRANSCRIPTS/0604/23/le.01.html, January 13, 2008.
16. Thomas Friedman, interviewed on *Hardball with Chris Matthews,* MSNBC, May 11, 2006, retrieved from http://www.fair.org/index.php?page=2884, December 1, 2007.
17. Duncan Black (Atrios), "F.U.," October 6, 2006, retrieved from http://atrios.blogspot.com/2006_10_01_atrios_archive.html#116014885846435492, December 1, 2007.
18. "Undersecretary Feith Remarks to the Center for International Studies," July 9, 2003, retrieved from http://www.defenselink.mil/transcripts/transcript.aspx?transcriptid =2815, December 1, 2007.
19. "President Bush Discusses Freedom in Iraq and the Middle East," November 6, 2003, retrieved from http://www.whitehouse.gov/news/releases/2003/11/2003/1106-2.html, December 1, 2007.
20. "President Salutes the Military at Macdill Air Force Base in Tampa; Remarks by the President to Military Personnel," June 16, 2004, retrieved from http://www.whitehouse.gov/news/releases/2004/06/20040616-4.html, December 1, 2007.
21. William Kristol, "After 1/30/05," *The Weekly Standard,* March 7, 2005, retrieved from http://www.weeklystandard.com/Content/Public/Articles/000/000/005/292bhhzj.asp, December 1, 2007.
22. "Secretary of Defense Message to the Armed Forces on the Iraqi Elections," February 2, 2005, retrieved from http://www.defenselink.mil/news/newsarticle.aspx?id=25995, December 1, 2007.
23. "President Discusses War on Terror and Upcoming Iraqi Elections," Office of the Press Secretary, December 12, 2005, retrieved from http://www.whitehouse.gov/news/releases/2005/12/20051212-4.html, December 1, 2007.
24. "President Discusses Recent Visit to Iraq by Secretary of State Rice and Defense Secretary Rumsfeld," Office of the Press Secretary, May 1, 2006, retrieved from http://www.whitehouse.gov/news/releases/2006/05/20060501.html, December 1, 2007.
25. "President Bush Discusses Global War on Terror," Office of the Press Sec-

retary, May 22, 2006, retrieved from http://www.whitehouse.gov/news/releases/2006/05/20060522-1.html, December 1, 2007.

26. Press Conference of the President, June 14, 2006, retrieved from http://www.whitehouse.gov/news/releases/2006/06/20060614.html, December 1, 2007.
27. Eric Schmitt, "After the War: Official Tour; Wolfowitz Sees Challenges, and Vindication, in Iraq," *The New York Times*, July 22, 2003, retrieved from http://query.nytimes.com/gst/fullpage.html?res=9805E3D6163FF931A15754C0A9659C8B63, December 1, 2007.
28. "The Final Word Is Hooray!" Fairness and Accuracy in Reporting Media Advisory, March 15, 2006, retrieved from http://www.fair.org/index.php?page=2842, December 1, 2007.
29. Ibid.
30. Ibid.
31. Ibid.
32. Ibid.
33. Daniel Pipes, "Why the Left Loves Osama [and Saddam]," *New York Post*, March 19, 2003, retrieved from http://www.danielpipes.org/article/1040, November 2, 2007.
34. Ann Coulter, *Treason: Liberal Treachery from the Cold War to the War on Terrorism* (New York: Crown, 2003), page 16.
35. Patrick D. Healey, "Rove Critizes Liberals on 9/11," *The New York Times*, June 22, 2005, retrieved from http://www.nytimes.com/2005/06/23/politics/23rove.html?_r=1&oref=slogin, December 1, 2007.
36. "President Addresses Veterans of Foreign Wars on the War on Terror," White House press release, January 10, 2006, retrieved from http://www.whitehouse.gov/news/releases/2006/01/20060110-1.html, October 20, 2007.
37. Ibid.
38. Dana Milbank, "A Reprise of the Grand Old Party Line," *The Washington Post*, September 13, 2006, page A02.
39. "Fox Brings Ann Coulter on to 'Gauge Reaction' to Petraeus' Testimony," September 10, 2007, retrieved from http://www.newshounds.us/2007/09/10/fox_brings_ann_coulter_on_to_gauge_reaction_to_petraeus_testimony.php, November 3, 2007.
40. Quoted in Ian Buruma, "His Toughness Problem—and Ours," *New York*

Review of Books, September 27, 2007, retrieved from http://www.nybooks.com/articles/20590, December 1, 2007.

41. "Remarks by Secretary of Homeland Security Tom Ridge at a Press Conference Announcing the Raising of the National Threat Level," Office of the Press Secretary, December 21, 2003, retrieved from http://www.dhs.gov/xnews/releases/press_release_0889.shtm, December 1, 2007.
42. "As Ashcroft Warns of Qaeda Plan to Attack U.S., Some Question the Threat and Its Timing," *The New York Times*, May 27, 2004, retrieved from http://query.nytimes.com/gst/fullpage.html?res=9D06E5DD133EF934A15756C0A9629C8B63, December 1, 2007.
43. "Chertoff Warns of Higher Risk of Terrorism," Associated Press, July 11, 2007, retrieved from http://www.nytimes.com/2007/07/11/us/nationalspecial3/11terror.html?_r=1&oref=slogin, December 4, 2007.
44. "Al Qaeda Weaker, President Insists," *Weekend Australian*, July 14, 2007.
45. "Remarks by the President at People for Ganske Dinner," White House Press Office, April 15, 2002, official transcript, retrieved from http://www.whitehouse.gov/news/releases/2002/04/20020415-10.html, November 6, 2007.
46. "Oscars Will Not Be Beaten by Terror," *BBC News*, October 17, 2001, retrieved from http://news.bbc.co.uk/1/hi/entertainment/film/1603303.stm, December 1, 2007.
47. Richard Weizel, "What Would John Philips [sic] Sousa Have Done?" *The New York Times*, November 4, 2001, retrieved from www.nyt.com, October 8, 2007.
48. Roy Rivenburg, "A Phrase That Turns Routine Acts into Acts of War," *Los Angeles Times*, November 27, 2001.
49. *Meet the Press,* NBC, September 10, 2006, transcript, retrieved from http://www.msnbc.msn.com/id/14720480/, December 1, 2007.
50. Michael Abramowitz, "Bush Says America Loses Under Democrats," *The Washington Post*, October 31, 2006, page A01, retrieved from http://www.washingtonpost.com/wp-dyn/content/article/2006/10=30/AR2006103000530.html, December 1, 2007.
51. Quoted in Nancy A. Youssef, "U.S. Officials Exclude Bombs in Touting Drop in Iraq Violence," McClatchy newspapers, April 25, 2007, retrieved from http://www.mcclatchydc.com/staff/nancy_youssef/story/16047.html, December 1, 2007.

52. "President Bush Holds Press Conference," White House, Office of the Press Secretary, official transcript, March 13, 2002, retrieved from http://www.whitehouse.gov/news/releases/2002/03/20020313-8.html, November 22, 2007.
53. "Third Presidential Debate," *washingtonpost.com,* October 13, 2004, transcript, retrieved from http://www.washingtonpost.com/wp-srv/politics/debatereferee/debate_1013.html, November 22, 2007.
54. *Hannity & Colmes*, Fox News, August 24, 2006, *mediamatters.org,* August 25, 2006, partial transcript, retrieved from http://mediamatters.org/items/200608250012, November 17, 2007.
55. Ibid.

VOLUME VI: TRIUMPH OR TRAGEDY?

1. "At O'Hare, President Says 'Get On Board,' " official White House news release, September 27, 2001, retrieved from http://www.whitehouse.gov/news/releases/2001/09/20010927-1.html, December 1, 2007.
2. Alasdair Roberts, "The War We Deserve," *Foreign Policy*, November/December 2007, page 47.
3. "President George Bush Discusses Iraq," Office of the Press Secretary, March 6, 2003, retrieved from http://www.whitehouse.gov/news/releases/2003/03/20030306-8.html, December 1, 2007.
4. "President's Message to America's Military and Their Families," April 14, 2003, retrieved from http://www.whitehouse.gov/news/releases/2003/04/20030414-3.html, December 1, 2007.
5. "President's Remarks at Talent for Senate Dinner," June 2, 2005, retrieved from http://www.whitehouse.gov/news/releases/2005/06/20050602-14.html, December 1, 2007.
6. John D. Banusiewicz, " 'As Iraqis Stand Up, We Will Stand Down,' Bush Tells Nation," American Forces Press Service, July 28, 2005, retrieved from http://www.defenselink.mil/news/newsarticle.aspx?id=16277, December 1, 2007.
7. Henry Kissinger, "The New Iraq Strategy," *Khaleej Times Online,* January 19, 2007, retrieved from http://www.khaleejtimes.com/DisplayArticleNew.asp?xfile=data/opinion/2007/January/opinion_January62.xml§ion=opinion&col=, December 1, 2007.
8. Quoted in Peter Eisner and Knut Royce, *The Italian Letter* (New York: Rodale Press, 2007), pages 18–21.

9. Tommy Franks, *American Soldier* (New York: ReganBooks, 2004), quoted in Thomas E. Ricks, *Fiasco: The American Military Adventure in Iraq* (New York: Penguin Press, 2006), page 115.
10. Thomas E. Ricks, *Fiasco: The American Military Adventure in Iraq* (New York: Penguin Press, 2006), page 115.
11. "John Negroponte's Nomination to Be Ambassador to Iraq; Hearing before the Senate Foreign Relations Committee," retrieved from http://www.iraqwatch.org/government/US/HearingsPreparedstatements/us-sfrc-transcript-042704.htm, November 1, 2007.
12. Elisabeth Bumiller and Douglas Jehl, "Bush Picks Longtime Diplomat for New Top Intelligence Job," *The New York Times*, February 18, 2003, retrieved from http://www.nytimes.com/2005/02/18/politics/18director.html?pagewanted=1, December 1, 2007.
13. "President Meets with Iraqis Who Received Medical Care in the U.S.," official White House press release, May 25, 2004.
14. "Under Armored," *Online NewsHour*, feature by Ray Suarez on Rumsfeld's town meeting remark, December 9, 2004, transcript, retrieved from http://www.pbs.org/newshour/bb/military/july-dec04/armor_12-9.html, November 11, 2007.
15. "Soldier Says He Asked Rumsfeld Armor Question Without Aid of Embed," *Editor and Publisher*, December 19, 2004.
16. "President Visits Troops at Brooke Army Medical Center, San Antonio, Texas," White House press office, January 1, 2006, retrieved from http://www.whitehouse.gov/news/releases/2006/01/20060101.html, December 1, 2007.
17. "Generals Speak Out on Iraq," *NewsHour with Jim Lehrer*, PBS, April 13, 2006, transcript, retrieved from http://www.pbs.org/newshour/bb/military/jan-june06/iraq_4-13.html, December 1, 2007.
18. "President Bush Nominates Rob Portman as OMB Director and Susan Schwab for USTR," April 18, 2006, retrieved from http://www.whitehouse.gov/news/releases/2006/04/20060418-1.html, December 1, 2007.
19. "Top U.S. General Says Rumsfeld Is Inspired by God," Agence France-Presse, October 19, 2006, retrieved from Lexis-Nexis, October 8, 2007.
20. "Press Conference by the President," November 8, 2006, retrieved from http://www.whitehouse.gov/news/releases/2006/11/20061108-2.html, December 1, 2007.
21. Jennifer Loven and Robert Burns, "Rumsfeld Gets Big Pentagon Sendoff,"

Associated Press, December 15, 2006, retrieved from http://www.sfgate.com/cgi-bin/article.cgi?f=/n/a/2006/12/15/national/w142117S14.DTL, December 1, 2007.

22. Ibid.
23. George W. Bush, in an excerpt from an interview with Matt Lauer, broadcast on the *Today* show on August 30, 2004, and quoted in "Bush Clarifies View on War Against Terrorism," *msnbc.msn.com,* August 31, 2004, retrieved from http://www.msnbc.msn.com/id/5865710/, December 1, 2007.
24. George W. Bush, in a speech to the national convention of the American Legion, Nashville, Tennessee, August 30, 2004, quoted in "Bush Clarifies View on War Against Terrorism," *msnbc.msn.com,* August 31, 2004, retrieved from http://www.msnbc.msn.com/id/5865710/, December 1, 2007.
25. George W. Bush, remarks at the American Legion National Convention, Nashville, Tennessee, August 31, 2004, quoted in "Bush Clarifies View on War Against Terrorism," MSNBC News Service, August 31, 2004, retrieved from http://www.msnbc.msn.com/id/5865710/, January 27, 2008.
26. Victor Davis Hanson, "What We Learned," *Hoover Digest,* no. 3, 2003, retrieved from http://www.hoover.org/publications/digest/3057056.html, November 9, 2007.
27. Dana Milbank, "At GOP Convention, Echoes of Sept. 11," *The Washington Post,* August 30, 2004, retrieved from http://www.washingtonpost.com/wp-dyn/articles/A45145-2004Aug29.html, October 12, 2007.
28. "Interview with Donald H. Rumsfeld," *ABC'S This Week with George Stephanopoulos*, ABC, November 20, 2005.
29. David Rose, "Neo Culpa," *Vanity Fair*, November 3, 2006, retrieved from http://www.vanityfair.com/politics/features/2006/12/neocons200612, December 1, 2007.
30. Ibid.
31. Michael Ledeen, "The Latest Disinformation from *Vanity Fair," National Review Online,* November 4, 2006, retrieved from http://corner.nationalreview.com/post/?q=MjQ0OTOQyNTdhNWE0NzAxNGMxYWQ2ODAxOTNjNWM4M2E=, December 1, 2007.
32. Michael Ledeen, "The War on Terror Won't End in Baghdad," *Wall Street Journal,* September 4, 2002, retrieved from http://www.aei.org/publications/filter.all,pubID.14216/pub_deta il.asp, December 1, 2007.
33. Kenneth M. Pollack, *The Threatening Storm: The Case for Invading Iraq* (New

York: Random House, September 2002) quoted in Michael Massing, "The War Expert: Wrong, Wrong, Wrong Again. But the Media Still Want Ken Pollack," *Columbia Journalism Review*, November/December 2007, retrieved from http://www.cjr.org/on_the_contrary/the_war_expert.php?page=all, December 2, 2007.

34. Bill Keller, "The I-Can't-Believe-I'm-a-Hawk Club," *The New York Times*, February 8, 2003, retrieved from http://query.nytimes.com/gst/fullpage.html?res=9A03E5D7123BF93BA35751C0A9659C8B63, December 2, 2007.
35. Michael Massing, "The War Expert: Wrong, Wrong, Wrong Again. But the Media Still Want Ken Pollack," *Columbia Journalism Review*, November–December, 2007, retrieved from http://www.cjr.org/on_the_contrary/the_war_expert.php?page=all, December 2, 2007.
36. Ann Coulter, "This Is War," *National Review Online*, September 13, 2001, retrieved from http://www.nationalreview.com/coulter/coulter.shtml, December 1, 2007.
37. "Remarks by the President upon Arrival," Office of the Press Secretary, September 16, 2001, official transcript, retrieved from http://www.whitehouse.gov/news/releases/2001/09/20010916-2.html, December 1, 2007.
38. "President's Remarks at White House Lighting of Menorah," Office of the Press Secretary, December 10, 2001, official transcript, retrieved from http://www.whitehouse.gov/news/releases/2001/12/20011210-7.html, November 11, 2007.
39. Elisabeth Bumiller, "Death on the Campus: The White House; Bush 'Furious' over U.S. Toll in Hamas Blast," *The New York Times*, August 2, 2002, retrieved from http://query.nytimes.com/gst/fullpage.html?res=9B03E6D61E3BF931A3575BC0A9649C8B63&sec=&spon=&pagewanted=print, November 7, 2007.
40. Daniel Pipes, "The Enemy Within (and the Need for Profiling)," *New York Post*, retrieved from http://www.danielpipes.org/blog/93, December 1, 2007.
41. Matt Gouras, "Burns Says Terrorists Drive Taxis by Day," Associated Press, August 31, 2006, retrieved from http://www.sfgate.com/cgi-bin/article.cgi?file=/news/archive/2006/08/31/politics/p070019D19.DTL, December 1, 2007.

42. Matt Gouras, Associated Press State and Local Wire, August 30, 2006.
43. Erika Howsare, "Goode Makes Complete Ass of Self," *C-ville*, Charlottesville, Virginia, December 19–25, 2006, retrieved from http://www.c-ville.com/index.php?cat=141404064431134&ShowArticle_ID=11041812060944420, December 1, 2007.
44. *Ha'aretz* (Tel Aviv), June 24, 2003, quoted in Dilip Hiro, *Secrets and Lies* (New York: Nation Books, 2004), page 1.
45. Cited in William G. Effros, *Quote Without Comment* (Greenwich, CT: Wee Press, 2004), page 65.
46. Jerry Falwell, "God Is Pro/War," *World Net Daily*, January 31, 2004, retrieved from http://www.worldnetdaily.com/news/article.asp?ARTICLE_ID=36859, December 1, 2007.
47. *Washington Post*, October 14, 2005, page A17.
48. Interview with *CBS News'* Dan Rather, quoted in "Iraqi Leader Says God on His Side," Associated Press, August 29, 1990.
49. Interview with ABC's John Miller, May 1998, retrieved from http://www.pbs.org/wgbh/pages/frontline/shows/binladen/who/interview.html, December 1, 2007.
50. Pepe Escobar, "Zarqawi—Bush's Man for All Seasons," *Asia Times*, October 15, 2004, retrieved from http://www.atimes.com/atimes/Middle_East/FJ15Ak$2.html, November 11, 2007.
51. "Wrath of God, Osama bin Laden Lashes Out Against the West," *Time*, January 11, 1999, retrieved from http://www.time.com/time/asia/asia/magazine/1999/990111/osama1.html, December 1, 2007.
52. "Iraq: A Year of War: Quotes," *The Independent* (London), March 17, 2004, retrieved from http://findarticles.com/p/articles/mi_qn4158/is_20040317/ai_n12774994, December 1, 2007.
53. Paul Johnson, "The Answer to Terrorism? Colonialism," *Wall Street Journal Online*, October 6, 2001, retrieved from http://www.opinionjournal.com/extra/?id=95001283, November 9, 2007.
54. Max Boot, "The Case for American Empire," *The Weekly Standard*, October 15, 2001, retrieved from http://www.weeklystandard.com/Utilities/printer_preview.asp?idArticle=318, November 9, 2007.
55. Quoted in Jonah Goldberg, "Baghdad Delenda Est, Part Two," *National Review Online*, April 23, 2002, retrieved from http://article.nationalreview.com/?q=YTFhZGQ4Y2IyZmNIY2QyNDkwZTlkZjFkYjZiNWY0YzU=, December 1, 2007.

56. Peter Beinart, interviewed on "Buying the War," *Bill Moyers' Journal*, PBS, April 29, 2002, transcript dated April 25, 2007, retrieved from http://www.pbs.org/moyers/journal/btw/transcript1.html, November 11, 2007.
57. Francis Fukuyama, "After Neoconservatism," *The New York Times*, February 16, 2006, retrieved from http://www.nytimes.com/2006/02/19/magazine/neo.html, December 1, 2007.
58. Jonah Goldberg, "The Cowboy Way," *National Review Online*, January 29, 2003, retrieved from http://www.nationalreview.com/goldberg/goldberg012903.asp, November 10, 2007.
59. John Ibbitson, "If Push Comes to Shove, Trust the English, Not the Continentals," *Globe and Mail* (Toronto), January 25, 2003, page A23.
60. Max Boot, "American Imperialism? No Need to Run Away from Label," *USA Today*, May 5, 2003, retrieved from http://www.usatoday.com/news/opinion/editorials/2003-05-05-boot_x.htm, December 1, 2007.
61. Larry Schweikart, "Why We Will Win the War on Terror," July 10, 2006, retrieved from http://hnn.us/articles/27494.html, December 1, 2007.
62. "President's Remarks at Victory 2004 Luncheon," Office of the Press Secretary, September 17, 2004, retrieved from http://www.whitehouse.gov/news/releases/2004/09/20040917-4.html, December 1, 2007.

SPECIAL BONUS SECTION

1. Interview with Bush while on NATO tour of Europe, February 22, 2005, retrieved from http://www.cbsnews.com/stories/2005/02/22/world/main675340.shtml, December 1, 2007.
2. White House Press Conference by the President, March 13, 2002, retrieved from http://www.whitehouse.gov/news/releases/2002/03/20020313-8.html, December 1, 2007.
3. Henry Kissinger, "The Next Steps with Iran," *The Washington Post*, July 31, 2006, page A15.
4. Michael Ledeen, "Just Like the Mullahs," *National Review Online*, March 27, 2007, retrieved from http://www.aei.org/publications/filter.all.pubID.25847/pub_deta il.asp, December 1, 2007.
5. Interview on *Fox News*, July 19, 2006, retrieved from http://thinkprogress.org/2006/07/19/kristol-iran/, December 1, 2007.
6. William Kristol, "It's Our War," *The Weekly Standard*, July 24, 2006, retrieved from http://weeklystandard.com/Content/Public/Articles/000/000/012/433fwbvs.asp?pg=2, November 2, 2007.

7. "Interview with John Bolton," *Fox News*, August 22, 2007, transcript, retrieved from http://thinkprogress.org/2007/08/22/bolton-iran-six-months/, November 1, 2007.
8. "Press Conference by the President," official White House transcript, October 17, 2007, retrieved from http://www.whitehouse.gov/news/releases/2007/10/20071017.html, November 1, 2007.
9. "Vice President's Remarks to the Washington Institute for Near East Policy," official transcript, October 21, 2007, retrieved from http://www.whitehouse.gov/news/releases/2007/10/20071021.html, November 1, 2007.
10. Toby Harnden, "We Must Bomb Iran, Says Republican Guru," *Daily Telegraph* (London), November 1, 2007, retrieved from http://www.telegraph.co.uk/news/main.jhtml?xml=/news/2007/10/27/wbomb127.xml, November 2, 2007.

PROGRESS REPORT

P1. Donald Rumsfeld, speech, February 7, 2003, retrieved from http://www.defenselink.mil/transcripts/transcript.aspx?transcriptid =1900, December 1, 2007.

P2. "Interview with Senator John McCain," *Meet the Press*, NBC, March 23, 2003, retrieved from http://www.msnbc.msn.com/id/10266650/, December 1, 2007.

P3. Quoted in Dana Milbank "The Time Is (Perpetually) Now," *The Washington Post*, November 30, 2005, retrieved from http://www.washingtonpost.com/wp-dyn/content/article/2005/11/29/AR2005112901283_pf.html, December 1, 2007.

P4. Quoted in Dana Milbank, "The Time Is (Perpetually) Now," *The Washington Post*, November 30, 2005, retrieved from http://www.washingtonpost.com/wp-dyn/content/article/2005/11/29/AR2005112901283_pf.html, December 1, 2007.

P5. Thomas Friedman, "The Chant Not Heard," *The New York Times*, November 30, 2003, retrieved from http://www.fair.org/index.php?page=2884, December 1, 2007.

P6. Quoted in Dana Milbank, "The Time Is (Perpetually) Now," *The Washington Post*, November 30, 2005, retrieved from http://www.washingtonpost.com/wp-dyn/content/article/2005/11/29/AR2005112901283_pf.html, December 1, 2007.

P7. Max Boot, "Democratic Candidates Find Themselves Caught in a Hole of Their Own," *Los Angeles Times*, December 16, 2003, retrieved from http://www.cfr.org/publication/6601/democratic_candidates_find_them selves_caught_in_a_hole_of_their_own.html?breadcrumb=default, December 1, 2007.

P8. Tony Blair, speaking during a surprise visit to Iraq, January 4, 2004, retrieved from http://www.iol.co.za/index.php?sf=2813&art_id=qw1160 316001316B262&click_id=2813&set_id=1, December 1, 2007.

P9. George W. Bush, remarks, March 24, 2004, retrieved from http://www .cpa-iraq.org/transcripts/20040524_bush_carlisle.html, December 1, 2007.

P10. Victor Davis Hanson, "Western Cannibalism," *National Review Online*, April 8, 2004, retrieved from http://www.nationalreview.com/hanson/ hanson200404080815.asp, December 1, 2007.

P11. Victor Davis Hanson, "American Cannibalism," *National Review Online*, April 8, 2004, retrieved from http://www.nationalreview.com/hanson/ hanson200405140838.asp, December 1, 2007.

P12. "President Bush's Address to the AIPAC Policy Conference," May 18, 2004, retrieved from http://www.jewishvirtuallibrary.org/jsource/US-Israel/bushaipac2004.html, December 1, 2007.

P13. Quoted in Alastair Macdonald, "Iraqis Skeptical on Bush Speech, Want U.S. Out," Reuters, May 25, 2004, retrieved from http://www.common dreams.org/headlines04/0525-06.htm, December 1, 2007.

P14. Interview on *Special Report with Brit Hume*, Fox News, June 1, 2004, retrieved from http://www.prospect.org/cs/articles?articleId=10113, December 1, 2007.

P15. Interview on *Fresh Air*, NPR, June 3, 2004, retrieved from http://www.fair .org/index.php?page=2884, December 1, 2007.

P16. Bryan Bender, "U.S. General (Casey) Says Next Few Months Key to Iraq's Future," *Boston Globe*, June 25, 2004, retrieved from http://www.boston .com/news/nation/articles/2004/06/25/us_general_says_next_few_months _key_to_iraqs_future/ , December 1, 2007.

P17. Richard G. Lugar, "Statement to the Senate Foreign Relations Committee," July 22, 2004, retrieved from www.senate.gov/~foreign/testimony/ 2004/LugarStatement040722.pdf, December 1, 2007.

P18. David Petraeus, "Battling for Iraq," *The Washington Post*, September 26,

2004, retrieved from http://www.washingtonpost.com/wp-dyn/articles/A49283-2004Sep25.html, December 1, 2007.

P19. *Face the Nation*, CBS News, October 3, 2004, retrieved from http://www.fair.org/index.php?page=2884, December 1, 2007.

P20. Thomas Friedman, "The Last Mile," *The New York Times*, November 28, 2004, retrieved from http://www.fair.org/index.php?page=2884, December 1, 2007.

P21. Max Boot, column, *The Montreal Gazette*, December 9, 2004.

P22. Quoted in "Australia Boosts Its Military Commitment to Iraq," *The World Today*, February 22, 2005, retrieved from http://www.abc.net.au/worldtoday/content/2005/s1308325.htm, December 1, 2007.

P23. White House press briefing, June 24, 2005, retrieved from http://www.whitehouse.gov/news/releases/2005/06/20050624-3.html, December 1, 2007.

P24. *All Things Considered*, NPR, June 29, 2005, retrieved from http://www.washingtonpost.com/wp-dyn/content/article/2005/11/29/AR2005112901283_pf.html, December 1, 2007.

P25. Quoted in Dana Milbank "The Time is (Perpetually) Now," *The Washington Post*, November 30, 2005, retrieved from http://www.washingtonpost.com/wp-dyn/content/article/2005/11/29/AR2005112901283_pf.html, December 1, 2007.

P26. "News Briefing with Lt. General David Petraeus," Department of Defense, October 5, 2005, retrieved from http://www.defenselink.mil/transcripts/transcript.aspx?transcriptid=1497, December 1, 2007.

P27. "Hagel: Iraq Growing More Like Vietnam," *CNN News*, August 18, 2005, retrieved from http://www.cnn.com/2005/POLITICS/08/18/hagel.iraq/, December 1, 2007.

P28. Hoshyar Zebari, "Iraq Timeline: The Broken Record on 'the Next Few Months,' " Center for American Progress, August 8, 2007, retrieved from http://www.americanprogress.org/issues/2007/08/timeline.html, December 1, 2007.

P29. John Bolton, Statement to the UN Security Council, August 4, 2005, retrieved from http://www.globalsecurity.org/security/library/news/2005/08/sec-050804-usia04.htm, December 1, 2007.

P30. Interview on *Meet the Press*, NBC, September 25, 2005, retrieved from http://www.fair.org/index.php?page=2884, December 1, 2007.

P31. Thomas Friedman, "The End Game In Iraq" *The New York Times*, September 28, 2005, retrieved from http://www.fair.org/index.php?page=2884, December 1, 2007.

P32. David Petraeus, briefing, October 5, 2005, retrieved from http://www.defenselink.mil/transcripts/transcript.aspx?transcriptid=1497, December 1, 2007.

P33. Interview on *Meet the Press*, NBC, November 27, 2005, retrieved from http://www.msnbc.msn.com/id/10154103/, December 1, 2007.

P34. Interview on *The NewsHour with Jim Lehrer*, November 30, 2005, retrieved from http://www.pbs.org/newshour/bb/middle_east/july-dec05/iraq; sf11-30.html, December 1, 2007.

P35. Interviewed on *Meet the Press*, MSNBC, December 18, 2005, retrieved from http://www.msnbc.msn.com/id/10266650/, December 1, 2007.

P36. Quoted in "Lieberman: Bush Turned Corner on Iraq," Associated Press, December 17, 2005, retrieved from http://www.usatoday.com/news/washington/2005-12-17-lieberman-iraq_x.htm, December 1, 2007.

P37. Interview on *Face the Nation*, CBS, December 18, 2005, retrieved from http://archive.salon.com/politics/war_room/2006/11/15/six months/, December 1, 2007.

P38. Interview on *Face the Nation*, CBS, December 18, 2005, retrieved from http://www.fair.org/index.php?page=2884, December 1, 2007.

P39. Interview on *The Charlie Rose Show*, PBS, December 20, 2005, retrieved from http://www.fair.org/index.php?page=2884, December 1, 2007.

P40. Thomas Friedman, "The Measure of Success" *The New York Times*, December 21, 2005, retrieved from http://www.fair.org/index.php?page=2884, December 1, 2007.

P41. Quoted in Mark Sappenfield, "U.S. Sees Iraqi Progress, but Key Test Ahead," *Christian Science Monitor*, December 27, 2005, retrieved from http://www.csmonitor.com/2005/1227/p01s02-usfp.html, December 1, 2007.

P42. "Geopolitical Diary: Al-Zarqawi and the Tipping Point," Statfor, June 9, 2006, retrieved from http://www.stratfor.com/products/premium/read_article.php?id=267394, December 1, 2007.

P43. "Lieberman, Lamont Spar in Connecticut Primary Debate," *The Washington Post*, July 7, 2006, transcript, retrieved from http://www.washingtonpost.com/wp-dyn/content/article/2006/07/07/AR2006070700029.html, December 1, 2007.

P44. "Iraq Timeline: The Broken Record on 'the Next Few Months,' " Center for American Progress, August 8, 2007, retrieved from http://www.americanprogress.org/issues/2007/08/timeline.html, December 1, 2007.

P45. Interview on *The Oprah Winfrey Show*, January 23, 2006, retrieved from http://www.fair.org/index.php?page=2884, December 1, 2007.

P46. "Daily Press Briefing by the Office of the Spokesman for the Secretary General," March 15, 2006, retrieved from http://www.un.org/News/briefings/docs/2006/db060315.doc.htm, December 1, 2007.

P47. Interviewed on *Hardball with Chris Matthews*, MSNBC, May 11, 2006, retrieved from http://www.fair.org/index.php?page=2884, December 1, 2007.

P48. Stratfor, "Core Issues in Iraq," May 22, 2006, retrieved from http://www.lebanonwire.com/0605MLN/06052220STR.asp, December 1, 2007.

P49. George Friedman, "Breakpoint," Stratfor, May 23, 2006, retrieved from http://www.stratfor.com/products/premium/read_article.php?id=266594, December 1, 2007.

P50. Quoted in Joe Klein, "Why Bush Is (Still) Winning the War at Home," *Time*, June 1, 2006, retrieved from http://www.time.com/time/columnist/klein/article/0,9565,1205323,00.html, December 1, 2007.

P51. Associated Press, June 7, 2006.

P52. "The Next Six Months Will Be Critical," interview in *Der Spiegel*, June 7, 2006, retrieved from http://www.spiegel.de/international/spiegel/0,1518,419978,00.html, December 1, 2007.

P53. Stratfor, "Geopolitical Diary: Al-Zarqawi and the Tipping Point," June 9, 2006, retrieved from http://www.stratfor.com/products/premium/read_article.php?id=267394, December 1, 2007.

P54. Interview on *Meet the Press*, NBC, June 11, 2006, retrieved from www.mccaffreyassociates.com/pdfs/MTP_Transcript_061106.pdf, December 1, 2007.

P55. Quoted in Jim Garamone, "Window of Opportunity Opens for Iraqi People, Official Says," American Forces Press Service, June 16, 2006, retrieved from http://www.defenselink.mil/news/newsarticle.aspx?id=16028, December 1, 2007.

P56. Mark Udall, press release, June 22, 2006, retrieved from http://markudall.house.gov/HoR/CO02/Newsroom/Columns/UDALL+SEEKS+BIPARTISAN+PLAN+FOR+REDEPLOYING+TROOPS+FROM+IRAQ.htm, December 1, 2007.

P57. Quoted in Sabrina Tavernise, "Iraqi Premier Offers 'Reconciliation,' but No New Plans for Amnesty," *The New York Times*, June 26, 2006, retrieved from http://www.nytimes.com/2006/06/26/world/middleeast/26iraq.html?_r=1&oref=slogin, December 1, 2007.

P58. "Lieberman, Lamont Spar in Conn. Primary Debate," *The Washington Post*, July 7, 2006, retrieved from http://www.washingtonpost.com/wp-dyn/content/article/2006/07/07/AR2006070700029.html, December 1, 2007.

P59. Ibid.

P60. Quoted in Joshua Partlow and Jonathan Finer, "Iraqi Troops Clash with Shiite Militia," *The Washington Post*, July 8, 2006, retrieved from http://www.washingtonpost.com/wp-dyn/content/article/2006/07/07/AR2006070701250_pf.html, December 1, 2007.

P61. Quoted in "Top U.S. General: Iraqis Can Take Over Security within 18 Months," *USA Today*, August 30, 2006, retrieved from http://www.usatoday.com/news/world/iraq/2006-08-30-iraq-security_x.htm, December 1, 2007.

P62. Quoted in Deborah Block, "U.S. Special Commission Says Next Three Months Are Critical in Iraq," Globalsecurity.org, September 22, 2006, retrieved from http://www.globalsecurity.org/wmd/library/news/iraq/2006/09 /iraq-060922-voa01.htm, December 1, 2007.

P63. Quoted in Dave Clark, "Next Six Months 'Critical in Iraq'—Again," *Independent Online*, October 8, 2006, retrieved from http://www.int.iol.co.za/index.php?sf=2813&art_id=qw1160316001316 B262&click_id=2813&set_id=1, December 1, 2007.

P64. Interview with Reuters, October 26, 2006, retrieved from http://www.alertnet.org/thenews/newsdesk/HOL661955.htm, December 1, 2007.

P65. Quoted in "White House Rebuffs Call for Troop Withdrawal in Iraq," CNN.com, November 14, 2006, retrieved from http://www.cnn.com/2006/POLITICS/11/13/iraq.next/index.html, December 1, 2007.

P66. Interview on *Late Edition with Wolf Blitzer*, CNN, November 26, 2006, retrieved from http://transcripts.cnn.com/TRANSCRIPTS/0611/26/le.01.html, December 1, 2007.

P67. Interview on *Meet the Press*, NBC, November 26, 2006, retrieved from http://www.msnbc.msn.com/id/15850729/page/5/, December 1, 2007.

P68. Quoted in Dennis Gale, "SD Senator Thinks Iraq Policy Will Change,"

Associated Press, December 17, 2006, retrieved from http://www.bismarcktribune.com/articles/2006/12/17/news/state/125648.txt, December 1, 2007.

P69. Nina Kamp, Michael O'Hanlon, and Amy Unikewicz, "The State of Iraq: An Update," *The New York Times*, December 20, 2006, retrieved from http://www.nytimes.com/2006/12/20/opinion/20ohanlon.html, December 1, 2007.

P70. Quoted in Michael Duffy and Elaine Shannon, Interview with Condoleeza Rice, *Time*, January 12, 2007, retrieved from http://www.state.gov/secretary/rm/2007/78683.htm, December 1, 2007.

P71. Interview on CNN, January 23, 2007, retrieved from http://transcripts.cnn.com/TRANSCRIPTS/0701/23/cnr.05.html, December 1, 2007.

P72. Interview on *This Week*, ABC, February 4, 2007, retrieved from http://thinkprogress.org/2007/02/04/mccain-flip/, December 1, 2007.

P73. Interview on *Saturday Morning News*, CNN, February 24, 2007, retrieved from http://transcripts.cnn.com/TRANSCRIPTS/0702/24/smn.02.html, December 1, 2007.

P74. Quoted in Charles Babington, "Congressional Republicans Increasingly Worry about Iraq War," Associated Press, May 4, 2007, retrieved from http://www.boston.com/news/local/new_hampshire/articles/2007/05/04/congressional_republicans_increasingly_worry_about_iraq_war/, December 1, 2007.

P75. William Kristol, "Why Bush Will Be a Winner," *The Washington Post*, July 15, 2007, retrieved from http://www.washingtonpost.com/wp-dyn/content/article/2007/07/13/AR2007071301709.html, December 1, 2007.

P76. Michael O'Hanlon and Kenneth Pollack, "A War We Just Might Win," *The New York Times*, July 30, 2007, retrieved from http://www.nytimes.com/2007/07/30/opinion/30pollack.html, December 1, 2007.

P77. Interview on *Fox News*, August 5, 2007, retrieved from http://thinkprogress.org/2007/08/06/ohanlon-six-months/, December 1, 2007.

P78. Interview on *The Daily Show*, Comedy Central, August 13, 2007.

P79. Victor Davis Hanson, "All Eyes on Baghdad," May 2, 2007, retrieved from http://pajamasmedia.com/xpress/victordavishanson/2007/05/02/the_crazy_middle_east.php, December 1, 2007.

P80. Interview on *The Colbert Report*, Comedy Central, September 24, 2007.

P81. Quoted in Phillip Coorey, "By George: Now It's All the Way with

Howard J," *Sydney Morning Herald*, September 6, 2007, retrieved from http://.smh.com.au/news/national/by-george-now-its-all-the-way-with-howard-j/2007/09/05/1188783320123.html, December 1, 2007.

P82. John McCain, blogger conference call, September 12, 2007, retrieved from http://race42008.com/2007/09/12/john-mccain-blogger-conference-call-recap/, December 1, 2007.

INDEX

Abbas, Mahmoud, 184
Abdullah, King of Jordan, 183
Abizaid, John, 77, 119, 149
  on insurgency's modest numbers, 92
  on Iraq's new untrained military, 133
Abrams, Floyd, 33
Abu Ghraib, 115–21
  ill-fated reconstruction plan for, 120–21
  as misstep and setback, 160
Adelman, Kenneth:
  Baghdad celebrations expected by, xxvi
  on the coming Iraqi cakewalk, 45
  on that dysfunctional national security team, 181
  walk in the park anticipated by, 45
Aegis Defence Systems, 147
Afghanistan, 23
  as going swimmingly, 169
  liberation in, 178
airline industry, war on terror as aid to, 173
Ajami, Fouad, kites and boomboxes envisioned by, xxvii
Al-Ani, Ahmed, 27
al-Haideri, Adnan Ihsan Saeed, 31, 32
Allah, 186
  see also God
Allawi, Ali:
  on the brevity of occupation, 29
  on stability as only months away, 134
al-Qaeda, 111, 154
  anthrax obtained by, 16
  Bush instructed by God on, 184
  Iraqi links with, 6, 22–26, 28
Al Qaeda in Iraq (al-Tawhid wal-Jihad), 186
Al Rashid Hotel, 90
al-Sahaf, Mohammed Saeed, "Comical Ali" briefings of, 67–69
al-Tawhid wal-Jihad (Al Qaeda in Iraq), 186
aluminum tubes, 9, 30
al-Yawir, Ghazi, 121
American Enterprise Institute, 191–92
anthrax, 3, 11, 16–20
Anton, Michael N., 102
Arabs, confusing alikeness of, 150
Armenia, Coalition contribution of, 66
Armitage, Richard, on the price to be extracted for Fallujah, 138
Ashcroft, John, on when terrorists will strike next, 165

atomic bomb, 30
Atrios (Duncan Black), 158
Atta, Farhan, nonexistence of, 27, 28
Atta, Mohamed:
anthrax obtained by, 16, 17, 18, 20
in Prague, 16, 17, 18, 20, 27, 28
Australia, 66
Axis of Weasel, 38

Ba'ath Party, 26, 125, 126, 132
Baghdad:
al Qaeda in, 23
joy in, xix, xxvi, xxvii
records in, 26
as safe as any American city, 93–94
WMDs in, 96
see also Iraq; *specific experts*
Baghdad Airport, 130
Baghdad stock market, 122
Barnes, Fred:
on the casualty sensitive press weenies, 162
on democracy-building vs. war-winning, 89
on the desperation of guerrillas, 91
on improvements in Iraq, 105
on WMDs, xix
Bartlett, Dan:
cheaper gas as war motive unknown to, 52
on imminence of threat, 28
Bartley, Robert L., scales-from-the-eyes moment of, 20
Basra, eruptions of joy in, xxvi, xxvii
Bayh, Evan, Bush's ultimatum supported by, 22
BBC, 74, 130
Beck, Glenn, Representative's loyalty questioned by, 184
Beinart, Peter, on the benefits of siding with angels, 187
Berman, Paul, on logic of Iraq War, xx
Bertelli, Chris, honor and dignity as paramount concern of, 140
Biden, Joseph, prospect for keeping a large force in Iraq not seen by, 137
bin Laden, Osama:
Bush's indifference about hunt for, 168
capture as irrelevant, 169
context for criminality of, 186
God's Jihadist orders to, 185
joy of Hanukkah not grasped by, 183
Saddam partnership rejected by, 26
Saddam's relationship with, 23
biological weapons, 3, 4, 10, 11, 12, 13, 14, 15, 18, 21, 28, 31, 34, 98
see also anthrax
Birnbaum, Jeff, on the amazing Iraq victory, 79
Black, Duncan, 158
Blackwater USA, 137–45, 148
Blair, Tony:
as ready to meet his Maker, 186
on speed of WMD deployability, 4
on a very critical six months, 19
vision of Iraq nearly realized by, 131
on WMDs, 4, 97
Blitzer, Wolf, 28
Blix, Hans, xviii, 35
Boehner, John, on his Democratic friends' loyalties, 164
Bolton, John, on the critical next months, 69
Boot, Max:
on America's paramountcy, 188
on Fallujah as turning point, 49
on improvements in Iraq, 17
on what troubled lands cry out for, 186
Border Enforcement Department, Iraqi, 136
Boston Globe, 35, 173
botulism toxin, 3
Boykin, William, bigger God of, 185
Bragg, Rick, rise and fall of, 74
Bremer, L. Paul:
attempted assassination of, 130
de-Ba'athification ordered by, 125, 132
immunity granted to contractors by, 141, 144
on insurgents posing no strategic threat, xix, 91
on Iraq's money, 127, 128
New York and Baghdad compared by, 130
on normality of Iraq, 130
on those false stories about chaos, 90, 130

on why the Iraqi military were disbanded, 133
Brokaw, Tom, anthrax mail sent to, 16
Brooks, Vincent, on the unanticipated looting, 87
Browne, Daniel, on failed security arrangements at Fallujah, 139
Browning, Stephen, 126
Brubaker, Jack, 185
Bureau of Diplomatic Security, 145
Burns, Conrad, on the day job of terrorists, 184
Bush, Barbara, a beautiful mind not wasted by, 48
Bush, George H. W.:
on Iraqi friendship, xxiv
on Iraqi threat, xxiv
Bush, George W.:
alternatives to Guantánamo sought by, 109
ass kicking delivered by, 187
benchmark achievement of, 131
bin Laden as worry of, 169
bin Laden not a preoccupation of, 168
on biological weapons, 11, 12, 98
on Brits, Africa, and uranium, 9, 10, 101
casualties unforeseen by, 48
civil war called pure evil by, 150
civil war declared nonexistent by, 150
on Coalition of the Willing, 65, 67
in combat with a cedar, 178
connecting Iraq to war on terrorism as hardship for, 25
crusade of the patient launched by, 183
on dealing with leakers, 104
as decider who decides what is best, 178
on Democrat loser approach in Iraq, 168
demolition of Abu Ghraib proposed by, 120
disarmament as mission of, 173
on eliminating torture, 114
on ending Saddam's regime, 174
on the end of major combat operations in Iraq, xix, 79
false religion denounced by, 183
on finding the WMDs, 4, 98
on fluctuating Iraqi battalion numbers, 134–35
on free societies, 189
God's advice to, 184
as God's spokesperson, 185
on his unprecedented human rights record, 105
on how history will record the statue toppling, 80
on how we hand victory to suicide bombers, 168
on the inapplicability of Geneva Convention, 111
on Iraq's critical moment, 21
on Libby's sacrifices, 104
Libby's sentence commuted by, 105
on the "Mission Accomplished" banner, 151
on our wartime unity, 164
on patriotic airline travel, 173
on possibility of nuclear attack, 8
on revisionist historians, 103
Rumsfeld's position secure with, 178
Rumsfeld's resignation accepted by, 179
on Saddam's attempted purchase of aluminum tubes, 9
on Saddam's gleeful celebration of 9/11 attacks, 23
on Saddam's terrorizing himself, 24
on shaking a hand, 176
"16 little words" of, 9, 10, 101
on smoking gun as mushroom cloud, 8
on speed of Iraq's possible attack, 28
on strategy of Iraqis standing up, 132
tide's turning as puzzling to, 160
on the total transparency of Guantánamo, 108
troop levels defended by, 48
truth as virtue for, vii
turning points as viewed by, 159, 160
on understanding the joy of Hanukkah, 183
on various goals of Iraq mission, 173–74

Bush, George W. (*cont.*)
vision of Iraq nearly accomplished by, 131
war avoided by, 39, 40
war casualties not expected by, 48
on why we are there, 174
on winning too much too soon, 180
Butler, Richard:
on Atta's obtaining anthrax, 17
on Iraq–al Qaeda connection, 23
on Iraq's WMDs, 4
Bybee, Jay:
on the A through D of murder, 112
on the constitutionality of torture, 112

Caldwell, Bill, on the next few months, 127
Card, Andrew, on marketing of Iraq War, 1
Carlson, Tucker, on how weakness was signaled in Fallujah, 138
Carr, David, on the lack of terrible consequences, 76
Casey, George W., Jr., 77, 139
on the decisive next few months, 35, 143
on Iraqi security, 135
on the one effective Iraqi battalion, 134
casualties, irrelevance or nonexistence of, 48
Cavuto, Neil, 109
CBS News, 157
Central Intelligence Agency (CIA), xvi, 5, 10, 15, 26, 30
Atta-Iraq connection disproved by, 28
in Valerie Plame affair, 33, 104–5
Chalabi, Ahmed, 29
on Iraq oil, 50
Judith Miller's stenographic services for, 33
Chandrasekaran, Rajiv, 122
Charen, Mona, on our luck with Bush, 76
chemical weapons, 3, 4, 10, 11, 12, 21, 28, 31, 34, 162
Cheney, Dick:
on allied billions for Iraq, 56
on a campaign of weeks rather than months, 58
on confirming the al Qaeda–Iraq link, 25
on debate as validating terrorist strategy, 168
extraordinary foresight of, 191–93
Halliburton years of, 193
on how we will, in fact, be greeted, xxviii
on insurgency's last throes, 92
on the joy about to erupt in Basra and Baghdad, xxvi
on Rumsfeld as finest defense secretary we ever had, 179
on 2005 as turning point and watershed, 160
WMDs not doubted by, 3, 10, 98, 99
Chennelly, Joseph R., on the slapping of Jessica Lynch, 72
Chertoff, Michael, gut feeling of, 166
Christian Science Monitor, xxiii
Clinton, Bill, on brevity of war, 58
Clinton, Hillary, on critical next few months, 15
Clinton, Hillary Rodham:
on Saddam's WMDs, 22
Simone Ledeen's crazy impulse to spit at, 124
CNN, 108
Coalition of the Willing, 65–67
Coalition Provisional Authority (CPA), xxix, 88, 90, 121, 122, 123, 124, 125, 126, 127, 128, 131, 132, 138
Cohen, Richard:
on havoc-wreaking biological weapons, 18
on those incredulous fools and Frenchmen, xvii, 6
Collier, Robert, cheap oil predicted by, 51
Colmes, Alan, on Hollywood's responsibilities, 77
conservatives, war preparations of, 163
Cornyn, John, on next six months, 149

Costa Rica, Coalition membership renewal declined by, 66
Coulter, Ann:
  convert-or-kill strategy of, xxi, 183
  Iraq-California analogy of, 93
  on irrelevance of capturing bin Laden, 169
  on liberal traitors and idiots, 163
  on student benefits of looting, 88
  on troop-hating Democrats, 164
Czech Republic, as nexus of Iraq–al Qaeda connection, 16, 17, 18, 20, 27, 28

Damascus, overwhelming support for liberation in, xxvi
Daniels, Mitchell, sustained aid to Iraq not foreseen by, xx, 56
Daschle, Tom, anthrax mail received by, 16, *17*
Dearlove, Richard, 41
de-Ba'athification, 125, 126, 132
Defense Department, U.S., 72, 88, 111
Delahunty, Robert, on criteria for torture, 110
Democrats:
  troop-hating and defeatism ascribed to, 164
  warped priorities of, 164
Dempsey, Martin, on security in Baghdad, 94
Downing Street Memo, 41
Dunleavy, Steve, on French wimpiness, 38

Edwards, Bob, on end of war, 77
El Baradei, Mohamed, 9
Ellison, Keith, proof of innocence demanded of, 184
Energy Department, U.S., 9
experts:
  definition of, xvi
  minds changed by, xvii–xviii
  the one who was right, xviii, 191–93
extraordinary rendition, 114

Face the Nation, 156
Fairness and Accuracy in Reporting (FAIR), 155
Fallujah, 23, 49, 135, 137–38
Falwell, Jerry, God's pro-war politics proclaimed by, 185
Federal Bureau of Investigation (FBI):
  anthrax mailings investigated by, 20
  Atta-Iraq connection disproved by, 28
Federal Reserve, 126
Feith, Douglas:
  Atta's brother invented by, 27
  destruction of Saddam's regime announced by, 125
  on the Iraq turning point, xx, 158
Fiasco (Ricks), 175
Fisher, Marc, on Judith Miller's reporting, 33
Fitzgerald, Patrick, 33
Fitz-Pegado, Lauri J., 73
507th Ordnance Maintenance Company, 69, 70
Fleischer, Ari:
  on decline in looting, 85
  on Everest-like evidence of WMDs, 3
  on getting to the bottom, 103
  on Iraq shouldering its own reconstruction, 56
  moving on urged by, 102
  on revisionist bull, 103, 104
  on WMDs, 4, 97
Foley, Alan, intelligence gathering methods of, 174
Foley, Tom, on safety of contracting in Iraq, 136, 137
Foreign Policy, 173
France, xxviii, 34–38
  cheese-eating surrender monkeys of, 35, 36
Franks, Tommy, 76, 89, 96
  on excellence of war plan, 175
Freedom Fries, 36
Friedman, George, on who will or will not control the insurgency, 115
Friedman, Thomas:
  patience of, 33
  on what the next six months, more or less, will tell, xvii, xix, 13, 41, 47, 71, 73, 95, 111, 135, 155–58
  WMDs not an issue to, 100
Friedman Units, 155–58

Frum, David:
  on "the rush to peace," 61
  on a very, very fast war, 58
Fukuyama, Francis, 187

Garner, Jay, "Damn, we're Americans!" as catchphrase of, 79
Gates, Robert, 147
Gelman, Barton, on serendipitous finds during WMD search, 97–98
Geneva Convention, 111, 112
  inapplicability of, 110
  unread by administration, 105–6
Germany, wimping out of, 38
Gibson, Charlie, 7, 130
Giuliani, Rudy, Iraq–New York comparison of, 93
God:
  American stomachs grilled by, 68
  bin Laden ordered by, 185
  Bush advised by, 184
  Bush as conduit for, 185
  Bush blessed by, 48
  as pro-war, 185
  Saddam's partnership with, 185
  size of, 185
  see also Allah
Goldberg, Jonah, 187
  on euphemisms, 188
  on how to describe the French, 35, 36
Gonzales, Alberto, failure of memory of, xx
Goode, Virgil H., Jr., immigration position of, 184
Good Morning America, 7, 130
Gordon, Michael, 30
Gore, Al, on Saddam's WMDs, 21
Graham, Lindsay, in guided tour of Baghdad, 94
Graner, Charles, on pleasure of making a grown man piss himself, 118
Greenspan, Alan, on what the Iraq war is about, 52
Green Zone, 90, 130
Guantánamo, 106–10
  alternatives considered or rejected for, 109
  as gulag of our time, 107
  as resort, 108, 110
  suicides at, 109
  total transparency promised at, 108
  Yoo and Philbin on, 106
Gulf War, 58, 65, 191–92

Hagel, Chuck, on the next six critical months, 61
Hallen, Jay, on Baghdad's new stock market, 122
Halliburton, 128, 193
Hamilton, Lee, on the next three critical months, 141
Hannity, Sean, on what the naysayers were saying, 162
Hansen, Liane, 90
Hanson, Victor Davis:
  on forces of change, 25
  on Iraq's consensual government, 23
  on next six months, 183
  on problems of success, 180
  on responsibility for Abu Ghraib's excesses, 120
Hardball, 155
Harris, Harry B., Jr., on suicide as asymmetric warfare, 109
Harrison, George, on Bush's avoidance of war, 40
Haveman, James, 123
Heritage Foundation, 124
Hersh, Seymour, 116
Hitchens, Christopher, Iraq not a big enough enemy for, xxvii
Hitler, Adolf, Saddam as modern incarnation of, 38
Hoagland, Jim, on Powell's rectitude, 6
Hoon, Geoff, Umm Qasr and Southampton compared by, 96
Horowitz, David, on the bloody hands of antiwar activists, xx, 161
House Committee on Oversight and Reform, 127, 128, 139, 140, 148
Howard, John, 51
Hubbard, Glenn, on cheapness of war, 53
Hunter, Duncan, on comforts of Guantánamo, 107

Hussein, Saddam:
bin Laden's partnership with, 23
candor of, xxiv
Cheney's concerns about replacement of, 193
as elephant standing in the corner, 191
foreign Arab fighters seen as threat by, 26
on God's grilling of American stomachs in hell, 68
God's partnership with, 185
Ledeen on terrible evil of, 182
Left's fondness for, 162, 163
peacefulness of, xxiv
predicted downfall of, xxviii
Rumsfeld's meeting with, xxiii
as threat to U.S. oil supply, 50
toppled statue of, 80

Ibbitson, John, on English nations banding together, 188
Iceland, Coalition troop strength of, 66, 67
Ijaz, Mansoor, on end of WMD trail, 100
Independent Commission on the Security Forces of Iraq, 136
Ingraham, Laura, on Blix's inability to find Rosie O'Donnell's stretch marks, xviii, 35
Inhofe, James:
as outraged by outrage over torture, 118
as outraged as well by humanitarian do-gooders, 118
Institute of Expertology, xvi–xviii, xix–xxi
Institute of Peace (USIP), 163
Interior Ministry, Iraqi, 136
Iran, imperialism of, 174
Iraq:
al-Qaeda's links to, 6, 16, 17, 18, 20, 22–26, 28
army disbanded in, 132–33
army rebuilt in, 133–36
budget of, 124, 127–29
contractors in, 136–38, 146–48
critical time in, 53, 55
liberation in, xxvi–xxix, 178
looting in, 85–88, 123
military of, 133–35
missing money in, 127–29
oil in, 49–52
reconstruction of, 52–56, 125–26
2005 election in, 159
Iraq Dossier, The (Blair), 4
Iraqi National Congress, 30, 31
Iraqi National Museum, 85, 87
Iraqi Security Forces (ISF), 136
Iraq Survey Group, 15, 30, 32
Iraq War:
brevity of, 5, 7, 56–59
as cakewalk, 45
casualties of, 48, 162
Coalition of the Willing in, 65–67
cost of, 52–56
expertology and, xv–xviii
as five-day World War II, 58
justifications for, xviii, 173–74
Left's moral turpitude revealed by, 162
plausible deniability in, 181
predictions of easy victory in, xxvi–xxviii
resistance and insurgency in, xix, 88–92, 125–26, 147
troop levels in, 46–47
turning points in, 157, 158–61
victory in, 76–81
see also specific expert opinions
Israel, 18

Joan of Arc, surpassed by Jessica Lynch, 71
Johnson, Paul, on colonialism as answer to terrorism, 186
Jones, Walter, on Freedom Fries, 36
Justice Department, U.S., 111

Kagan, Robert:
on Atta's pre-9/11 movements, 28
on morality of U.S. foreign policy, 187
Kamp, Nina, on make or break time, 159
Kaplan, Fred, on war games, 84
Kaplan, Lawrence, on Iraq's easy democratization, 46
Karpinski, Janis, on comfort in Abu Ghraib, 115
Kay, David, on WMD evidence, 15
Kazakhstan, Coalition contribution of, 66

Keller, Bill, on Kenneth Pollack's war role, 182
Kennedy, Edward, on Saddam's WMDs, 21
Kerry, John, on Saddam's miscalculations, 22
Khalilzad, Zalmay, 176
  on the critical months ahead, 55, 121, 131
Khan, Irene, on Guantánamo, 107
Killip, Hamish, 15
Kimmit, Mark, on the safety or danger of traveling through Fallujah, 137
King, Peter, on Baghdad's similarity to Manhattan, 93
Kingston, Jack, on next two crucial months, 169
Kirkpatrick, David D., on Jessica Lynch's story, 73
Kissinger, Henry:
  on Shia-Sunni civil war, 150
  on U.S. interest in Iraq, 174
Knight, Bobby, on Jessica Lynch vs. Joan of Arc, 71
Koppel, Ted, 54–55
Krauthammer, Charles:
  on bad news, 31
  on being morally compelled to torture, xx, 112
  on those purblind Upper West Siders, 77
Krepinevich, Andrew, on the actual crucial year, 99
Kristol, William:
  on anthrax, 20
  on Atta's pre-9/11 movements, 28
  on the hopeful signs of Iraqi pluralism, 150
  on Iraq as the big unspoken elephant, 22
  Iraq's democratization as seen by, xx, 46
  on Iraq War odds, 175
  on morality of U.S. foreign policy, 187
  on pop sociology about Iraqi discord, 149
  on vindication of Bush Doctrine, 159
  on war's clarity, 38
  on war's end, 78
Krongard, Alvin "Buzzy," as Blackwater employee and brother of "Cookie," 148–49
Krongard, Howard J. "Cookie," as not his brother's keeper, 148–49
Kurds, 13, 69
  liberation of, xxvii
Kuwait, 73

Lamont, Ned, 135
Landay, Jonathan S., 32
Late Edition with Wolf Blitzer, 157
Leahy, Patrick, anthrax mail received by, 16
Ledeen, Michael, 124
  on Bush's procrastination, 60
  on the need to throw crappy little countries against the wall, 187
  on popular support for liberation, xxvi
  on regime change, 181, 182
  on the warlike American character, 49
Ledeen, Simone, Hillary Clinton as target of opportunity for, 124
Levin, Carl, on phased redeployment, 147
Libby, I. Lewis "Scooter":
  commutation of sentence of, 105
  conviction of, 105
  on preserving access to oil, 49
  as source of CIA leak, 33
  tireless work of, 104
liberals:
  as always against America, 163
  Soviet Union defended by, 163
  therapy for terrorists offered by, 163
  of Upper West Side, 77
Lieberman, Joseph:
  on improvement in Iraq, 167
  on Iraq–al Qaeda connection, 23
  on Iraqi military, 135
  on last two weeks as turning point, 89
  on progress in Iraq, 103
  on upcoming withdrawal of troops, 135
Limbaugh, Rush:
  on female torturers receiving NEA grants, 116, 117

on Guantánamo, 108, 110
on torture as emotional release, 117
Lindsey, Lawrence:
cheap oil predicted by, 50
on war's economic benefits, 52
Livingston Group, 73
Loeb, Vernon, on Jessica Lynch, 70
Los Angeles Times, 76, 80
Lott, Trent, on those look-alike Arabs, 150
Lowry, Rich, troop levels unimportant to, 48
Lugar, Richard G., on the critical next few months, 37
Lynch, Jessica, rescue mission for, 69–74

McCaffrey, Barry, on next six months, 151
McCaffrey, Barry R.:
on the crucial next few months, 57, 125
on truncated World War II, 58
McCain, John:
on the critical time, 11
on next few months, 165
on next six months, 189
on the next six months to a year, 87
on our expected Iraqi greeting, xxviii
on a relatively short war, 7
in safe walking tour of Baghdad, 94, 95
McClellan, Scott:
on critical period in Iraq, 53
"imminent" disdained by, 29
on "Mission Accomplished" banner, 147
on Rumsfeld's fine job, 178
McPherson, Peter, on lootings as privatization, 123
Majid, Ali Hassan al-, 69
Makiya, Kanan, on Iraq's longing for the war, xxvii
Maliki, Nuri al-:
on killing of civilians, 142
on poor security situation, 145
on when Iraqi forces will be ready, 135
Maltseya, Nelja N., 31
Marsden, Rachel, on one man's torture, 113
Marshall Islands, Coalition regrets sent by, 66
Massing, Michael, 182
Matthews, Chris, 157
Meet the Press, 156
Metzenbaum, Howard, on Saddam's peacefulness, xxiv
Michaels, Jim, on improvements in Iraq, 185
Micronesia, as Coalition no-show, 66
Miller, Judith, 29–33
"Mission Accomplished" banner, xix, 79
justification for, 151
Moldavia, Coalition troop deployment of, 66
Mongolia, annual defense budget of, 66
Moritz, Owen, on Jessica Lynch's injuries, 72
Morrell, Geoff, 147
Morris, Dick, on the soon-to-be-found chemical weapons, 162
Murdoch, Rupert, 73
Murdock, Deroy, on waterboarding as source of pride, 113
mushroom cloud, smoking gun as, xix, 8
mustard gas, 3
Myers, Richard B., 120
on Guantánamo as model facility, 107, 108
on short, short conflict, 59
short war never promised by, 59
Mylroie, Laurie:
on bin Laden–Iraqi friendship, 23
on Saddam's impending large attacks, 19

Nasiriyah, 69, 72
Nation, 76
National Police, Iraqi, 136
National Priorities Project, 56
National Review, 122
National Review Online, 35
Natsios, Andrew, on Iraq reconstruction costs, 54–55
Nazis, Red Cross hoodwinked by, 34
negative expertology, xviii

Negroponte, John:
  on resolve, constancy, and unity of purpose, 176
  on wish to depart from Baghdad ASAP, 176
NewsMax, 19
New York, Iraq compared to, 93, 130
New Yorker, 76, 116, 126
New York Times, xvii, 73, 95, 101, 143, 144, 145
  Judith Miller at, 29–32
  on Rumsfeld's "Army you have" principle, 177
  staying in and leaving Iraq advised by, 154
Ney, Bob, on Freedom Fries, 36
Niger, uranium of, 100, 101, 102
Nightline, 54–55
Nightly News, 95
9/11 Commission, 28
Novak, Robert:
  Geneva Convention evidently unread by, 105–6
  Valerie Plame outed by, 104
  on WMDs as elitist issue, 100
nuclear weapons, 8, 28, 31
  aluminum tubes for, 9
  Rumsfeld vs. Cheney on, 10

O'Beirne, Jim, 122
O'Beirne, Kate, 122
Observer, 16
Odeh al-Rehaief, Mohammed, 72, 73
Odierno, Ray, on insignificance of resistance, 89
O'Donnell, Rosie, easily found stretch marks of, xviii, 35
O'Hanlon, Michael:
  on dearth of dead-enders, 91
  on importance of picking right adversary, 177
  on Iraq's American-style violence, 90
  on make or break time, 159
  on next six or nine months, 179
  waiting four to six months advised by, 167
O'Hare Airport, 173
oil, 49–52
  price of, 50
  as vital to U.S. national security, xxiv, 174
"oil-for-food" program, 126
Oliver, David, on unimportance of fiscal responsibility, 129
Operation Desert Storm, 73
Operation Vigilant Resolve, 138
Oprah Winfrey Show, 156
O'Reilly, Bill, 150
  apology promised by, 7
  on brevity of war, xx, 57, 58
  enemies of the state decided by, 161
  on final solution for Fallujah, 138
  oil as bottom line to, 50
  war plans improved by, 81

Pace, Peter, on the good Lord's advice to Rumsfeld, 179
Palau, good wishes sent to Coalition by, 66
Parshall, Janet:
  on French and German WMDs in Iraq, 38
  on hidden smoking guns, 35
Paul H. Nitze School of Advanced International Studies, 146
Pelosi, Nancy, on Saddam's WMDs, 21
Pence, Mike, 94, 95
Perle, Richard:
  on brevity of the war, 56
  Bush Square in Baghdad envisioned by, 79
  on eye-opening of doubters, xxviii
  on futility of inspections, 33
  on imminence of threat, 28
  on Iraq's self-reconstruction, 52
  on the joint downfall of Saddam and the UN, xix, 60
  on the seriously deceived UN, 34
  troop levels lite suggested by, 46
  war architect role denied by, 181
  the war's happy ending pictured by, 78
  on what one whiff of gunpowder will do, 45
Petraeus, David, on the critical next several months, 59, 77
Philbin, Patrick F., on Guantánamo, 106
Pierson, Frank, on not giving in to fear, 167

Pipes, Daniel:
the Left as viewed by, 162, 163
Muslim profiling favored by, 183
Plame, Valerie, 33, 104–5
Podhoretz, Norman, on the bloody war of ideas, 164
Pollack, Kenneth:
on the affordable Iraq reconstruction, 52
invasion once supported by, 182
Pollack, Kenneth M., on importance of picking right adversary, 177
Powell, Colin:
on biological weapons, 4, 15
books not cooked by, 15
on chemical weapons, 4, 11, 12
on inadvisability of rumor mongering, 18
on Iraq–Al Qaeda connection, 6, 24
on mobile factories, 12, 13, 14, 15
as oracle, xvii, 6, 7, 13, 14, 24, 25, 98
at UN, xvii, xix, 6, 7, 11, 13, 14, 15, 24, 25, 98
on war as last resort, 39
on WMDs, xvii, xix, 4, 6, 13, 14, 98
Powers, Kirsten, 169
Prince, Erik, on insurgents attacking Blackwater, 142

Qazi, Ashra, on the critical next six months in Iraq, 109

Raheem, Amir, on sniper fire in Baghdad, 95
Ready, Christopher, 167
Reid, Harry, on correctness of Bush's methods, 20
Research Institute for Viral Preparations, 31
Rice, Condoleezza:
on distinguished cast of experts, xvi
extraordinary rendition denied by, 114
on "Mission Accomplished," 151
on mobile trailers, 14
on mushroom cloud as smoking gun, xix, 8
on next six months, 161
on trained Iraq forces, 134
Ricks, Thomas E., 175
Ridge, Tom, on terrorism in the holiday season, 161
Risen, James, 26
Ritter, Scott, 34
Roberts, Pat, on the crucial next few months, 9
Robertson, Pat, 48
Robson, Eleanor, on the scale of Baghdad looting, 86
Rodgers, Walt, 88, 89
Rove, Karl, on the liberal offer of therapy for terrorists, 163
Rumsfeld, Donald, 65, 120
on the Army you have, 177
on attempts to avoid war, 41
on biological weapons, 3, 12, 14, 28
on brevity of coming war, 5, 57, 58
on chemical weapons, 3, 10, 12
on contractors, 146–47
on dead-enders, 89, 91
as finest secretary of defense in the nation's history, 179
on Guantánamo, 109
hundreds of thousands of troops not needed by, 47
invasion not advocated by, 181
on Iraq–al Qaeda connection, 24
Iraq-Niger story ended by, 102
on Iraq's nuclear and biological weapons, 10, 28
known knowns, known unknowns, and unknown unknowns distinguished by, 26
on location of WMD mobile facilities, 4, 14
looting viewed stoically by, xix, 86
on oil, 51
on payment for reconstruction, 53
resignation of, 178–79
Saddam's meeting with, xxiii
on torture photos, 117
on turning point in Iraq, 159
on TV's repetitive looting coverage, 87
on the untidiness of freedom, 86

Saddam Hussein, *see* Hussein, Saddam
Saddam Hussein Hospital, 31

Safire, William, on undisputed fact of Atta's trip to Prague, 27
Salman, Hassan Jabar, on Blackwater, 143
Sanchez, Ricardo, 119
  Abu Ghraib interrogation role of, 120
sarin, 3
Satan, American partnership with, 185
Sawyer, Diane, 73
Schieffer, Bob, 155, 157
Schmidt, Susan, on Jessica Lynch, 70
Schwartz, Eric, on the natural process of looting, 85
Schweikart, Larry, on what we Americans do, 188
Senor, Dan, 131
September 11, 2001, terrorist attacks of, 19, 23, 28, 159
  Left's moral turpitude exposed by, 162
  liberal vs. conservative response to, 163
  Saddam's connection to, 27
  weakness as cause of, 138
Sessions, Jeff, on Guantánamo as beautiful resort, 108
Sforza, Scott, "Mission Accomplished" banner created by, 151
Shaalan, Hazin, strict punishments by, xx
Shahwani, Mohammed Abdullah, on strength of the Iraq resistance, 92
Shinseki, Eric, troop level calculations of, 44
Shorja market, 94, 95
Simpson, Alan K., on Saddam's candor, xxiv
Simpsons, The, 35
Slate, 84
Slocombe, Walt:
  on Iraq troop training, 133
  on protection from hypothetical looters, 88
smallpox, 3, 31
Smerconish, Michael, on Ritter-Saddam footsie game, 34
smoking gun as mushroom cloud, xix, 8
Snow, Tony, on bloodless victory, 76
Solarz, Stephen J., on the few remaining dead-enders, 91
Solomon Islanders, membership in Coalition as news to, 66
Southampton, Umm Qasr likened to, 96
Soviet Union, liberal defenders of, 163
Special Republican Guard, 19
Spicer, Tim, 147
State Department, U.S., 9, 19, 145
Staton, D. R., on the ambushed contractors in Fallujah, 139
Stevens, Bob, 16
Stewart, Martha, on why terrorists prevail, 168
Strategic Forecasting Inc., 113, 123, 153
Streisand, Barbra, O'Reilly's fair and balanced warning to, 161

Taft, William H., IV, on inapplicability of Geneva Convention, 110
Taguba, Antonio, 119
Taliban, 25, 111
Tate, Joseph, 33
Taylor, Chris, on Blackwater Kool-Aid, 141
Tehran, popular support for liberation in, xxvi
Tenet, George, arresting basketball metaphor of, xix, 5
terrorism, 165–66
  see also war on terror
Thomas, Cal, on the duped, dumb, and desperate, xviii, 7
Thompson, Tommy, on isolated anthrax incident, 16
Thune, John, on next six months, 157
Tikrit, WMDs in the area around, 96
Time, 125
Times (London), 18, 41
Today, 157
Tonga, deployment and withdrawal of 49 Coalition troops by, 66

torture, 105–21
  photos of, 117
Travel Industry Association, 173
Turkey, nerve-sparing drug ordered from, 32
Tyrrell, Anne E., on insurgents attacking Blackwater, 142, 143

Udall, Mark, on the decisive next six months, 129
United Nations, 38
  Bush's address on preemptive war at, 8
  "oil-for-food" program of, 126
  Powell at, xvii, xix, 6, 7, 11, 13, 14, 15, 24, 25, 98
  predicted downfall of, xix, 60
  the 17 Security Council resolutions of, 65
  weapons inspectors of, 19, 34
UN Monitoring, Verification and Inspection Commission (UNMOVIC), 14
uranium, 9, 30, 100, 101, 102
USAID, 54–55

Vietnam, 88

Wallace, William, on war games, 84
Warner, John, on the next six, or four to six, or two to three months, 79, 81
war on terror:
  Bush's views on winnability of, 180
  Bush team's efforts in linking Iraq to, 22–25
  U.S. victory inevitable in, 188
  see also Afghanistan; Iraq War; *specific experts*
Washington Post, xvii, 97, 114, 122, 131
  on Bush's vindication for going to war, 13
  on Rumsfeld's "Army you have" principle, 177
waterboarding, Americans justifiably proud of, 113
Waxman, Harry, on what were the facts, 21
weapons of mass destruction, 3–21, 28, 96–104
  anthrax, 3, 11, 16–20, *17*
  Democrats' supportive views on, 19–21
  as elitist issue, 100
  Everest-like evidence for, 3
  expert testimony on, 4
  45-minute deployability of, 4
  Iraq's outsourcing of, 38
  Judith Miller's reportage on, 29–33
  marketing of evidence for, 1
  mobility of, 4, 12, 13, 14, 15, 98
  the now dead and buried buriers of, 100
  Powell's UN speech on, xvii, xviii, xix, 6, 7, 11, 13, 14, 24, 25
  world owed no explanation for whereabouts of, 100
  see also biological weapons; chemical weapons; nuclear weapons
Weisberg, Jacob, on pessimism, xx
Whitman, Bryan, on the BBC's ridiculous report about the Jessica Lynch rescue, 74
Willis, Frank:
  on attempts to get the right people into CPA, 124
  on how to play football with packets of cash, 129
Wilson, Joseph:
  on the administration's selective use of intelligence, 102
  Niger trip of, 101
Wolfowitz, Paul:
  cheering crowds of Iraqis hesitatingly predicted by, xxvii
  on the clear-cut al Qaeda–Iraq links, 25
  in dangerous Green Zone, 90
  on exaggerated ethnic differences in Iraq, 149
  on foreign interference in Iraq, 161
  Iraqi and French liberations compared by, xxviii
  on Iraq's ability to finance reconstruction, 53

Wolfowitz, Paul (*cont.*)
on which way the oil wind should blow, 49
on why Iraqi POWs appreciate us, 115
on wildly overstated troop requirements, 46, 47
WMDs not a concern of, 101
World War II, Iraq War as five-day version of, 58

Yarsinske, Amy Waters, 71
Yoo, John:
on the inapplicable Geneva Convention, 112
on tieing the President's hands on torture, 113
on what reasonable people think about torture, 110, 113
on what the great weight of legal authority says about Guantánamo, 106

Zarqawi, Abu Musab al, handy little prayer for the destruction of the Bush kingdom by, 186
Zimansky, Paul, on the historic Iraqi looting, 86

THE INSTITUTE OF EXPERTOLOGY

☆

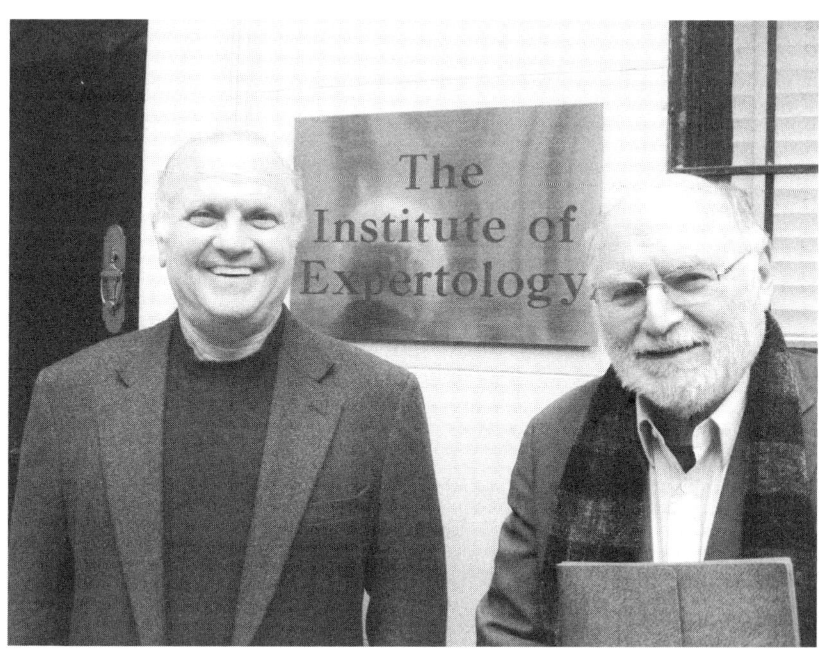

OFFICERS, DEPARTMENT HEADS, AND FELLOWS

Chairman of the Board: Christopher Cerf[1]
President: Victor S. Navasky[1]
Vice Presidents and Directors of Expertological Research: Eugene Ashton-Gonzalez and Susannah Vila
Vice President, Curator, and Chief Archivist: Bill Effros
Vice President and Director of Taxonomy: Richard Lingeman
Artist-in-Residence: Robert Grossman
Chairman of the Committee on Acquisitions: David Rosenthal
Director of Editorial Services: Dedi Felman
Director of Indexology: Sydney Wolfe Cohen
Managing Editor: Phil Metcalf
Public Affairs Director: Lizzy Mason
Office of the Secretary-Treasurer: Victoria Chiaro, Tina Marie Keane, and Mary Schilling
Visiting Director of Internet Services: Peter Rothberg
Non-Visiting Scholar: Dilip Hiro
Director of Human Resources: Lindy Hess
Chief Librarian-in-Absentia: Linda Amster
Director, Office of Peripheral Research: Paige Matthews Peterson
Peripheral Research Adjutant: Alexandra Peterson
Liaison to the Nation Institute: Hamilton Fish
Director of Development: Amanda "Binky" Urban

EMERITI

Publisher Emeritus: André Schiffrin
Editors Emeriti: Wendy Goldwyn Batteau and Phil Pochoda
Research Fellow Emeritus: Christopher Power
Founding Expertologist: Joseph Aidlin

[1] In 2004, on the occasion of the twentieth anniversary of the Institute of Expertology, the Institute's Board of Directors voted Christopher Cerf, who had served as president of the Institute for the life of the organization, to the Chairmanship of the Board, and conferred the presidency on the Institute's twenty-year chairman, Victor S. Navasky. The new titles were officially conferred at a gala anniversary investiture ceremony at the Institute's New York City headquarters.

ABOUT THE AUTHORS

CHRISTOPHER CERF is the coeditor of *The Official Politically Correct Dictionary and Handbook* and *The Iraq War Reader.* He is a former contributing editor to *National Lampoon,* an Emmy- and Grammy-winning composer/lyricist for *Sesame Street,* and an executive producer of *Between the Lions,* the literacy education series his company, Sirius Thinking, Ltd., created for PBS.

VICTOR S. NAVASKY is the publisher emeritus of *The Nation* and chairman of *The Columbia Journalism Review.* He is the author of *Kennedy Justice; Naming Names,* which won a National Book Award; and *A Matter of Opinion,* which won the George Polk Award. He lives in New York City. In 1984, with Mr. Cerf, he cofounded the Institute of Expertology and coauthored *The Experts Speak: The Definitive Compendium of Authoritative Misinformation.*

ABOUT THE ILLUSTRATOR

ROBERT GROSSMAN is a New York artist whose work has appeared in *The New York Times, The Nation, The New Yorker, The New York Observer, Rolling Stone,* and many other publications.

SPECIAL BONUS SECTION

A Sneak Preview of Our Forthcoming Book, *THE EXPERTS SPEAK ABOUT IRAN*

This notion that the United States is getting ready to attack Iran is simply ridiculous. Having said that, all options are on the table.

President George W. Bush, February 22, 2005[1]

IN FACT

This is not the first time that all options have been on the table. Here is Bush in 2002: "Again, all options are on the table, and—but one thing I will not allow is a nation such as Iraq to threaten our very future by developing weapons of mass destruction."[2]

If Tehran insists on combining the Persian imperial tradition with contemporary Islamic fervor, then a collision with America . . . is unavoidable. Iran simply cannot be permitted to fulfill a dream of imperial rule in a region of such importance to the rest of the world.

Henry Kissinger, former U.S. Secretary of State, July 31, 2006[3]

We should undertake the legitimate self-defense to which we are entitled, by moving against the terrorist training camps, and the improvised explosive device assembly lines and manufacturing sites inside the Islamic Republic [of Iran].

Michael Ledeen, Freedom Scholar at the American Enterprise Institute, March 27, 2007[4]

We have to be ready to use military force against Iran. . . . We have to stop them from getting nuclear weapons. We can try diplomacy. I am not hopeful about that. We have to be ready to use force.

William Kristol, *Weekly Standard* editor, July 19, 2006[5]

We might consider . . . a military strike against Iranian nuclear facilities. Why wait? Does anyone think a nuclear Iran can be contained? That the current regime will negotiate in good faith? It would be easier to act sooner rather than later. Yes, there would be repercussions—and they would be healthy ones, showing a strong America that has rejected further appeasement.

William Kristol, *The Weekly Standard*, July 24, 2006[6]

I don't think there's any doubt, based on the information we have, that Iran is interfering in Iraq and is posing a direct threat to our troops. So I think if President Bush as commander in chief believes that information is accurate, he is fully entitled to take defensive measures, which could include going after the Revolutionary Guards inside Iran.

John Bolton, former U.S. Ambassador to the United Nations, August 22, 2007[7]

We got a leader in Iran who has announced that he wants to destroy Israel. So . . . if you're interested in avoiding World War III, it seems like you ought to be interested in preventing them from hav[ing] the knowledge necessary to make a nuclear weapon.

President George W. Bush, October 17, 2007[8]

Given the nature of Iran's rulers, the declarations of the Iranian President, and the trouble the regime is causing throughout the region—including direct involvement in the killing of Americans—our country and the entire international community cannot stand by as a terror-supporting state fulfills its most aggressive ambitions.

The Iranian regime needs to know that if it stays on its present course, the international community is prepared to impose serious consequences. The United States joins other nations in sending a clear message: We will not allow Iran to have a nuclear weapon.

Vice President Dick Cheney, October 21, 2007[9]

None of the alternatives to military action—negotiations, sanctions, provoking an internal insurrection—can possibly work. They're all ways of evading the terrible choice we have to make which is to either let Iran get the bomb or to bomb them. . . .

We've got three carriers in the region and a lot of submarines. . . . It would take five minutes. You'd wake up one morning and the strikes would have been ordered and carried out during the night. All the president has to do is say go.

Norman Podhoretz, editor of *Commentary* and senior political advisor to Rudy Giuliani's Republican 2008 presidential campaign, November 1, 2007[10]